RELEVANCE OF TRADITIONAL CULTURES FOR THE PRESENT AND THE FUTURE

RELEVANCE OF TRADITIONAL CULTURES FOR THE PRESENT AND THE FUTURE

Edited by

K. Raghunath and Nalin Surie

India International Centre
in association with
Konark Publishers Pvt Ltd
New Delhi · Seattle

Konark Publishers Pvt. Ltd
206, First Floor,
Peacock Lane, Shahpur Jat,
New Delhi-110 049.
Phone: +91-11-41055065, 65254972
e-mail: india@konarkpublishers.com
Website: www.konarkpublishers.com

Konark Publishers International
8615, 13th Ave SW,
Seattle, WA 98106
Phone: (115) 109 9900
e-mail: us@konarkpublishers.com

Cataloging in Publication Data—DK

Courtesy: D.K. Agencies (P) Ltd. <docinfo@dkagencies.com>

International Conference on "The Relevance of Traditional Cultures for the Present and the Future" (2014 : India International Centre)

Relevance of traditional cultures for the present and the future / edited by K. Raghunath and Nalin Surie.

pages cm

Conference papers.

Includes bibliographical references.

ISBN 9789322008802

1. Civilization--Congresses. I. Raghunath, K. (Krishnan), 1939- editor. II. Surie, Nalin, editor. III. India International Centre, host institution. IV. IIC-Asia Project, organizer. V. Indian Council for Cultural Relations, organizer. VI. Title.

CB69.R45 2014 DDC 909 23

Editor: Teesta Guha Sarkar

Typeset by Saanvi Graphics, Noida

Printed and bound at Thomson Press (India) Ltd.

Contents

Preface

KAPILA VATSYAYAN

THE IIC-ASIA PROJECT HAS BEEN set up to give a distinctive focus and direction to the realization of the Centre's basic vision—in regard to the specific aspect of promoting the substantive study of Asia led by the countries of Asia, accompanied by purposeful intra-Asian dialogue, so as to reinforce the larger effort to build cultural understanding and amity within Asia. This initiative was inspired by the recognition that, notwithstanding the considerable progress made since the end of the colonial era, in the discovery of Asia by its people, and in nurturing Asian cultural interaction, much remains to be done in this regard.

The core of the IIC-Asia Project's endeavour in fulfilling this mandate is the bringing together of scholars from Asian countries (though not exclusively so), in a sustained, long-term series of programmes of seminars, conferences and publications. This mode of engagement helps stimulate rigorous scholarship and research on Asia, and also provides a productive forum for dialogue and cross-cultural interaction. The process is intended to go beyond academia and to help create greater public awareness of renascent scholarship on Asia and the deeply significant affinities and commonalities among the cultures of Asia.

In the first six years of the project since its inception in 1997, its programmes centred on the cultures of specific geographical regions, individual nation states, societies and political formations in Asia and the interactions among them—an approach in some ways akin to area cultural studies. The experience of this phase underlined that there was a truly rich variety of themes and issues relating to the cultures of Asia and their interactions, cutting across regional and national boundaries, which were waiting to be explored through scholarship and research. It was felt that one could best do justice to this demand and exciting prospect, through a thematic approach.

A brief recounting of the principal themes taken up in this framework helps clarify the thinking behind the present compilation. The essence of the thematic approach is to explore the many manifestations of dialogue within and between Asia's diverse cultures, and the activities and processes that unite them.

In this larger dimension, among the subjects explored first was a complex of fundamental overarching interactions—relating to ideas, ways of thinking and reasoning, aesthetic perceptions, knowledge systems, skills, and other kindred categories, and their outcomes in shaping Asia's cultural heritage and tradition—and its cultural accomplishments. This was the inspiration for the international seminar on "Asian Encounters: Networks of Cultural Interaction". The three large issues chosen for scholarly examination on this occasion, that is, "Exploring Connected Histories", "Asian Aesthetic Theories and Art Forms", "Exploring Epigraphic Sources", give some sense of the rich substance and flavour of the exercise. This event interfaced seamlessly with another large set of ideas, notably the common religious and architectural legacy of Asia. One must also draw attention to two other major seminars held in 2012 and 2013 respectively, that is, "Mind and Body in Health and Harmony in Asian Systems of Medicine" and "Remembering Raimundo Panikkar"—especially because they illustrate the diversity and eclectic character of the themes for research which grow out of the long contact and conversation among the cultures of Asia.

Central Asia described evocatively as the "lost heart of Asia" has been a major area of geographical and thematic interest to the IIC-Asia Project. Following up on earlier discussions on this subject, including one predating the project, it was felt that a renewed examination of the role of Buddhism in shaping the culture of the region would indeed be timely. Hence, the 2008 seminar on "New Discoveries about Buddhism in Western Central Asia". West Asia—though geographically located some distance away from the heartland of the Asian continent, but very much within the IIC Asia Project's ken—has also received due attention, through the conference on "The Arabian Nights in World Literature". This was a scholarly exploration of a well-known theme which offers yet another timely and telling recapitulation of the depth and authenticity of the interaction between the Arab world and Iran and the rest of Asia—especially India.

Another outstanding instance of a rich shared cultural heritage is the long and thriving contact across the seas and oceans among the coastal communities on the Indian Ocean Rim, involving the hinterlands as well; it was celebrated rightly in the 2015 international seminar on "Maritime Cultural Heritage of the Western Indian Ocean—Bridging the Gulf."

Besides the large dimensions of arts, architecture, religion, history and even politics, the exploration of Asian cultural affinities and interconnections also involves more immediately human concerns—in education, learning and the unique contribution of women through their voices, expressed notably in poetry and the crafts. Reference may be made to the symposium on "Transmission and Transformations: Learning through the Arts in Asia", "Speaking for Myself—An Anthology of Asian Women's Writing", and the "Festival of Documentary Films by Asian Women Filmmakers".

A specially imaginative example of this vital human level of cultural exploration is the humble needle and thread—appropriately taken up in the seminar, "Embroidery in Asia: Sui-Dhaga—Crossing Boundaries through Needle and Thread".

Reflecting the same principle and spirit, though in a different vein was the focus on "The Culture of Indigo—The Asian Panorama", a multidimensional exercise which revealed the astonishingly far-reaching role of this innocuous botanical entity in shaping not only culture but history and politics in Asia and beyond.

The immersion in the "Needle and Thread" and "Indigo" themes, opens one's eyes to the fact that embedded in culture and cross-cultural interaction is a multiplicity of what could be called "Micro Themes", which do not *prima facie* have the grand profile of the larger themes, but are nonetheless of fundamental, archetypal import growing out as they do of elements of a given culture that constitute the hub and nodal and focal points of large cultural processes and activities: they make up the warp and woof, and the basic pattern and structure of the fabric of culture in its entirety. Exploring and teasing out the many layers and implications of these elements is not merely deeply enriching, but is indeed an essential part of the study of Asian cultures and cultural interactions.

The experience with the long series of events recounted above made it clear that while the "Asian" focus was necessary for coherence and identity, it was, at the same time, in the nature of things, that the Asian cross-cultural dialogue would transcend the boundaries of Asia and encompass cultural territory in Africa, Latin America, Oceania and elsewhere in the non-occidental world. Recognition of this perspective is implicit in the renaming of the project as "IIC—International Research Division."

Regarding the genesis and rationale of the seminar which is the basis for the present compilation, an attribute common to the entire series of programmes scanned here is that this study of Asian cultures and cross-cultural dialogue inescapably leads one back to "Traditional Culture" both in the sense of a natural return to the beginnings, to the roots—as well as its continuation into the present, this construct emerges as a key reference point and baseline of enquiry. Further, as this is taking place in a modern, contemporary context, the relevance of traditional culture to the present and future is a key question that must be addressed.

The defining and organizing concept may be summed up thus: All nations and societies have considered it crucial to evaluate the role and relevance of tradition to their own generation and beyond. This discourse has a fundamentally different content and quality in non-western societies as against the shape it takes in the West. Indeed, because of the differing trajectories of historical evolution in the Western and non-Western world, the "Relevance" question itself applies essentially to the latter. That is because in striking contrast to the West, the Eastern world has preserved/ retained a substantial part, indeed the core, of their tradition, with a remarkable continuity in mores and value systems. Their experience of the anticolonial struggle—which uniquely distinguishes them from the West—has consolidated this difference in the tone of the discourse of the relevance of tradition. An added dimension of vital importance is the fact that the inexorable process of globalization, and the large and bewildering complex of global challenges and threats (as well as the tantalizing opportunities) which it represent impinges with much greater force on non-Western societies.

It is the ensemble of fascinating and thought-provoking questions growing out of this situation that provided the driving impulse for this event. Accordingly, the IIC-Asia Project sounded out several scholars, in Africa and Latin America, and in Asia as well, coming together with their interest in joining in collectively addressing this subject. The response was resoundingly positive and supportive. The participating scholars came from Benin, Ghana, Ethiopia, Egypt, Mauritius, Senegal, Lebanon, Mexico, Argentina, as well as Greece, Russia, Germany, the UK and the USA, besides some countries in Asia. All the papers read on the occasion have been brought together in this volume. The record would be incomplete without recalling the event itself—for its uplifting atmosphere and the all-round enthusiasm of the participants. One of the many memorable indicators of this quality was the spontaneous call by the delegate from Ghana for holding the next conference on this subject in Africa.

I must reiterate our sincere thanks to all the delegates, both from abroad as well as home, for their dedicated participation. The IIC-Asia Project also puts on record our acknowledgement of the generous financial assistance of the Indian Council for Cultural Relation (ICCR), which was essential to enabling the foreign participants to attend. I am grateful to the Hon'ble Vice President, M.H. Ansari, for inaugurating the event, to N.N. Vohra for chairing the inaugural proceedings, and Karan Singh for his valedictory address. The texts of their addresses as well as the summary of proceedings by Nalin Surie are included in the text. Lastly, our thanks are due to the Editors, K. Raghunath and Nalin Surie, for their contribution and assistance in organizing the seminar.

Introduction

NALIN SURIE

THERE IS NOW AN OVERALL consensus that a shift is taking place in the structure of power from the West to the East; not simply to Asia but also via select parts of South America and Africa. The older civilizations have not only maintained their continuity in spite of their turbulent trajectories and the political and economic dominance that they have been subject to over time but they have also been able to retain and sustain their inherent values and traditions together with knowledge systems that are alive. Now they are poised to re-articulate the relevance of their values in contemporary times to the shaping of the future.

The old civilizations of Asia, South America and Africa predate the rise of Western civilization. The latter has been influenced by the intellectual and cultural aspects of the older civilizations over a long period of history. Asian civilization is characterized from the very beginning as having certain common elements, but with centrifugal and centripetal forces. It has a commitment to plurality, plurality of perception and plurality with a capacity for dialogue. It has a very distinct Asian sensibility, a sensibility which can contain multi-identities. In different parts of Asia, very distinct cultures have emerged but they have all been like honeycomb, attached to each other.

Similarly, or differently, Egypt has played a very important role in terms of its antiquity and a distinct Egyptian civilization; it has a long history of both continuity and change which has affected that part of what is today called Africa. Within the African continent, there are a number of countries which can be grouped together as forming another network, like a honeycomb, which may be called the African civilization. Whether it is in Ethiopia, Central Africa or Western Africa, there is an African sensibility. That African sensibility and its civilizational and cultural aspects have not received the kind of attention they deserve.

Latin America or South America is the home of one or more ancient civilizations. Most important among these are Peru, Mexico and Brazil. In each of these, there is a distinct Latin American sensibility and it has been observed that in all these there has been a long history of accretion—layers upon layers—and the question to be asked is how have these civilizations been able to absorb and also maintain their character through the many historical moments which naturally includes the history of the world post-Renaissance and post-Enlightenment.

There has been a sizeable body of scholarship on these civilizations in the last 200 years in the West. However, no longer are these civilizations studied only as relics of the past but have been re-assessed for their pertinence today in shaping a new global architecture that takes into account the global shift in power balances that is underway.

The purpose of the conference is to bring together intellectuals from different countries of Asia, Africa and Latin America, who have reflected and will reflect on the fundamental questions of whether the long civilizational histories of these countries, with their rich and varied knowledge systems and cultural traditions, have a meaningful and significant role to play in the contemporary world and certainly the world of the future. The discussion will necessarily have to take into account the existing economic models of development and the evolving more viable models. There have been conferences in the past decade on the study of civilizations and relevance of ancient civilizations in the modern world. But this is the right time to assemble scholars and thinkers to address themselves to the crisis that faces the modern civilization. Select scholars from Europe and the USA will also be invited.

Inaugural Address

M. HAMID ANSARI, VICE PRESIDENT OF INDIA

A THEME THAT DWELLS SIMULTANEOUSLY on the past, the present and the future is not to be trifled with by the uninitiated. I consider myself in the latter category and can only attribute my presence on this podium to Kapila Vatsyayan's non-negotiable imperative.

A first reading of the Concept Note of the Conference suggests a focus on the geopolitical changes in our times and their implications for cultural perceptions. These could be extended to include phenomena like modernity and globalization.

It is a truism that long periods of alien dominance impart slanted or distorted perceptions. In an epic work, Edward Said demonstrated the way cultural domination operated resulting in what he called a failure "to identify with human experience", leading to a "seductive degradation of knowledge".

And yet, the compendium of knowledge collected in the process, exemplified by accounts of travellers, ancient and modern, is in many ways invaluable. The task for contemporary scholarship is to correct the slant, not to junk it.

Take the case of India. We have the travelogues of Chinese Buddhist monks Faxian, Xuanzang and Yijing that tell us a good deal about Indian living and religious habits, and religious practices. A few centuries later, Alberuni after noting that Indians differ in everything from other nations, went on to diligently record observations on every aspect of Indian life, religion, philosophy, sciences and legal system. Ibn Battuta wrote that when he entered India, he was told of the rule that anyone coming from Khurasan had to execute an undertaking that he had come with the intention of staying here. The fact that Ibn Battuta was able to continue his travels shows that even then, all rules were not enforced!

Other travellers, Asian and European, followed. All made comments on Indian practices and traditions. In our society, therefore, there is a surfeit of recorded and remembered traditions that can be scanned with benefit, emulated or rejected. No effort has yet been made to disown them wholesale.

The classic Western study is, of course, Arnold Toynbee's majestic survey of 21 societies, past and present. He pointed out the overwhelming numerical preponderance of primitive societies (650 by his count in the early 20th century), over those classified as civilizations. Toynbee's study, however, had a different focus: to trace the contrast between the diversity of growth of individual societies and the uniformity of their disintegration.

For our purposes today, both civilizations and primitive societies can yield elements of traditional cultures that may be of relevance. It has been said that differences of conditions among people are the result of the different ways in which they make their living. As a result, custom causes human nature to incline towards the things to which it becomes used. The challenge is to identify and retrieve from them the "inherent values and traditions" and "to re-articulate the relevance of [these] values in contemporary times to the shaping of the future".

Some questions arise. What constitutes a tradition? What do we mean by designating a behaviour pattern as traditional? Is it simply chronological or is it imbued with certain values that the collective memory of a society holds precious? How do we assess their worth for the present and the future?

In its simplest meaning, a tradition is anything which is transmitted or handed down from the past to the present. It includes material objects, beliefs, images, practices and institutions. They are not independently self-productive or self-elaborating. The sociologist Edward Shils had drawn up a comprehensive list of "what is not tradition". He notes that "although mankind cannot live without traditions and although it cannot live contentedly with the traditions it receives, traditions are both persistent and disrupted. They survive, nevertheless, in some form. The particular configuration of persistence and disruption are not matters of indifference to the societies in which they occur".

Shils added that the existence of a tradition is at least as much a consequence of limited power to escape from it as it is a consequence of a desire to continue and to maintain it. Human societies retain much of what they have inherited not because they love it, but because they grasp that they could not survive without it. Traditions are indispensable. They do not impede the forward movement of societies. They lend authenticity to them.

A good example is our approach to indigenous medicine. It is defined by the WHO as "the health practices, approaches, knowledge and beliefs incorporating plant, animal and mineral-based medicines, spiritual therapies, manual techniques and exercise, applied singularly or in combination to treat, diagnose and prevent illnesses or maintain well-being".

Indigenous medicine represents an alternate knowledge system, based on a holistic and traditional understanding of the human condition. Its efficacy and utility are being increasingly recognized the world over.

Other examples relate to dispute-settlement practices. These exist in all societies and can be usefully adapted and implemented as alternate, inexpensive, methods of dispensing justice speedily. Many more models would undoubtedly be cited at this conference.

It is important to note that tradition and modernity are not antipodes. Neither are they static, consistent, homogenous, mutually exclusive, or in perennial conflict. The endeavour of locating what is of value in the past, and adapting it into the framework of modernity, has to be inductive rather than deductive. The examination of the past, therefore, has to be critical rather than adulatory. It has to steer clear of imagined glory and must not be an incentive for chauvinism.

Ours is a world characterized by a globalization of values and to some extent of culture. One aspect of it is alienation from one's roots; another is benefit derived from the experience and practices of others. How then is traditional culture, which is by definition space- or location-specific, to be integrated in the value system or larger spaces? What would be its methodology and limits? How would values that compete be accommodated in these spaces?

Two factors compel attention. In the first place is the sheer diversity of traditions across the globe. For the sake of convenience, these could be grouped into broad categories relating to personal behaviour, familial norms, birth, marriage, death, inheritance and value judgements attached to these. Similarly, norms pertaining to civic and market behaviour would be of relevance.

The second is the question of globalization. It is said that it erodes national cultures, and therefore traditions. It is further asserted that contemporary migratory flow of people are introducing greater complexity and heterogeneity to societies that leads them to becoming progressively multicultural and poly-ethnic.

Both need to be encapsulated in our approach. Perhaps we need to rethink modernity by criticizing it from within, in its own terms, and thereby enriching it.

I venture to hope that this conference would help give shape to a theory of cultural values, inclusive of relevant traditional norms, on the global stage.

Jai Hind!

Presidential Speech at the Inaugural Session

N.N. VOHRA

Hon'ble Vice President of India, M.H Ansari, Kapila Vatsyayan, Chairperson of the IIC-Asia Project, President and members of the Board of Trustees of the IIC, Director IIC, Satish Mehta, distinguished participants, ladies and gentlemen.

Kapila Vatsyayan has lucidly commented on the theme of the conference and M.H. Ansari has spoken at some length on some of the more important aspects, particularly internal insurgencies, militancies, terrorist activities and varied other disturbances which are presently plaguing many parts of the world. I think it is a good occasion, and an opportune time, to hark back to our hoary past and to seriously ponder whether all that has happened in the past several centuries in the name of industrial, scientific and technological revolutions has actually produced the kind of outcomes which the people had expected and deserved.

M.H. Ansari has recalled some of our invaluable inheritances which comprise very high levels of learning and expertise in the arenas of languages, philosophy, mathematics, astronomy, medicine and the sciences.

In this context, it may be mentioned that some efforts have been made in the past years to revive our traditional scientific knowledge sources, most of which were virtually obliterated by the colonial paradigm, the so-called Macaulayan school, which propounded that there is nothing to be learnt from the non-West civilizations. This reminds us that the colonial goal in large parts of Asia, Africa and Middle-East was merely to earn fortunes, to earn revenues and send them back home, and destroy all that was indigenous, all that was valuable, so that nothing at all came in the way of securing the imperial objectives which were publicized to bring us, the natives, "out of backwardness" and, under the cover of this explanation, anything which "appeared to be conservative" was ruthlessly done away with.

The Concept Note touches upon various important aspects of the theme of this Conference. It also briefly states that there are indications of a global power shift. I am not particularly sure whether such a shift is in the making or is it merely that in the past decades several European nations have started taking greater interest in the contributions made by some of the older civilizations.

Considerable work has been done on our cultural traditions and some very valuable books have come out, as well as translations of our ancient literature. However, I am unsure whether all this adds up to the beginning of a shift in the global power structures.

The traditional cultures in Asia can boast of having the most philosophical, the most penetrating, and the most lasting cultural traditions and values, knowledge systems, thought processes and life styles. Unfortunately, particularly during the period of colonial rule, our knowledge centres and sources were damaged and destroyed and a great deal of work shall need to be done to restore and rebuild the ancient centres of learning.

M.H. Ansari made reference to the enormous storehouse of scientific knowledge which lies embedded in our traditional systems of medicine. It is indeed a great tragedy that the vast majority of our scientific learning, particularly the documentation comprising the bedrock of our ancient medicine systems, was systematically destroyed and the practitioners were not allowed to freely practice their arts and sciences. Therefore, a great deal of resurrection would have been required. While this has not been publicized, it is gratifying to note that the Indian Council of Cultural Relations has, over the period of time, particularly during Karan Singh's tenure, done a great deal of good work in this direction.

And I learnt only this morning that my former colleague, Lalit Mansingh, has also joined this prestigious council. A lot of work still remains to be done and I am sure it is possible. As Vatsyayan mentioned, the IIC has, in the last six decades, done excellent work to bring together notable intellectuals, thinkers and scholars, from within our own country and from various parts of world, to discuss important issues of common interest.

I would like to recall that, in early 1997, the IIC set up the IIC-Asia Project. While this was done with a very modest investment, it is a matter for considerable satisfaction that, under the aegis of this project, we organized a series of international conferences to which we invited known scholars to discuss the people, history, culture, society, politics and other important aspects of countries in South, South East, Central, West and Far East Asia, covering the entire continent and far beyond. I had the privilege of being associated with the work of the Asia Project for over eight years.

It is relevant to note that, right from its inception, the Asia Project decided consciously, and very sensibly, to exclude discussions on geo-political and security aspects as, in our experience, these would have merely resulted in generating avoidable disharmony in our debates.

As considerable time has passed since the Asia Project carried out its initial studies in respect of Asian countries, perhaps the time has come for Vatsyayan to consider doing another round of conferences, in today's much changed regional and global environment. Also, recognizing how much the world has changed, we need to re-look the views which were expressed in the days before the onset of religious radicalization and global terrorism. Today, we must think, and most critically, about all that we need to do to keep the world together, free from the daily fear of terror strikes.

Apropos the varied other questions that arise from the concept paper, we need to seriously consider how best we can utilize the rich historical traditions and value systems of the non-Western world, the civilizational values, the knowledge systems, the ways of life and thought, and the vast overall wisdom which lies embedded in our civilizational foundations. Can this—all this wisdom, all this knowledge, all these approaches and all these philosophies—be put together and brought to bear on the most worrisome global environment that obtains today, to find insights and answers to the frightening serious challenges which continue to face the world—poverty, hunger, illiteracy, disease, religious radicalisation, communal conflicts and, more recently, terrorism.

I would urge all the distinguished participants to please deliberate on some of these issues in the next two days and evolve some pragmatic approaches which show how the wisdom of our ancient past can be utilized to look at the present and the future and enlightened approaches pursued for establishing a humane and peaceful world order. Whatever else is done, as may be possible, it is most urgently essential to contain and stop the very many conflicts that continue to shatter peace and normalcy in many parts of the world.

It is necessary to revive our pluralistic foundations, deeply rooted in our ancient civilization, and restore humane traditions and amity among our diverse societies. From my own experience, I would like to mention that such an objective could be attained only if we have the requisite will and the capability to engage in sustained dialogues with all those who have contrary beliefs.

I compliment Vatsyayan for taking the valuable initiative of organizing this conference on a theme that is both important and increasingly relevant in today's context. I wish the participants fruitful deliberations.

The Struggle for Egypt's Soul

MOHAMED SALMAWY

I PROPOSE TO TAKE YOU to the land of the Nile, land of the Sphinx and the pyramids, land of Al-Azhar University and the seat of Islamic learning. Indeed also to the land of one of the oldest Christian churches in the world which we share with our good neighbours in Ethiopia; the oldest church before the Vatican was even thought of. This is the very old church that was built on the remnants of a cave in which the Virgin Mary and her son hid when they fled from Palestine from the Roman rule over there.

The reason I mention the Nile, the Sphinx, the pyramids, the Al-Azhar, the Christian church and the deserts of Egypt, which form 95 percent of its surface area, is that these are the main factors that make what we can call the traditional culture of the country. Egypt's traditional culture has been formed by a number of factors, first among which are these sort of touristic landmarks that I have pointed out: The river Nile with its eternal flow which has created stability and has filled people with confidence and security. The pyramids, the architecture and the civilization were built along the banks of this river; Christianity and the fact that Egypt protected the Virgin Mary and her son when they were threatened by the Roman rule in Palestine. Perhaps if this had not happened, the history of Christianity might have been different. But, this is the nature of Egypt: protecting whoever visits. And of course, Al-Azhar and Islam with its very strong imprint on daily life, the identity and traditional culture, of the country.

In making this presentation, I find that I have ended up speaking not only about traditional culture in Egypt but about the soul of Egypt itself.

Hence my presentation is entitled "The Struggle for Egypt's Soul". This is the subtitle to this big subject we are addressing when we apply it to Egypt. The story becomes the story for the struggle for Egypt's soul.

In a country as ancient and as old and as far removed in time as Egypt, it was not difficult to reach some kind of consensus among its people. It is not a land that has emerged out of diversity like India but rather the opposite, out of similarities and from common traits that have held these people together in an oasis surrounded by desert from all sides, the desert which kept it secure for thousands of years. It may be strange to imagine or to learn that in the early stages of Egypt's history there was no such thing as an army because there was no sense of danger. There was no feeling that interchange with another people or another culture could pose some kind of threat to Egypt. All the great wars and victories that have taken place in later stages were in defence of this soul, in defence of this sense of identity and in defence of this traditional culture that was Egypt.

Egypt perhaps is very peculiar among old civilizations in the sense that it did not have an empire. Unlike Rome or Athens or many of the other great civilizations that we have known even in Asia, Egypt did not seek to have an empire, did not need to have an empire and the civilization that we now know of was built within the boundaries, the very same boundaries that we know today. Egypt has a long coastline along the Mediterranean and the Red Sea but it never had any real wartime fleet. The boats, the famous Pharaonic boats that we know of, were no more than a means of transportation along the Nile or were a means of transportation for the soul of the dead to the other world. But there was no fleet as you would have thought in a country with such a long coast along the seas.

By virtue of historical and geographical factors, this "seclusion" for want of a better word, helped to create a kind of tradition, a kind of culture that was not easy to destroy later on when Egypt opened up to the rest of the world. And through many invasions from abroad, by the Persians, the Romans, the Greeks, the Turks, and, more recently, the British, and lately the French, the sense of identity has always remained. Each of us has this because of our long history and because of this sense of isolation in the middle of the desert. Due to vast deserts on all sides, Egypt was able to maintain its identity. Not only that, it was also able to import and assimilate the new conquerors into its own tradition.

It is not insignificant that when Alexander the Great conquered Egypt, he was immediately affected and influenced by the culture of Egypt. It is known that he wore Pharaonic costumes and called himself the son of Amon, not in an attempt to ingratiate himself with the public but because that is how he felt. The proof of that is that when he died years later in Babylon, he willed that he should be buried in Egypt. And I think it is historically suggested that his body was actually taken from Babylon to Egypt in order to be buried there. Some accounts by travellers in Roman and Greek times speak of their having visited Alexander's tomb in Egypt. Nobody knows where it is now but it appears that his will was indeed executed after his death.

The same thing happened to Napoleon hundreds of years later following the French invasion. The influence of Egypt on Napoleonic France extended all the way from the design of furniture to that of costumes. Egyptomani or Egyptomania had infiltrated France to the extent that one may well ask who was the actual invader: Was it the French who invaded Egypt or Egypt that invaded France?

This sense of identity extended through the Coptic period, the Islamic period and up to the present. Anybody who examines the manners and customs of modern-day Egyptians would easily relate many of those patterns to the time of the Pharaohs, especially when it comes to rituals that have to do with birth and death. We call them Islamic but they have nothing to do with Islam. They were inherited from the Pharaohs. For instance, you mark the fortieth day of the death because forty days after the process of embalmment you pass through a different stage. My good friend Wafaa El-Saddik, who was the former director of the Egyptian museum, is an expert on Egyptian history, and knows more about it than I do. But I can tell you that all this lives on till this very day. Strangely enough, many Islamic countries, especially in the Arab world, have taken over all these traditions from Egypt and still call them Islamic and they, too, celebrate the fortieth day since the death and many other rites and rituals that were mainly Egyptian and part of our heritage.

This heritage carried over into the Coptic period, a very important period in our history between the Pharaonic and the Islamic eras, which was brought forward to the Islamic period as well. Of course, I do agree entirely with what the Chairman said that the West has carried on a crusade against our traditional culture.

But what I want to concentrate on here is not the foreign influences on traditional culture in Egypt but the internal struggle that took place during periods of retreat where, like in the Dark Ages and the Middle Ages, there was an attempt by religion to take over and influence traditional culture, to make it subservient to religion. Religion is definitely a component of Egyptian traditional culture but there is a difference between the two. And the use of religion or the substitution by religion of traditional culture was one sign of these periods of regression that we have known throughout our history. Every time there was an attempt to separate the two was invariably a time when a new renaissance was unleashed to bring about a period of progress and modernity. The first such attempt happened in the nineteenth century after a long period of darkness. This happened with the advent of Mohammed Ali, the Viceroy of Egypt, who created for the first time secular learning, secular schools in Egypt, at a time when all schooling and learning was religious. And by so doing he was able to see the difference between the two, and a period of renaissance came about at a time that marks this period as the beginning of the modern state in Egypt.

The same thing happened under Nasser when he secularized Al-Azhar and we were able to learn medicine and agriculture and engineering and literature in Al-Azhar side by side with Islam and Shariat. But we reached a very strange situation at the time of Mubarak, when we were faced with a very clear choice between a secular, be it a dictatorial, authoritarian, backward regime, and an Islamic, rather fundamentalist alternative. And in between you had nothing. You were to choose between one or the other. We Egyptians were faced with that choice. The whole world bought the theory and they had to choose between supporting the Mubarak government in Egypt or have it replaced with an Islamic alternative because there was no third alternative available.

And now I come to the Arab Spring. We have this luxury in Egypt that you can jump thousands of years if you like and you will still be talking about the same history. So in 2011, lo and behold, a new alternative springs in Egypt like a new flower and maybe that is why it was called the Arab Spring, because something bloomed out of this stagnant situation as though, after winter, spring was bringing flowers into being. The third alternative was personified by a younger generation that was not Islamic in the ideological sense, that was secular, that believed in progress, democracy and modernity, and was unhappy with the regime of Mubarak at the time. But strangely enough, rather than cultivate this new alternative that came into being and hence save Egypt's soul from dictatorship on one hand and fundamentalism on the other and restore its traditional culture, as we have always known it for the past thousands of years, this alternative was hijacked, and at the end of two years of revolution, a very unstable and turbulent revolution, we were faced with the same choice once again; that we vote for either an old general like Mubarak or a representative of the Muslim Brotherhood. We were back to square one where there were only those two choices and the third choice was gradually lost in the process.

People could not go back to the regime they had revolted against, so Mohammed Morsi was voted into office. I am not talking politics, I am still talking of traditional culture, but in Egypt when you talk about traditional culture, especially when you talk about the present and the future, you mix everything up together with politics and all these other things.

We in Egypt are facing a situation where we have to find ourselves another alternative. We have to go back to our traditional culture. We brought down the usurpers of our soul, of our Egypt's secular, cultural, traditional soul and are now facing a new future. We hope that during that future we would be able to restore the soul of Egypt, which has come to us as a result of our heritage, our civilization, our belief in the good in this world and our belief also in religion, which is a very strong force in Egypt but very far removed from the violent fundamentalist trends that are now around us.

So I think Egypt is in the process of finding itself again. It is on the verge of a new period which hopefully will end up in our restoring our traditional culture. After one year of Islamic rule, the people have risen against it and have liberated the country from it.

On the Role and Significance of Cultural Heritage for a Positive National Identity

Some Educational Remarks on Museum Education

WAFAA THA EL-SADDIK

THE POPULATIONS OF EGYPT AND other developing countries are currently involved in a struggle to overcome the problems of everyday life—money, food, jobs, health and, increasingly, security. Hardly any time or energy remains for them to concentrate on their cultural heritage, and that includes visits to their local museums and archaeological sites. The danger looms large, that the nation could lose awareness of its own cultural heritage. It is our task to re-educate the people as accurately as possible on their own cultural history. We hope in Egypt to found a sort of museo-pedagogical centre or museum education department in every city and town, in order to aid the population in enhancing its national identity, and broadening its horizons.

Museum education has two components: the matter of the museum and the task of education. Therefore, museum education is not only an affair for scientists and museum people. The perspective of the educators also has to be considered.

In modern times, museums have become a relatively young expression of human life. As such they comprise two aspects. They are a collection of a certain area to document something of cultural importance. The second aspect is that museums are collections for the public; this is one of the results of enlightenment: the public, "the people", should possess such a collection.

One might say the collection, conservation and exhibition of artefacts is the museum's primary task. But in fact all museums are first of all places of learning. Museums offer different types of learning opportunities. Visitors who go through an exhibition may experience a personal kind of learning, but there is a need to learn more as well and this can be achieved through the formal services museums offer, such as guided tours, gallery talks, lectures and learning through activities. Such programmes help museums become more attractive and interactive. That is why museums are becoming centres of learning. Many educational institutions use museums as an additional teaching resource. Other initiatives try to take the museum out into the community. The aim of such activities is to make museums more accessible to different parts of the population. Cultural collection and the public are to come together, and even more than that: they have to be mediated to each other. The mediation is necessary because the public is not knowledgeable about the collection like the owner is. The task of a museum is mediation between a cultural collection and the public. This is the educational task.

The definition of museum education as the task to mediate between collection and the public may sound very abstract. One might elaborate on this through a famous quote from the German poet Goethe: "What you inherit from your father, acquire it to possess it!" Superficially taken, this sentence does not make sense. For why shall I acquire something which I have inherited already? It already belongs to me, so why to try to possess it again? For sure, Goethe knew this, too. Therefore we have to look more carefully for the meaning of his sentence. The three main statements of Goethe's sentence are: to inherit, to acquire and to possess. When we relate the heritage to our topic, that is, to museums, then the heritage comprises the goods and traditions which stem from ancient times. These traditions and goods of culture and civilization are supposed to be present in a museum. Museums document the heritage. But Goethe demands from us that we acquire the heritage. Obviously, for Goethe, pure presence is not enough; it needs the active participation, the activity of the individual. On the other hand, a museum has to make the heritage available for the public; the average citizen needs a good presentation of the exhibits through a skillful selection of exhibits by an expert and a calm presentation which enables meditation.

The active participation in their heritage by citizens must be supported by the museum. However, acquiring the heritage must not be mixed up with information. This is a fatal misunderstanding in our schools. They feed the children with information, with superficial data about, for example, history. The result is that those children, later as adults, will be fed up of history, they will be bored and will even hate it. Therefore, acquiring one's heritage must be more than information; it requires an encounter with it.

Museums have to arrange the encounter; they have to provide the opportunity for it and encourage it. However, they cannot make the encounter happen without the active participation of people, which is the key to real encounter. This brings us back to the individual who should actively address his heritage. In which way has he/she to be active? There must be, first of all, a personal question, interest, curiosity. We can call it motivation or interest.

Is interest sufficient? We know that a superficial interest may quickly disappear; therefore, it must be serious. The more serious and deeper the motivation is, the more powerful and sustainable the interest will be in order to bring an individual and his heritage together. The more we are able and ready to relate our heritage to our present or even a personal situation, the deeper and the more existential our questions are, the more we are ready to encounter a historic figure, event, etc.

An existential acquirement is not only based on motivation, but also on the involvement of the senses. Also, "information" needs eyes and ears, though, in a very superficial way, just for the transfer of abstract knowledge. Real involvement of our eyes would mean, for example, to watch a painting carefully and draw it. Who has drawn it has a different kind of "knowledge" than the one who has read only the description. The more senses are actively involved the more existential is the encounter with the subject matter. Drawing is only one simple possibility of involving the senses. It can also be painting, forming in clay, in paper, other materials, describing it in words and by reflecting on it; it can be a role or a dramatic performance. Thus, our senses can be activated in many forms in order to take the subject matter into our hands and not only in our brain, i.e. learning by doing.

Thus, we can reformulate Goethe's statement in a new way: What is presented to you as your heritage, actively acquire and encounter it with all your senses, in order to possess it. One important aspect is related to this: Without a personal relationship to an object or a sensual encounter, there is no *real love* for it. Because of the importance of museum education, the UNESCO designed a programme, which offers an ideal setting for site-related museums to play a pivotal role as a mediator for peace and intercultural understanding, a provider of quality educational content for local and international communities, as well as an agent for development. The UNESCO project was designed as a pilot project to accompany the process of revitalizing the World Heritage site museums and interpretation centres dedicated to archaeological sites. The programme is aimed primarily at the development of professional skills of museum staff, not only curators and conservators, but also archaeologists and managers of the World Heritage sites. The participants are to re-scope the mission of the World Heritage site museums in the contemporary world, by means of collective reflection and practical exercise for the enhanced and holistic interpretation of collections, collection management, development of participative approach for local communities, and museum visitor studies. The aim of museum education's activities is to make museums more accessible to various parts of the population and more responsive to the visitors' needs and interests.

Learning around museum objects can be an effective way to provide education to people who do not have easy access to the written word or do not speak the dominant language. The current relationship between Intangible Cultural Heritage, museums and educational organizations that together play a role in safeguarding Intangible Cultural Heritage, is one that is still evolving. Museums and other public institutions have keenly promoted UNESCO's Convention, 2003, for the Safeguarding of Intangible Cultural Heritage. Our goal is to help children, and also adults, in looking at original exhibits and monuments to have a better understanding of their history and their environment. In taking into consideration the interests and needs of our youth, our goal of making the ancient cultural heritage tangible for them requires us to provide programmes with a clear overall view of the materials used and the roles people played in the past. This would mean that we must make ancient cultures "come alive". We must awaken new understanding and excitement in the young people of our countries, in order to enhance their cultural identity and increase their awareness of the world they live in.

Awareness of the role and significance of cultural heritage helps make a positive future for children and their family a reality.

Ethiopian Christian Art: A Rich Aesthetic Tradition

ELIZABETH W. GIORGIS

BACKGROUND

ETHIOPIAN PAINTINGS OF ILLUSTRATED MANUSCRIPTS, church murals, and paintings on wood have been produced over 10 centuries, and much of this heritage is preserved in old churches and monasteries. The most important source of Ethiopian Christian painting is the introduction of Christianity into Ethiopia in the fourth century. For centuries, Christianity has been the most dominant factor in Ethiopian political life and an important component of Christian education was the art of painting. What makes Ethiopian church paintings unique is that paintings are believed to possess the power of intercession in that the saint or the holy person represented can communicate with the individual. For centuries, the nobility financed the construction and decoration of churches in order to attain salvation.

Apocryphal texts, such as the *Miracles of Mary*, homilies, and hagiographies of saints dictated rules of paintings, according to which colours had to be made from plants and soil. Paintings were also ways of conveying stories of saints as well as the theology of the Church. Painters worked by moving from place to place, which led to the similarity of styles of paintings of particular periods. To become pure and spiritually superior, the Ethiopian Orthodox Church supports chastity and abstinence specifically through fasting, and this austere ideal is central in the workings of the image. Goha Tsbeha, a professor of theology, remarked: "The rule is that the painter must not be a sinner; he must be pure, religious.

If someone prays on such painting, God can work miracles. The painting speaks and it also cures." (Tsbeha as quoted in Mercier, 1997) An image given to the Church must be blessed by an abbot, monk or priest known to be pure.

Wall paintings in the Church are covered by cloth except for special occasions like a particular saint's monthly feast when the priests show the image of that particular saint to the sick to be kissed and touched. There are over 200 original hagiographies in Ge'ez (the liturgical script) about Ethiopian saints. Most of these hagiographies have not been translated to Amharic (the official language of Ethiopia), making them inaccessible to Ethiopian scholars who do not understand Ge'ez, let alone European scholars who do not understand either Ge'ez or Amharic. It is these hagiographies that the painter narrates in the paintings. The hagiographies of saints are not mere translations from other Christian texts, but are adaptations to Ethiopian particularities, and they stand as literary works of art in their own right. According to Ullendorff (1967), these hagiography texts "are conveyed into the spirit and ambiance of Christian Abyssinia". Writing lines are cyclical and recurring in all apocryphal and hagiographic texts, and one has to understand its layered meaning, the Wax and Gold of the language, which I will discuss below, if one is to indulge in the visual component of its narrative.

Ethiopian myths have multiple meanings, and are many times mutually constitutive, one becoming necessary for the other's existence, and they regulate the pace, range and distribution of values. However, their subtle and nuanced harmony and cohesion that simultaneously incorporates its enigmatic dimension has been complicated by the lack of written academic scholarship by local scholars who can relate to the fine distinction of the language that frames it. While pictorial and iconographic documentation are important reflections of the values and attitudes of Ethiopian society, the deficiency of written scholarship has often reduced these monumental art forms to shadows of their former selves. Instead, written scholarship had been dominated by scholars in an approach that pays little attention to the codex's meaning, often-times with problematic translations based on purely pragmatic grounds and in some cases on Eurocentric stereotypes.

While understanding the vernacular is crucial to translating, the obscurity, the ambiguity and the secrecy of these texts, being part of the culture, and its intricacies, also become important. Understanding Ge'ez, the liturgical script, is the best way to understand Ethiopian traditional art or Ethiopian religious script since the narrative of the paintings is solely based on hagiographies and apocryphal texts. Although some texts like the *Miracles of Mary* have been interpreted into Amharic, most still remain in Ge'ez. The script and the image are continuous, in that they are one while at the same time different. They come from the same source of mythic conceptions and beliefs. It is extremely difficult for secular people who are solely Amharic language speakers, a language that is directly derived from Ge'ez, to interpret liturgical scripts or meanings. It is also important to note that speaking and fully comprehending the deep layers of Amharic is by far preferable than not speaking at all if one is ever going to indulge in the analysis of Ethiopian Christian art.

The Amharic language itself is full of puns, wits and layered meanings. The Wax and Gold is the most dominant form of the poetic expression of the Amharic language. The apparent figurative meaning is called the Wax, while the hidden and significant meaning is called the Gold. "Wax and Gold," said philosopher Messay Kebede (1999), "is the art of discovering and reinstating the truth." Kebede believes that the Wax and Gold corresponds with the Ethiopian conception of the divine. "For the Ethiopian," Kebede (ibid) has said, "there is a fundamental duality in the nature of God and that the mystery of God and his omnipotence constitute the dyad appearance/essence."

Therefore, essence and appearance are fundamental in the conception of things. The Wax and Gold is prevalent in the everyday language of Amharic and is especially ubiquitous in the Ge'ez liturgical script. The concept of Wax and Gold is intrinsic in the images of Ethiopian traditional art, but the ontology of knowledge implicit in the paintings that is derivative of Ethiopian Orthodox religious studies is absent in the scholarly works of Ethiopian traditional art.

CURRENT SCHOLARSHIP OF ETHIOPIAN CHRISTIAN ART

As mentioned earlier, the academy that has framed Ethiopian traditional art is not organized by Ethiopian scholars, but by many Europeans, with Stanislas Chojnacki, a Pole who came to Ethiopia as a librarian in the early sixties, leading the discourse. Chojnacki is mainly concerned with formalist interpretations of classifications and techniques as well as Ethiopian paintings' influences from Western and Eastern art, rather than the mythology of the theosis. Although Chojnacki has lived in the country for over 40 years, he did not speak Amharic let alone understand the liturgical script Ge'ez. His scholarship is primarily object-centred, hence making it difficult for him to actually grasp the dyad of essence and appearance.

His foundational narrative is generally based on traveller's documents and colonial archives. Nevertheless, he remains to be the only scholar who has widely dealt in Ethiopian traditional art and his scholarship is the primary document that has set the introductory account of the subject.

WHY STUDY ETHIOPIAN CHRISTIAN ART IN CONTEMPORARY TIMES

The symbols that communicate the complex knowledge of good and evil, and the abstract truths and ideas about life and its meanings are major components in African aesthetics and particularly in Ethiopian Christian art. One sees in these images the existence of a whole different world that comes through mythological cryptograms that situates agency in the core of past analysis and that sheds light on present-day knowledge. Moreover, exploring these images opens up new possibilities against marginal perceptions and promotes conscious models of modernity that valorize those aspects of intellectual and creative activity that are excluded from mainstream art projects. Although scholarly works of Ethiopian Christian traditional art are predominantly based on the assumption that it lies outside the circle of African aesthetics, I believe that it is important to critically look at Ethiopian Christian art within an African experience. It is this fundamental link between African cultures that scholars should explore to bring a new insight into and interpretation of Ethiopian traditional art within African aesthetics and the integration of these two fields of knowledge into one discourse.

Investigating Ethiopian Christian art mediates the space between tradition and modernity, particularly that of the tradition of the Orthodox Church, its mysterious journey of the soul, and the understanding of the modern world within this theosis. The Orthodox icon, which elucidates the incarnation for humanity and the world and the possibility to attain union with God, is one of history's most sophisticated analyses of the nature and function of art. For many Ethiopian believers, icons of the Orthodox Church strictly serve as the link between the human and the divine and are only worshipped as instruments of miraculous intervention. They provide valour and strength in a world marked by tragedy and suffering. Yet for a few others in the same Orthodox Church, they serve as the antithesis of the immaculate and as medicine, or a mere synthesis of the pre-Christian vision of ancestors whose pristine purpose is to ward off evil with the power of devotional Christian texts. It is this unique blend of Ethiopian Orthodox Christianity that unifies pre-Christian indigenous practices with Orthodox religion that is fascinating. What is intriguing is the juxtaposition of fantasy and reality that is rooted in the cultural and historical reality of Ethiopia. Moreover, it is an aesthetic that best represents the intangible aspects of place and the religious naturalizing of the supernatural.

REFERENCES

Kebede, M. (1999). *Survival and Modernization: Ethiopia's Enigmatic Present: A Philosophical Discourse.* New Jersey: Red Sea Press.

Mercier, J. (1997). *Art That Heals, The Image as Medicine in Ethiopia.* Amsterdam: Prestel-Verlag.

Ullendorff, E. (1967). *Ethiopia and the Bible.* UK: Oxford University Press.

Relevance of Indigenous Languages and Oral Traditions of Africa

AKOSUA ANYIDOHO

INTRODUCTION

For several centuries, many African indigenous structures, systems of knowledge and practices have been branded barbaric and inferior to those of other cultures with which the continent has come into contact. Various religions and systems of education that have their origin in foreign societies and which the continent has embraced, have waged intense and continuous assault on African civilizations and sensibilities. However, in spite of the denigration, many African systems and practices have shown remarkable resilience and continue to be relevant in African societies. These enduring aspects of African cultural heritage include tangible and intangible elements such as religion, governance, judicial system, kinship, inheritance, rituals, customs, values and beliefs as well as languages. In this paper, we focus on the oral traditions of Africa to illustrate the preceding point.

LANGUAGE AND ORAL TRADITIONS

Language is the main resource in the creation, dissemination, storage and retrieval of oral traditions. Therefore, in this discussion we must first look at language, which is inextricably linked to most aspects of human life. The centrality of language in the cultural heritage of societies is well articulated by Kwesi Prah as follows:

> Of all these, that is, both material and non-material elements of culture, language is the central pillar and the transactional medium through which culture is created, shaped, adapted and adopted. As such, language is also a register of the records of humanity. It is indeed a representation of the history of humankind. It is the collective memory *par excellence* of its owners and users. That is why language is so crucial to development.[1]

Anyidoho in a recent paper[2] continues this argument in these words:

> Culture, it has been suggested, is not only a force of creativity but also the utilization of human intelligence for social development. But culture cannot achieve its creative and utilitarian potential without the vehicle of language. The fruits of human creativity and intelligence cannot be accumulated and disseminated without the vehicle of language.

From time immemorial, Africans have used oral traditions to document their systems of knowledge, histories and other invaluable resources. Since arguably there can be no oral tradition without language, the survival, maintenance and augmentation of the latter also depends on the effective use and development of the former. However, several centuries of education that employ mainly colonial languages has resulted in a tacit belief that African languages are not capable of "handling the full range of experiences associated with modernity."[3] This scholar and others have pointed to the inherent falsehood in such arguments. In the same paper mentioned above, Anyidoho provides an interesting observation of an early German missionary scholar, Jacob Spieth (1906), who made the following recommendation to the German colonial authorities and policymakers regarding the Ewe language used in West Africa. He quotes:

> Such a rich language, which is capable of further enrichment, would be highly suitable as a language of culture, education and trade and the greatest crime that Europe can commit against that tribe would be to suppress their most valuable native inheritance under European languages or even as much as declaim against it. If we want the Ewes to retain their valuable intellectual individuality, then we must seriously ensure that this language remains, and that the up and coming youth of that country develops an insight into the beauty and worth of their mother tongue.[4]

Needless to say that in many African countries, the indigenous languages were not given much attention during the colonial era and are still suffering from neglect as language policies in education continue to privilege colonial languages. One of the repercussions of this situation is that many educated Africans are unable to use their native languages proficiently. This sad fact, in turn, has negative consequences for oral traditions in that the youth are unable to acquire the relevant high-level language skills required for their sustenance and recreation. Furthermore, the role that oral traditions could play in socialization, societal cohesion, knowledge creation and dissemination and in development in general is neither fully appreciated nor exploited by the elite policy makers. Consequently, Africans lose out on the positive contribution that this cultural heritage could make in their lives.

THE IMPORTANCE OF ORAL TRADITIONS IN SOCIETY

Oral traditions are invaluable in societies that create them. A few examples of the benefits of oral traditions in the education of children would be relevant here.

Development of linguistic competence

Language development starts very early in life, and according to child language acquisition experts, by age five, children have already acquired their first language or mother tongue. Even though this view is generally accepted, it is known that children continue to acquire high-level linguistic skills after this period. For example, they continue to develop extensive vocabulary, listening skills, accurate pronunciation, variety of sentence structures, idioms, metaphor, euphemisms, etc. In societies where verbal skills are highly valued, linguistic competence must be linked with communicative competence, and exposure to a variety of oral traditions, such as storytelling, provides young people the opportunity to observe, practise and perfect their verbal skills.

Observational skills

Njoroge[5] has observed that oral artistic forms such as riddling depend a great deal on keen observation of plants, animals, insects, human life, colour, shape, size, similarity, oppositions and natural phenomena. One such oral tradition that fosters observation skills in children is the Akan verbal game called "epee" (verbal abuse, for want of a better word). The essence of the game is for the two contestants to take turns to compare parts of the opponent's body or something associated with or related to her/him to something else in the environment. The object of comparison must not be complementary and must have something in common with the named body part. The observational skills that young people acquire through their own creation and performance of riddles and other forms could stay with them throughout their lifetime.

Knowledge of societal norms, beliefs and expectations

Chesaina[6] has commented that each genre of oral literature has a part to play in the education of a particular society. While expressing the philosophy of a people and playing a therapeutic role, an oral text may satirize unacceptable behaviours and warn members against misdemeanour. Proverbs capture various elements of a people's wisdom, expressing a value in a terse, but vivid manner. Furthermore, characters in oral narratives are presented in such a way as to highlight strong qualities that members of a society value and to ridicule weaknesses that they are encouraged to avoid. In the context of storytelling, for example, children not only acquire communication strategies, but also learn morals and ethics through praise and criticism. "Oral literature, therefore, enshrines people's traditional culture"[7].

Memory and intellectual skills

Oral traditions provide training in recall and assist in the development of intellectual skills. As Njoroge has pointed out, the opportunity that oral texts provide for recall and re-narration of stories and riddles, for example, enhances memory, and the ability to construct new riddles or respond to opponents also engenders wit and speed in thinking. Furthermore, some oral traditions are based on the ability to understand double meaning. These and other intellectual skills that participation in oral traditions can bring about are of great value to individuals.

Personal development: self-esteem/self-confidence

Many children are often unsure of themselves when they have to talk in the presence of other people, apart from their parents and close relatives. However, as they grow and participate and excel in the performance of oral traditions within their peer group, and thus gain the respect of their friends, they gradually develop a positive image of themselves. Thus, participation in children's language games prepares young people for public speaking in the future.

Access to social history and worldview of society

In addition to the values discussed above, oral traditions afford young people the means of accessing knowledge about their cultural heritage, so that they can hand down its traditions and customs to new generations.

Entertainment

Oral performances also offer relaxation and interaction with others that, by and large, make the learning of norms of social interaction possible. As already indicated, mass media (mainly radio and television) now join, in the provision of this education to young people.[8]

Outlet of social criticism and commentary

In some African societies, the performance types of oral genres contribute to social cohesion and organization. The knowledge of these forms is therefore vital to young people in order that they would explore appropriate avenues to seek redress. Salm, et al.[9] inform, us that *halo* (poetry of abuse) of the Ewe people of Ghana is used to settle disputes or reduce hostilities within communities. As it is not appropriate to criticize people directly, *halo* offers a means to reduce aggression and provide social sanction. This verbal event is also a source of historical information about the families of the individuals involved in the contest.

Augmentation of local and global knowledge

In a general sense, the creation and recreation of knowledge give new generations the opportunity to add to the existing local corpus of knowledge, and, by implication, to global knowledge. Young people can play this vital role when they have deep insight into their cultural heritage and understand the modes of construction of the art forms. The knowledge needed to build on what is bequeathed to succeeding generations can come through exposure and participation.

In modern times it appears that the enterprise of education has been entrusted largely to the formal school system where most children spend a large part of their waking hours. One would expect that the school curriculum would make it possible for children living in oral cultures to get the exposure cited above. However, this does not seem to be the case. Some writers have lamented that oral forms are infrequently brought into the purview of academic institutions, thereby creating unequal exchange between local knowledge and global knowledge.

RESILIENCE OF ORAL TRADITIONS IN AFRICA

In relation to the preceding point, I hasten to add that despite this neglect in formal education, oral traditions are very much alive at the grassroots. These traditions have remained resilient as many of them have been adapted and re-configured in different forms and contexts.[9] For example, various forms of panegyrics are still important in the indigenous political life of several African societies. The *izibongo* of the Zulu and Xhosa of southern Africa have received extensive investigation and commentary. *Apae, the* royal appellation of the Akan of Ghana, performed in celebration of the achievements of kings, chiefs, nobles and leaders, is still treasured. Other forms that are highly utilized include songs and chants that belong to clans, family songs, love lyrics, children's forms, lullabies, work songs, personal praises, funeral dirges, and songs of divination. Various types of oral traditions also feature prominently in celebratory events that mark the arrival of babies, naming of infants, puberty, marriage and annual festivals. The survival of sophisticated traditions of storytelling and historical narratives is in evidence in South Africa, Mali and Senegambia.

Even as the socio-cultural, religious, political and economic contexts that gave rise to these verbal traditions continue to change, their inherent adaptability makes them relevant for today and tomorrow. This fact highlights contemporary understanding of "tradition," which emphasizes that traditions are not reified and fixed objects and ideas that are passed on from generation to generation. Rather, the concept embodies both continuity and change. Thus, oral traditions have the capacity for dialogic relationship with time and space. In this sense, many oral traditions in Africa continue to be useful to society through adaptation and adoption. For example, new religions, urbanization, Western-style political systems, print and modern technology have all influenced oral traditions and engendered new contexts, syncretic as well as new forms that have become part of the cultural capital of the people.[11] A few examples of the new forms and contexts are relevant here.

Even though the early Christian missionaries viewed many African oral performances as anathema to their faith, ironically, the survival and propagation of this religion in contemporary Africa have been enhanced by the use of the same forms that were once denounced. Among the Akans of Ghana for example, *Abibinnwom* (African melodies) features prominently in the liturgy of the Methodist Church. These songs combine indigenous Akan melody and Biblical texts. Similarly, in order to attract the youth, fast-paced, danceable African tunes, handclapping and backchannel cues are employed not only by the Pentecostal and the Charismatic churches, but the Orthodox ones as well. It appears that the Western-style hymns are unappealing to many contemporary African Christian congregations.

In the same vein, rather than these traditions disappearing as people migrate into cities and towns for work and commercial purposes, it has been observed that the migrants often take these resources along and adapt them to suit the changing industrial, urban and political environments. In Ghana, for example, there are numerous well established, commercialized urban "musical and cultural dance troupes", whose clients are often the elite. At another level, the performances provide avenues for the migrants to achieve psychological and emotional balance and healing amidst the multiple tensions and stress associated with city life. Modern technology, such as radio and television, has also engendered a shift in the contexts in which oral traditions were originally performed, just as "*ananse*" stories, which are part of the storytelling traditions, are now available on CDs and DVDs.

CONCLUSION

The discussion in the preceding paragraphs has highlighted the resilience of oral traditions and by extension other aspects of African cultural heritage in the face of the socio-cultural, religious, political, economic and educational changes taking place on the continent. This fact also points to the view that indigenous forms and practices of societies everywhere in the world are invaluable resources for understanding the present and for constructing the future. The task of nation-building and progress in Africa would be meaningful and sustainable when the cultural heritage and traditions of the people form the foundation blocks. Anyidoho[12] uses the following metaphor to emphasize this point.

> The fertilizer is indeed very helpful for the enrichment of our crops. But for it to work well, the crop must first take root in its native soil, and even after that, the fertilizer must be applied in carefully regulated measures and only when and as needed. Any overdose results in avoidable death for the crop. Unfortunately, even with the greatest care, constant application of the fertilizer soon leads to lower and lower yields, and in eventual exhaustion of the fertility of the soil.

In conclusion, it is important to observe that when the cultural heritage of each society informs its present and guides its future path(s), the potential result would be a healthy conglomeration of ideas and practices, all being part of the global arena and enriching human existence.

NOTES

1 Kwesi Kwaa Prah, *African Languages, African Development, and African Union*. CBAAC Occasional Monograph. No. 14, 2009, p. 18.

2 Kofi Anyidoho, "Culture: The Missing Link in African Development Planning" Presented at the Abant Platform Forumon AFRICA Between Experience in Inspiration. June 2013, Abant, Turkey. Unpublished, p. 19.

3 ibid.

4 Jacob Spieth, *The Ewe People: A Study of the Ewe People in German Togo*. Dietrich Reimer (Ernst Vohsen), 1906. Translated by Marcellinus Edorh, Emmanuel Tsaku, Raphael Avornyo. Accra: Sub-Saharan Publishers, 2011.

5 Njoroge, Joseph. 1994. "Oral Traditions in Education." In Austin Bukenya, Wanjiku M. Kabira and Okoth Okimbo (eds.) *Understanding Oral Literature*. Nairobi: Nairobi University Press, pp. 49–57.

6 Chesaina, Ciarunji. 1994. "Images of Women in African Oral Literature: A Case Study of Kalenjin and Maasai Oral Narratives." In Austin Bukenya, Wanjiku M. Kabira and Okoth Okimbo (eds.). *Understanding Oral Literature*. Nairobi: Nairobi University Press, pp. 85–92.

7 ibid.

8 Anyidoho, Akosua. 1994. "Tradition and Innovation in *Nnwonkoro*, An Akan Female Verbal Genre." *Research in African Literatures*, 25.3, pp. 142–159.

9 Salm. Steven J. and Falola, Tonyin. 2002. *Culture and Customs of Ghana*. Westport, Connecticut, London: Greenwood Press.

10 Anyidoho, Akosua. 1998. "Cross-cultural influences on Akan folklore." *Legon Journal of the Humanities*. Vol. X1, pp. 49–65.

11 Anyidoho, Akosua.1999. "Influence of Socio-Political Changes on Akan Royal Praise Poetry." In *Beyond Survival: African Literatures and the Search for New Life*. (African Literature Association Annual Selected Papers Series) Kofi Anyidoho, Abena P.A. Busia and Anne V. Adams (eds.). Africa World Press, pp. 85–108.

12 ibid., p. 1.

Senegalese Traditional Culture

Response to the conceptual note

OUSMANE SENE

WHEN THE TOPIC WAS SENT to me, I was just saying, of course, of course, of course and of course. As if you had a clear answer to the topic which is given for you to think about. And especially when you come from Africa because you say "tradition"—of course Africa. Unanimously in the world everybody will say yes, tradition and Africa go hand in hand although sometimes people will ask you to show them the real Africa. That is interesting. They come to Dakar and you make them visit the capital city. They will stop, scratch their head and ask you, "Can you show us the real Africa?"

Somebody else asked me a question in university: "What is Africa to you?" But these young overseas students will just tell you, give us the real Africa. What is exactly that? The Africa of drums, the Africa of mud huts or that of the proverbs? If you give them the drums and the mud huts, they will just enjoy it but if you pull them in the intricacies of proverbs, they will be hard put to decipher meanings!

And I was just thinking about a proverb. In one of his celebrated novels, *Arrows of God*, the famous Nigerian writer Chinua Achebe has one of his characters uphold the truth of his statement or pronouncement with the following proverb: "Wisdom is like a goatskin bag, everyone carries his own". It was his habit to spike his writings with proverbs. Proverbs are the palm oil with which words are eaten. Of course, if you have a gombo plus palm oil and you put a dash of it on your rice and you just gulp it in your mouth, it smoothly and beautifully slides in, no effort. And I was just thinking, this guy uses proverbs, and you look at the definition of proverbs, they are so old that you cannot date them. So very old that you cannot point out a date to proverbs except those that were coined during the colonial period because Africa was faced with an unprecedented situation and you had to clinch the new truth or realities by some new-fangled modern proverbs, but with the traditional ones, you have no dates. You have no author either. It is just produced by the community as they converse with nature and converse among themselves.

And I was just thinking about one that perhaps would be a good one to illustrate the new type of political rule that is democracy. And I relate democracy to what Achebe taking from his Yoruba ancestors relates to a goatskin bag, wisdom. Wisdom is like a goatskin bag, everyone carries his own. You have your goatskin bag. Among us present, we have 33 goatskin bags but each of us is wise. How come? That is a very interesting issue that through our goatskin bags we have diversity but each goatskin bag is a reality. Then you have diversity of reality because there are so many realities, each and every one of them absolutely real. This is perhaps how we illustrate democracy through African traditions. Those people who were born to speak English exclusively and who colonized Nigeria, I mean the British, if you ask them, how come wisdom is illustrated by a goatskin bag? How is the plurality of wisdom illustrated by a goatskin bag? That would be a task for them. This is where tradition comes in, because of how important it is in a time of modernity.

Indeed among Yoruba people a goatskin bag will always and forever be different. The skin of a particular goat has got patches and those patches are never the same from one goat to another. There are differences in colours. The goatskin among elderly Yoruba is hand-sewn. The pattern of hand-sewing will be always different from one person to another and even for the same person because if you sew two goatskin bags, there will be a moment when your hands are going to shake a little bit or a moment when you are going to call your child to send him somewhere, and when you begin again the pattern will never ever be the same. Also, if you belong to the group of my elder Olabiyi—I think he is Yoruba—you will fill your goatskin with what a Yoruba elder needs to survive, you will get many things but different things. One Yoruba elder will have a piece of chalk because he believes in peace and he travels in peace. So that when he visits you in your huts, he may use the chalk to trace two lines on the ground to just show you peace. This is going to be reinforced by the kola nut which may be red, which maybe white, it just depends, which he is going to share with you to illustrate peace. Well, he also wants to chew his tobacco, he may have a piece of tobacco. So not only the shape, not only the colour, but the content will always be different from one goatskin bag to another.

And we have here the illustration indeed of tradition, which is not only very old but also the instrument through which modern realities and modern truths can be experienced and can be implemented. For instance, there is an absolutely valid illustration of democracy which is a very old practice among African communities. Everybody has heard about the Palavra tree and under a Palavra tree if you want to clinch your truth, you will say, my father told me. Somebody else may say also, my father told me but it is a different story. Since in Africa elders never lie, your father will never ever lie one single minute. So no matter what my father told me, yes, because he is my father, and your father told you a different story, no matter how different it is, it is going to be the truth because it is your father.

So again you will ask me the question, who speaks in proverbs now? Yes, who speaks in proverbs? That is a question just like who speaks in tongues now. But it so happens that this is another dimension of Africa. We still speak in proverbs. And not only among older people who know the language, who know the tradition, but this way of speaking has been beautifully integrated by the youngest and apparently the most modern or, as they say, the most Westernized portion of our population. And this is exactly the instrument we are using in 2012 to change or to contribute to changing the political situation in Senegal. Because everybody knows that we had a presidential election in Senegal and it was rife with so many threats because we never had a president before like Abdoulaye Wade. A very complicated person creating problems every single day for Senegalese people although doing good things at the same time. But overnight one thing had to change because in the beginning he was told he would be voted in twice and not three times. He had a way of changing things that put us in a quandary. We did not know what to do. But it is young people and the very modern young people—you see them in their baggy trousers, in their basketball hats and they wear gold chains of course; you would say that they grew up in Harlem, they would dress like that—who had a way of creating songs into speeches with proverbs to tell us, if we are lost, let us go back to our true values, to the values coined, created by our ancestors, that is where the truth is. The proverbs were there and people woke up again and did the right thing, that is to say, voted in somebody else and asked Abdoulaye Wade, who was almost 85 years, to go to, not too early, to a well-deserved retirement home.

So we see these proverbs being used under different guises and different circumstances and also in a variety not only in shape but also in the content. These proverbs are in fact endowed with variety and originality. And talking of originality, some people's comments today have led me to think about another situation. As soon as they saw me, they congratulated me and said that I was wearing a very nice dress and they asked, is that your traditional dress? Even if they had said national dress, maybe it could relate to traditional. Yes, it was my traditional dress.

Yes, traditional dress is a very interesting issue. It does identify us as Senegalese because it stands as a representation of our tradition and culture. It is adapted from a garment which in the old days was brought in from Turkey (thus the local name of Turki). Even though an Egyptian brother participating in this conference said that they did not have a traditional dress because of the Turkey and Muslim factors, I should say that we, in Senegal, took the legacy we had from those same factors and turned it into something, an outfit, which really bears the stamp of the Senegalese genius, sartorial expertise and aesthetic inclination. Now, whether the dress is called Turki, Sabador or Wolof dress, it is recognized the world over as the Senegalese traditional outfit. Considering that in Senegal you are 95 per cent Muslim, so much so that the Christians sometimes hesitate to wear this. Or if they want to show that they are Christian but are as Senegalese as anybody else, they will wear it. What I am saying is that this dress, which looks like a Turkish way of dressing, of course represents Senegal because after all Islam came through Turkey, through the Middle East, and so on. What happened was that from the time this dress was introduced in Senegal, so many Senegalese seamstresses and tailors have shaped and reshaped it, adding, deducting, adapting, and adjusting to create something which is definitely Senegalese.

Another question, yes, this is the Senegalese dress. Fantastic, but do you know where this material comes from? Probably from some factories in Germany, very close to what you call Damask. And this is the most cherished material for any Senegalese to get their Senegalese dress made in. It is supposed to be rich, it is supposed to be the top of the top, it rustles when you move around, it smacks of opulence and stuff like that. So after Ramadan if you don't wear something like this, you do not count, you are nobody! So you should be wearing it.

Going to find fabric in a country which is so far away, going to select a design or adapt a design from a civilization which is so far away and working on it in such a way that you are going to be identified by it, not only you in the present but your ancestors as well—this boils down to something. That tradition after all may not be exclusive; it may be very inclusive because it is buried in the mists of time. We try to shape our identity in an exclusive manner but when we scratch the surface we see so many other contributions.

Cultural Identity and Social Development

A. PARSURAMEN

PEOPLE, COMMUNITIES, GROUPS AND INDIVIDUALS all over the world are striving for the preservation and protection of their cultural identity, to which they attach great value because they consider it an important part of their human dignity. Restricting or oppressing the expression and preservation of cultural identities may lead to a sense of confusion, alienation, exclusion and even violent conflict.

Asian culture or Indian culture or heritage is mostly composite in nature, variety and character. Traditional social values and thoughts provide a benign and supportive role to social change and development. In the history of Asia, especially that of India, outside intrusion and threat has always been a disturbance to the uninterrupted growth of traditional cultures and values. Safeguarding traditional cultures from these forces is essential. Tradition is inseparably linked not only with the present but also with the future. We have heard comments that our cultures and traditions are old-fashioned; they hold back progress in nation-building and that we should completely forget about them and adopt new ways of life. Many of us do not agree with all these comments because some of us are living examples of what our cultures and traditions did for us when we were young. They helped us develop and mould our attitudes and characters to be productive, useful, and live purposely and be progressive. T.S. Eliot in his very renowned essay entitled "Tradition and Individual Talent" stated that the present and future are tied together by many a tie with the past. The past influences the present and the present will exert influence on the past, too. The indigenous cultural heritage of most of the Asian countries became dormant after colonization which imposed a Western type of education and culture on them. In traditional Indian society, especially South Indian society, the aim of education was considered to be "soul-making". Since English education gave a lot of hope for government employment and other related services, the habit of studying the traditional texts written on palm leaves under the *gurukulam* (teacher and students living in one family) system started declining and the rare Tamil texts containing the rich experience and knowledge of the predecessors came to be considered as objects useless for an attractive worldly life.

Tamil society which has impressed the whole world by its excellence in the native systems of medical treatment and other arts has forgotten its heritage of medicine in due course. It is our responsibility to keep world history intact for tomorrow's children so that they may have the same opportunities to learn about the past and their own roots as we have. The example of Bharatanatyam which was not given due recognition even in the land of its birth in the so-called classical tradition has been recognized now globally. There is a great revival of herbal medicine of India. Indian yoga has become an attractive cultural commodity all over the world. When I speak about the relevance of traditional cultures for the present and future, I should make mention of the earliest Tamil grammar system *Tolkappiyam*, which was composed at least 2,000 years ago. It is still considered to be the first text written in Tamil.

Mauritius's, rich traditional cultures and indigenous systems would be lost if not regularly and with passion practised, properly recorded and preserved, and proudly and widely promoted. The young generations today need to practise the rich cultures of the country so that they are preserved for future generations. Our traditions and cultures will be lost if they are not passed on. Mauritius has very unique cultures and ways of life, but these were at high risk of Western influence. The blending of one culture with another also had the potential of killing off cultures. The challenge is to preserve our cultures by practising and making them a part of our lives. We must make an effort to sustain our cultures and not to depend on others.

Our culture is important to the future of our children and to our nation, because culture ensures a history, a past, present and certainly a future. It is therefore important, and absolutely necessary, to hand down such an important birthright and inheritance to an informed and prepared generation. The future of Mauritius lies in the hands of its children. They are our future! And they must carry our identity. They deserve to be cared for, directed, nurtured, and cultured, and prepared for the future of this nation.

By the way, what is culture? And why is it important? Culture has been defined generally as the totality of the way of life evolved by a people in their attempts to meet the challenges of living in their environment which gives order and meaning to their social, political, economic, aesthetic and religious norms and modes of organization, thus distinguishing a people from their neighbours. Culture should not be interpreted merely as a return to the customs of the past. It embodies the attitude of a people to the future of their traditional values faced with the demands of modern technology, which is an essential factor of development and progress.

Cultural policy is very important in order to incorporate such an essential part of our history into our general national development process because culture, as a force, has both its own economic and political consequences in the life of any nation. Culture is important because without it, a nation is as good as extinct, erased from the surface of the earth, blotted out, an existence without dignity or recognition. The only way to wipe out a people from the face of the earth is to take away their culture.

When we talk of self-reliance, self-sufficiency and national identity as the core of our national development, we refer to culture as the fountain spring of all policies, whether educational, social, political, medical or economic. Our strategies of national development would therefore depend on the understanding of the culture, the adaptation of its elements for political, educational and economic development as well as its strengths for social integration and development.

The importance of preserving our own cultural heritage escalates with each passing decade. As time goes on and people move from one country to the next or become too busy to reflect on their roots, the more it is at risk of endangerment. It is our responsibility to keep world history intact for tomorrow's children, so that they may have the same opportunities to learn about the past and their own roots as we have. At a time when we are all striving to be one people and minimize our differences for the sake of unity, we also need to understand the cultural heritage of other people and help each other celebrate our own uniqueness.

For a small country like Mauritius, preservation of its rich cultural heritage is critical to its very survival as a nation state. In addition to safeguarding a sense of identity in a rapidly globalizing world, the living cultural heritage is a source of human values and beliefs that are of eternal relevance and critical for sustainable development. The traditional beliefs and customs underpinned by a strong reverence for all sentient beings and an environment that promotes tolerance, compassion, respect and charity are fundamental values for harmonious co-existence between humankind and nature.

In addition to providing a strong sense of identity and values to all Mauritians, the preservation of the rich cultural heritage also provides a strong link and support between the individual and society at large acting as an effective social security net. The pursuit of individual self-interests during modernization often threatens the rich bonding of individuals as members of extended families and communities. It is necessary to preserve social bonds in which every one, whether children or elderly, are honoured and respected. The breadth and quality of social relations also lie at the root of happiness throughout a person's entire life, from childhood to old age.

UNESCO has responded to the warnings of researchers and anthropologists that intangible cultural expressions, such as oral traditions and literature, visual arts, music and performing arts, especially of minorities are fragile and easily lost. Among the actions taken by UNESCO was the recently formulated Convention for the Safeguarding of the Intangible Cultural Heritage. As stated in the convention, language is the main vehicle by which intangible cultural heritage, such as oral traditions and literature, is maintained. Thus, the safeguarding and preserving of languages is an important factor in the process of safeguarding cultures, especially among minorities whose cultural heritage is at greatest risk.

Due to their smaller populations and their lack of political influence, minority communities often face difficulties in achieving their goals, especially with respect to maintaining their own languages and cultures. One result of the large gap between indigenous and national cultures is that the majority population often perceives the minority groups among them as technically and economically backward. This has led to a certain blindness concerning the importance of safeguarding the less powerful languages and cultures (Condominas, 2003).

Traditional cultures provide us with ample data which enrich all our present and future studies. When poor communities preserve and develop their cultural assets, they are also generating new economic opportunities. It is possible for communities to generate income from cultural heritage and this creates employment, promotes tourism, stimulates micro enterprise development, fosters private investment and can reduce poverty.

The appreciation of people's own culture and heritage has important impacts on social development. Investment in cultural heritage can increase the awareness of a community's own identity, boost confidence and can be a factor in social mobilization and empowerment.

We are able to witness a rebirth of traditional value in most Asian countries and the West has now started coming to the East for gaining new knowledge. This has found powerful artistic expression in the poem entitled *Passage to India* composed by the American poet Walt Whitman. It was a vision or dream to Walt Whitman and Surbramania Bharathi in the early stages—now the dream has come to reality. This reality will establish the relevance of traditional cultures for the present and future and I am sure that India will be a leader in this direction.

Tradition: An African Overture

OLABIYI BABALOLA JOSEPH YAI

In my tradition, as arguably in all African traditions, a discourse on tradition is, by necessity, preceded and announced by a prolegomenon in two acts:

1. A ritual which may include a sacrifice;
2. A meta-discourse made up of incantations and magic or divinatory formulae. The function of this second part is specifically to inscribe, so to speak, the discourse to follow in a cartography and genealogy of discourses of its kind.

This prolegomenon should not be mistaken as a perfunctory formality. It is, quite to the contrary, of paramount significance. This is because tradition is conceived of as "very serious matter". Words to account for it are believed to be profound and heavy, only to be uttered by sages. A discourse on tradition is likened to "the head of an elephant" (àtàri àjànàkù in Yoruba), definitely not meant for the head or shoulders of youngsters.

The function of the second, metadiscursive part of the prolegomenon is, in addition, to remind its author that he or she is an element in a chain, a continuator of a long history in the collective enterprise tradition, however clever or creative he or she may be as an individual. Therefore, his/her contribution, whether knowledgeable and creative (*mimoonse*) or not-so-knowledgeable (ài moonse), is by force accepted by the ancestors as an accretion to their oeuvre.

The prolegomenon gives us a hint as to the nature and meaning of the concept of tradition in African philosophy and worldviews.

Since the advent of colonialism, it has been conventional and fashionable to oppose African tradition and modernity. This is, literally speaking, received wisdom, as it is foreign to African intellectual legacy.

Contrary to what some anthropologists have been saying, in chorus with uncultured Africans, African traditions are not reluctant to change and innovate. Indeed, in some African worldviews, change is an intrinsic part and a definitional element of tradition, so much so that the concept of modernity would be hard to translate into the language of such African cultures and worldviews, except through ultimately meaningless Europeanalizing linguistic acrobatics. Let me briefly exemplify with the Yoruba language.

In Yoruba, tradition is rendered by àsà. The word àsà derives from the verb *sà*, which means to choose, discern, discriminate, select, sort. When it is applied to a community, it describes a set of collective behaviours normally expected of individuals who have chosen it consciously and responsibly. In other words, in principle, àsà cannot be culture-imposed. Since àsà brings in the notion of choice, it can be said that Yoruba is part of a tradition open to innovation. Groups, lineages, ethnic groups, etc. have their own àsà, each forming a set that can be pictured as a chain with intersections. What is at stake in the context of African cultures is no change in itself. The concern of Africans is that, while changing, the social fabric remains whole, harmonious, holy, however drastic the elements of change. In that sense, tradition (àsà) is viewed as sacred. And colonialism is viewed as a desecration of African traditions precisely because it committed a rape on our ability to freely choose (*sà*).

To stress the relevance of traditions in our contemporary global world is therefore a most natural gesture in the intellectual tradition of Africans, considering the idea of tradition briefly explained above. To do so within the context of one single tradition is already a lofty enterprise. Envisaged at the level of the whole globe it takes on the features of a Herculean task. To use the Yoruba saying quoted earlier, our task can be likened to "lifting the head of innumerable elephants on our shoulders". A Herculean task no doubt.

But, in truth, this enterprise, however noble, would appear suspicious and even paradoxical in the eyes of cultured, non-alienated Africans. For, to begin with, given the nature and significance of tradition in Africa as briefly delineated above, how can one use for its adequate expression, the very instruments (languages) used by our colonial masters to demean it? This is a contradiction we, as bearers of African traditions, but using European languages to express them, should do well to acknowledge and keep in mind while we discourse on traditions.

It follows from the above observation that we owe to ourselves an additional debt of conceptual clarity and contrastive discursiveness as we talk of tradition in the global arena. From an African point of view, the concept of Tradition, one must insist, is a singularly plural concept, to use a deceptively facile oxymoron.

The very first issue, a gathering on tradition in the era of globalization, is confronted with is the unavoidable problem of translation and translatability of cultures. At the outset, a note of caution is particularly in order in this context. As, by necessity, we think between two or more languages and navigate between onomasiology (a method that starts from the referent and asks for the word) and semasiology (starting from the word and asking for its meaning) (Assman: 25) in our exchanges and discussions, we should endeavour to be and to remain individually and collectively, more of a *traduttore* than a *traditore* of our respective traditions.

The issue in this context is epistemological as it is ethical. Our exchanges and disquisitions are, "by accident of history", whatever meaning we read into that highly sibylline expression, conducted in imperial, hegemonic languages. Now, we do know for a historical fact that bearers of hegemonic languages and cultures are not exactly respecters, let alone preservers, of traditions they come into contact with. In the African context, their arrogance and intolerance largely accounts for the suspicion I identified earlier on in the minds of Africans. It will therefore appear that the African posture of doubt and suspicion about the ability of hegemonic languages to provide felicity conditions for the healthiest discourse on world traditions is ultimately a moral and epistemic posture. We must be acutely aware of these strictures on our disquisitions and their outcomes.

We live in a critical epoch. This is the major meaning of the 2008 global crisis which, sadly enough, has been under-analysed and underestimated as just another cyclical economic crisis of capitalism. Keeping in mind the theme of this meeting which is in itself an invitation to the principle of precaution, I prefer to apprehend the 2008 global crisis as a warning that Humankind, perhaps, is deteriorating. Our "global condition" as, Appadurai (Appadurai 2013) termed it, has ushered in a "hollow age", to borrow the words of Hölderlin. This poet, in his now celebrated poem titled "Brot und Wein" (Bread and Wine), asked the ever enduringly relevant question, in a line that has now become a wise and gnomic present to humankind:

"Und wozu dichter in durftiger zeit?" ("...and why poets in a hollow age?")

I suggest we adopt and reformulate Hölderlin's dictum to suit our preoccupation: "Why traditions in a hollow age?" Precisely because our "global condition" has neglected, undermined or killed traditions, these, in a manner of the "return of the repressed", are often manipulated by various groups to commit barbaric atrocities exactly antinomic to those values and principles that characterize traditions everywhere in the world. As a healthy and imperturbable reaction to the emergence of this parody of the concept of tradition and its use in pursuit of non-traditional values, many sages all over the world have been calling women and men of goodwill to "not commit the grievous sin of losing faith in Man". Tagore made this call in 1941, in an essay called "Crisis in Civilization" and in a context not dissimilar to ours. This is, *inter alia*, one reason for using the concepts of West and East in their Tagorean acceptations as an entry point to our discussion on Tradition. In his 1935 eponymous essay, Tagore had this to say:

> The modern age has brought the geography of the earth near to us, but made it difficult for us to come into touch with man. We go to strange lands and observe; we do not live there. We hardly meet men: but only specimens of knowledge. We are in haste to see for general types and overlook individuals.

Moving to cultural landscapes of the East, namely to Japan, he then added:

> And side by side, in the same soil, stands the modern world, which is stupendously big and powerful, but inhospitable. It has no simple-hearted welcome for man. It is living, yet the incompleteness of life's ideal within it cannot but hurt humanity.
>
> The wriggling tentacles of a cold-blooded utilitarianism, with which the West has grasped all the easily yielding succulent portions of the East, are causing pain and indignation throughout the Eastern countries. The West comes to us, not with the imagination and sympathy that create and unite, but with a shock of passion—passion for power and wealth. This passion is a mere force, which has in the principle of separation, of conflict.

To be sure West and East have evolved since Tagore's days and they have become more complex symbols, especially in our globalized world. Yet, it remains true that, as analytical tools, they have not altogether exhausted their respective entropies. Just to take, as an example, the central concept which is the object of our concern, most analysts will readily agree that traditions are more typical of the East than of the West, however we define East, West and tradition. Tagore characteristically does not pit a West against an East implied as the rest of us. His is not a reified West. He carefully avoids essentializing the West as a concept. This treatment of the West is reminiscent of a similar conceptualization of India in one of his letters to Andrews: "I love India, but my India is an Idea and not a geographical expression. Therefore I am not a patriot. I shall ever seek my compatriots all over the world". (Tagore 2009: 119).

Of importance is his distinction between general types as contrasted to individuals. The introduction of Japan as an element of comparison in this 1935 essay is no accident. It at once reinforces the non-essentializing nature of the concept of the West and anticipates our global world since Japan is geographically located in the East and shares many traditional cultural features with other elements thereof. East and West thus appear as heuristic tools used to understand human situations in constant change.

Certain ways of being, feeling or doing things, although they historically came into being in the geographical West, are now operating in the East along with Eastern ways of being, feeling and reacting.

Globalization has fractalized both West and East. West and East, both as ideas and as territories, have each become fractals. It may well be that what we call globalization is West-cum-East fractals work in progress. But progress towards what? That is the major question traditions must tackle.

An additional reason for colonials not to facilely jettison West and East as analytic categories is that the West, in its various ideological guises and disguises as progress, civilization, modernity, freedom, development, etc., has altered or suffocated many traditions, including in its geographical precincts. Their disappearance was often times presented as a prerequisite to progress and modernity conceived in the West but offered or imposed as universals of humankind.

Thus, the violence the West has imposed on its own traditions and traditional values, now ossified and folklorized, is offered to the entire humankind as a chreod.

Tagore, again:

> In India (and India is a synecdoche for what we now call the South) even when we are loudest in our denunciation of Europe, it is often her giant fortress that we long to build with awe and worship.

The West as fractals has now reformulated the world into "North" and "South". It is located in the hearts, minds and lifestyles of individuals, states and communities. Although a complex symbol, the "West" as fractals has enduring ingredients that characterize it, some among them being:

- Predilection for quantity over quality
- Profit for profit's sake
- Cold blooded utilitarianism
- Promotion of "having" over "being"
- Consumerism and individualism
- Indifference to environmental degradation

- Acceptance of war as a norm in the conduct of human affairs (culture of war)
- Debasement of spirituality and the sacred in general, resulting in ostentatious religiosity.

That West, as the 2008 cataclysm demonstrated, has exhausted its human/humane entropy. It risks taking humankind to the brink of suicide.

The question therefore is whether Tradition, the collective traditions of the entire world, can and should provide alternative redemptive resources to restore humankind. The first gesture towards providing a credible answer to that crucial question is a major intellectual investment in the restoration of traditions. The aim of this possibly lengthy and patient exercise is to have all world traditions dialogue and impregnate one another with a view to evolving a radically new set of values which will constitute a shared and credible foundation for a new human pact. This is a lofty agenda, based on the Tagorean rejection of "the grievous sin of losing faith in Man", a radically optimistic faith in the possibility of another world.

My guess therefore is that given the undeniable ability and propensity of the fractal West to resuscitate from the ashes of its victims, no patchwork on its robe will be the expected answer. What is needed, rather, is a rejection of the premises on which the governance of the world system is based and the search, in our traditions, of another set of premises that would inspire and guarantee the invention of new utopias in which solidarity, happiness, peace and emancipation are harmonized in and among individuals and communities.

To this end, I suggest we summon up our traditions and interrogate them about, *inter alia*, the following:

- The centrality of Values, including a critique of the concept of value and its avaricious avatars in the Global Condition
- The relevance and significance of such concepts as happiness in life, *sumak kwasa* (quechua) or *buenvivir*, *burkina*, *omoluabi*… etc., their contents and the possibility and felicity conditions of their emergence

- The conceptualization and actual treatment of the stranger, the strange and otherness in general
- Conceptualization and actualization of the woman-man interface, the status of women and the feminine principle in life
- Their ideas about other beings, Nature, the Environment and the relationships between them and human beings
- The status and role of poetry and the arts in general
- Spirituality
- The afterlife; life and death.

In conclusion of this African overture to our debates on tradition, I'd like to offer a few articles or principles of *Kurukan Fuga* or the *Mande* Chart as an illustration of one way Africans reacted to a crisis in civilization.

Between the 10th and the 12th centuries, the Ghanaian empire, a major West African polity, suffered wars and turmoil. It eventually disappeared, incapable of resisting the numerous invasions of intolerant Almoravid Muslim warriors. Another polity known as the Mali empire was born. The eventual victor emperor Sunjata, now converted to Islam, knew that it was far easier to win a war than to win the hearts of the people of the empire, thereby establishing a durable peace. In his wisdom, he now endeavoured to establish the new empire on new, solid and consensual principles. Hence the birth of the *Kurukan Fuga* Chart, named after the place where warriors and sages met to agree on the laws or principles that would be the foundations of the new polity. These principles were 44 in number. Here are a few among them:

PRINCIPLE/ARTICLE 3

The Nyamakala (literally those who are above all taboos) have a duty to tell the truth to the leaders and to be their advisers. Through the verbal arts, they shall be the advocates of established law and order throughout the territory.

PRINCIPLE/ARTICLE 5

Every person has a right to life, to the preservation of his/her physical integrity. Therefore, any attempt to take another person's life is punished with the death penalty.

PRINCIPLE/ARTICLE 7

Among the Mande, an institution called *Sunankuya* (teasing or humour parenthood) and *Tanamannyonya* (Blood Pact) were created. Consequently, no argument between these groups should degenerate; respect for the other being the rule. Between male and female in-laws, between grandparents and grandchildren, tolerance and humour should be the rule.

PRINCIPLE/ARTICLE 9

The education of the children is the responsibility of the entire society. Paternal authority is invested, consequently, in all citizens.

PRINCIPLE/ARTICLE 13

Never offend wordsmiths (the Nyamakala).

PRINCIPLE/ARTICLE 14

Never offend women. They are our mothers.

PRINCIPLE/ARTICLE 16

In addition to their daily duties, women shall be involved in all aspects of governance.

PRINCIPLE/ARTICLE 17

Lies that have survived 40 years should be regarded as truths.

PRINCIPLE/ARTICLE 22

Vanity is a sign of weakness and humility is a symbol of nobility.

PRINCIPLE/ARTICLE 23

Never betray each other. Honour your word.

PRINCIPLE/ARTICLE 31

Let us help those who need help.

PRINCIPLE/ARTICLE 36

Helping oneself with the produce in a farm to satisfy one's hunger is not stealing as long as one does not take produce away in a bag.

PRINCIPLE/ARTICLE 38

Before you set fire in a bush, do not look downwards, but raise your head towards the top of the trees and see whether they carry flowers or fruits.

Each of the enunciations quoted above deserves a thorough exegesis explaining the historical context of its emergence as well the extent of its enduring relevance. This is an exercise better left for a different forum.

In a celebrated essay, Talal Asad once suggested that peoples who live in the "East" in Tagorean acceptation may well be described as "Conscripts of Western Civilization" (Asad 1992; Scott 2004). In the same vein and before him, Friedrich Engels positively assessed and approved of French colonialism in Algeria and the tragic events that it ushered in because for him they precipitated Algeria from a pre-capitalist mode of production to capitalist mode of production, another variation on the theme of "conscription to modernity". The problem with these interpretations of history is that they invariably undermine local agency and traditions, then surreptitiously dubbed "subaltern". No doubt, this is seeing history through the lenses of the victor, or the hunter's narrative, as different from the lion's. Conscription is in essence an act of violence and no individual or community should choose to be a conscript under minimal conditions of freedom. This is precisely what all traditions of the world have been stridently suggesting; conscription to Western civilization cannot beget emancipation and peace. Before our eyes, the structure of power is shifting from West to East, from the North to the South. There are new emerging forces; they are called BRICS or Chindiafrica. It is too early to declare that this development is something to write home about. The pitfall to absolutely avoid is for the new polities to individually or collectively seek to "beat the West in its own game", while the majority of their populations crave a new world based on the values of their traditions.

Aimé Césaire, the visionary African poet, once wrote these words about renewal of traditions of Africa and the African diaspora, which I offer as an inspiratory viaticum for our discussions of Tradition.

"La relance ici se fait par le vent qui d'Afrique vient
La relance ici se fait par l'influx plus encore que par l'afflux".
(The resurgence here is achieved through the wind that comes
from Africa
The resurgence is achieved more through the influx than the afflux).

BIBLIOGRAPHY

Acosta, Alberto, Le BUEN VIVIR. *Pour imaginer d'autres mondes.* Les Editions Utopia, Paris, 2014.

Appadurai, Arjun: *The Future as Cultural Facts: Essays on the Global Condition.* Verso, London 2013.

Asad, Talal, 1993: "Conscripts of Eastern Civilization" in Christine Gailey, ed: *Dialectical Anthropology: Essays in Honor of Stanley Diamond,* Vol 1. University Press of Florida, Gainesville.

Assmann, Jan: "Translating Gods: Religion as a Factor of Cultural (Un) Translatability" in Sanford Budick and Wolfgang Iser: *the translatability of cultures*; Figurations of the space Between. Stanford University Press, Stanford, California, 1996.

Celhto: *La Charte De Kurukan Fuga: Aux Sources d'une Pensée Politique en Afrique.* l'Harmattan, Paris 2008.

Cesaire, Aimé: MOI, LAMINAIRE (Poèmes): *Editions du seuil,* Paris, 1982.

Hölderlin, Friedrich: *Œuvre Poetique Complete.* Edition bilingue. Editions de la Différence 2005, Paris.

Ogundeji, Adeotun & Akangbe, Adeniyi, eds. *OMOLUABI: Its Concept and Education in Yoruba Land.* Ibadan Cultural Studies Group. 2009, Ibadan.

Scott, David: *Conscripts of Modernity: The Tragedy of Colonial Enlightenment.* Duke University Press, 2004.

Tagore, Rabindranath, 2008 (1996): *The English Writings of Rabindranath Tagore* Vol II Plays Stories, Essays, Sahitya Akademi. New Delhi.

Tagore, Rabindranath, 2006 (1996): *The English Writings of Rabindranath Tagore* Vol III. Miscellary. Sahithya Akademi. New Delhi.

Yai, Olabiyi Babalola: "In Praise of Metonymy: The Concepts of "Tradition" and "Creativity" in the Transmission of Yoruba Artistry over Time and Space". in Abiodun, Rowland, Drewal Henry J & Pemberton III, eds: *The Yoruba Artist*: New Theoretical Perspectives on African Arts. Smithsonian Institution Press Washington and London 1994

Adapting Traditional Cultures to Modern Needs

MOHAMMAD AMIR KAMAWAL

AT THE START OF THE 21st century, we find ourselves caught between two contemporary cultures, the traditional and the Western. Most people find it difficult to accept both cultures. And the odds are that they will neglect the traditional ones in favour of the Western. Some people, especially the young, think that traditional culture is old-fashioned and that we should forget about it and adopt a new way of life.

A nation cannot be erased from existence, unless you destroy its culture. There are many examples in history of traditional cultures resisting and surviving cultural attacks. For instance, the rule over Bulgaria by the Turkish Empire for more than 500 years could not force the native people to forget their traditional culture. Some people fled to the mountains and tried to preserve their traditional culture and religion. They passed their knowledge to the next generations for nearly 500 years, and in doing so they proved that even a powerful army (Turkish Empire) cannot destroy your traditional culture by force.

Traditional culture and its consistency with globalization is considered an issue of historical and cultural importance. There is no doubt that today though the world is closely linked through modern technology and all countries are bound through globalization, it is a fact that ancient and traditional culture cannot be forgotten.

Human civilization is variously defined by famous scientists. Some people believe that the final stage of culture is called civilization. It follows from this definition that the basis of civilization was constructed by traditional culture in the ancient world, especially in centres of ancient civilizations (Egypt, Mesopotamia, Greece, Rome and the India region). Culture expresses the customs, traditions and attributes of a nation presented by folklore at a specific time.

The important issue of this international conference is this. In my opinion, there is no doubt that the people of the world are bound to join with one another through globalization and not remain backward. It is important though to bear in mind that no nation and country can forget its traditional and tribal culture. For instance, we are living in a century in which modern technology has reached a very high point of its development but it also seems that today, to advance, the world urgently needs to restore and respect its traditional cultures.

This discussion is a long discussion. In my opinion, the world today must endeavour to go forward step by step with globalization while considering how best to protect its culture, ensure that on the one hand it does not forget its culture and on the other be associated with globalization.

But advances in technology and modernization offer a different kind of threat. Since modernization improves quality of life significantly, its effect is more severe. But in many parts of the world we can see that traditional cultures have adapted well to modernization and have used modernization in a more sensible way while at the same time preserving the core of tradition and also passing it down to the next generation.

Over the course of history, Afghanistan has been subject to invasion by many great and mighty empires. The culture of Afghanistan has been influenced by those culturally rich empires such as the Greek, Persian, Indian and Arab.

Over the course of the last century and most recently as a result of civil war and globalization, the culture of Afghanistan has been influenced by Western cultures. The effect of Western culture and advancements in technology can be felt even in the smallest rural areas of Afghanistan. A more detailed study will, however, reveal that not only has Afghanistan retained its traditional culture but will also have its fair share of significance in the world of the future. If advancement of technology can reach and affect even the smallest rural areas of Afghanistan, then the same route can be of great significance for introducing traditional Afghan culture to the Western world.

The role and effect of great traditional non-Western cultures such as African, South American and Asian, can already be felt in the modern world, and they will be of huge significance in the future. As an example, Chinese acupuncture is practised in all countries and is also part of the anaesthesia department in many Western hospitals.

Another example would be the introduction of traditional Asian, African and South American food all over the world, like Afghani food in India and other countries and Indian food in Japan and other countries of the world. The fact that a 3,000-year-old Chinese or Indian dish is today served in many Western restaurants shows that traditional Asian, African and South American cultures have preserved their significance in the modern world.

Overall, modernization will have an effect on all traditional cultures. Advances in telecommunication and the Internet have made this effect more significant in recent years. Traditional cultures have been very flexible in adopting changes that improve the quality of life. Anything that improves the quality of life should be considered positive and should be adopted in a meaningful way in all traditional cultures.

We can look at some examples in Afghanistan. The traditional culture of Afghanistan has been very positive about the changes that modernization brings in areas of medicine, education and telecommunication. Those changes will improve the quality of life in Afghanistan, and we are ready to adapt to these changes. On the other hand, the impact on music and clothes has been of great concern in Afghanistan. From a detailed study, we can notice that although Western music and clothes have reached even the smallest towns and villages in Afghanistan, at the same time in large cities, such as the capital Kabul, we can notice that all Afghan people at least once a day still dress in our traditional dress and listen to traditional Afghan music.

Over the course of history, traditional cultures have maintained their character and have adapted well to the positive side of modernization. In the future not only will traditional cultures survive but will also have their say in the shaping of the new global order. Some elements of traditional culture will be lost, some will be modified and adapted to modern-day needs, but the core will always survive and serve their nations.

CONCEPTS

Culture: Culture is made of the characteristics of a particular group of people, defined by everything from language, religion, cuisine, social habits, music and arts.

Eastern culture: Eastern culture generally refers to the societal norms of countries in Far East Asia (including China, Japan, Vietnam, North Korea and South Korea) and the Indian subcontinent. Like the West, Eastern culture was heavily influenced by religion during its early development. In general, in Eastern culture there is less of a distinction between secular society and religious philosophy than there is in the West.

Western culture: The term Western culture has come to define the culture of European countries as well as those such as the United States that have been heavily influenced by European immigration. Western culture has its roots in the Classical Period of the Greco-Roman era and the rise of Christianity in the 14th century.

Latin culture: Many of the Spanish-speaking nations are considered part of Latin culture, while the geographic region is widespread. Latin America is typically defined as those parts of Central America, South America and Mexico where Spanish or Portuguese are the dominant languages. While Spain and Portugal are on the European continent, they are considered the key influencers of what is known as Latin culture, which denotes people using languages derived from Latin, also known as Romance languages.

Middle Eastern culture: The countries of the Middle East have some but not all things in common, including a strong belief in Islam and religion is a very strong pillar of this society. The Arabic language is also common throughout the region; however, the wide variety of dialects can sometimes make communication difficult.

African culture: The continent of Africa is essentially shaped by two cultures—North Africa and Sub-Saharan Africa. The continent comprises a number of tribes, ethnic and social groups. One of the key features of this culture is the large number of ethnic groups—some countries can have 20 or more—and have great diversity in beliefs as well.

Relevance of Traditional Culture—Facing the New Challenges

SAMIRA HANNA EL DAHER

IS TRADITIONAL CULTURE RELEVANT TO today's world and to the future? This is the question at the heart of the paper. But first, what is traditional culture, or ancient culture? It is, I believe, what centuries of wisdom and experience have built up block by block and left for us. But it is also surmised that traditional cultures are those that do not belong the First, economically developed world. In this context, their value is not considered significant.

Democracy, Dialogue of Civilizations, Dialogue of Religions—these are the catchphrases used to address today's problems: problems of insecurity, war, hate, terror. The last time anyone spoke of Love was at Woodstock. Today, we talk of Tolerance, which is not inclusive in the real sense, and is nothing more than mere acceptance of others. So how and with what are we going to meet the new challenges of this new century? What is democracy for most peoples of the world? How does it impact the way we think and act? Are acts of violence the voice of the right to free expression and to choose leaders? Or, are we not more ready to die to preserve our identity, our heritage, our culture?

The first and most well-known programme is UNESCO's identification and preservation of World Heritage Sites. But this does not mean only old stones, or manicured tourist spots. It is, instead, a realization of the relevance of traditional cultures today. Those living in so-called Third World regions of Africa, Asia and Latin America, are in fact, living richer lives that do not necessarily revolve around economic prosperity.

If we look around us today, war and terror have become endemic. Conventions after conventions have not been able to make a dent, offering lip service to the problem. It seems to me that the answer lies in going back to the basics. A computer cannot reach the soul of human beings! Technology cannot ensure that people live with dignity, a desire people the world over have. Connectivity is not everything. To answer the challenges of today's world, from globalization to war and conflict resolution, peace programmes, conferences and talks have only touched the surface of the problem. The world is in urgent need of working and workable solutions.

A few examples of the value of traditional cultures follow.

UNESCO's Culture of Peace Program aims for peace and strengthening of democracy, as also education and sustainable development. But isn't the concept of peace and non-violence as old as the hills, as Gandhi said? Are they not at the core of Indian and Buddhist traditions? Similarly, the Mesopatomians and the Arabs are heirs of the Natufian culture that valued mediation, negotiation and even consensus to prevent conflicts. The still well established institution of *Kaddy-al-Solh* attempts to judge and work towards an amicable way of preventing, solving or reconciling conflicts. The methods are still valuable, but rules and rituals are to be respected.

The Non-Aligned Movement, of which Jawaharlal Nehru, Gamal Abdel Nasser and Sukarno were an integral part, is the direct heir of the ancient tradition to seek peace and peaceful solutions, to save humanity and preserve the land—the fallow land system of old assured the fecundity, the fertility and fruitfulness of mother earth; it avoided the depletion of agricultural resources that is rampant today.

The Trace of God in the Christian Middle Ages gave spiritual sanctions to limit the violence of feuding. It gave a chance not only to the fighters and the wounded, but also created space for negotiations. Similar is the case with the modern form of Truce of the Gods in Africa.

The Code of Honour of Bushido of the Samurai too was based in a moral way of life: the Code of Donson-Ton focused on deep respect for human life; the Brotherhood of Hunters in Africa: the Griots of Manding in the Empire of Mali (1235) could be considered the first Human Rights charter, some seven centuries before the Universal Declaration of Human Rights. They have maintained a remarkably unified culture, and still rely on their Griots to remind them of their glorious place in history. This sets the basic yardstick for human behaviour. Solidarity in tribes and villages has for long avoided misery.

The Putin/US declaration for improving bilateral relations and honouring the dignity of people; or Khrushchev's visit to the US and his interaction with the Mayor of Los Angeles in 1959; US intervention in Somalia, initially for humanitarian reasons that were seen as American generosity—these are all examples of human dignity.

The Dialogue of Civilizations, the Dialogue of Religions, etc. are nourished by the Annals of Confucius, the teaching of Socrates, the Sumer and Indian traditions, and certainly by the cultural symbiosis of the three monotheist religions in the time of Al-Andalus between the 8th and 13th centuries AD in Europe. They lived together, not merely tolerated each other.

It was the time of the development of al-Ijtihad—or the process of reasoning and questioning in jurisprudence and of the questioning of all knowledge. It was used and taught by Middle Eastern Renaissance men, and the relevance of their teachings about science are quite modern. But science sans conscience will only lead to the destruction of the human being, overtaken and overridden by the virtual brain in the era of robots and the discoveries about the functioning of the human brain.

Respect and solidarity are the cement of living together in peace: they hold together human societies and our old civilizations; they help keep our culture, indeed all culture, alive.

Ancient cultures have put and kept human beings at the centre of life and today, more than at any other time, traditional cultures and old civilizations can point the way to solutions.

Significance of Chinese Thought in the Contemporary World

HAIMING WEN

WHILE SIGNIFICANT CULTURAL COMMUNICATION BETWEEN China and the West has only gone on for about 400 years, the impact of Chinese thought on the ancient world started more than a thousand years earlier. After Indian Buddhism first came to be accepted by Chinese people around two thousand years ago, Chinese thought began to communicate with Indian, and its influence on other civilizations continued to grow. In most historical periods, including the famous Tang (619-907), Song (960-1279) and Ming (1368-1644) dynasties, Chinese thought had a profound and persistent influence over China's neighbouring countries, especially Korea, Japan and Vietnam, and the Confucian cultural circle, lasted over a millennium. In ancient times, Chinese thought influenced the world through the channels for trade like the Silk Road, and other similar paths for communication between China and the West have increased over the last four centuries. However, as Ji Xianlin, a late leading scholar on Sino-Indian Studies, once mentioned,

> Sino-Indian relations suffered a major setback because of colonization by European powers. Their aggressive power shattered the basic social structure of Indian society, and hence their firm and solid culture could not develop further. After the mid-19th century, under the aggression of capitalist countries, China also turned into a semi-colonial, semi-feudal society. People of both countries

India, it is an everlasting tradition and deep-rooted belief that humans should live in a just society, and that people should fight for it if they find themselves living in unjust conditions.

Second, Chinese thought can bring universal values to our world. The Chinese civilization is one of the enduring ancient civilizations still in existence today, and its core is Chinese philosophy, which determines both Chinese people's thought paradigm and their social living patterns. In ancient Chinese philosophy, there are universally valid concepts like benevolence, righteousness, ritual, intelligence and trustworthiness, which were common truths in ancient times, and these humane values have proved to have universal importance across the millennia. Before China's communication with the West, China had remained a leading power and one of the most civilized nations for over a thousand years. People in other countries studied these values and incorporated them into their own thought. India and China share a history of cultural communication of more than a thousand years, with these two great civilizations devoting themselves to the journey of crossing the gap of the Himalayas to greater or lesser extents at different times and this communication can shed much more light on the contemporary world than any other historical time in human history. Today, Chinese universal values are still evident in Chinatowns and Chinese cultural circles around the world, and their influence should be extended to other communities. The traditional, universal ancient values are still rooted in the minds of today's Chinese people, and sustain their basic worldview. No matter where Chinese people go, they embrace a basic worldview of mutual benevolence, family values and filial piety, which effectively maintains the Chinese community as it moves forward and develops. Cultural ambassadors between China and India, like Xuanzang (596-664) in the Tang Dynasty and Poonam Surie, etc. have set a concrete foundation for future communications. Their works have showed that even when China as a nation suffered, her people still valued the universal values in their daily lives.[2] These universal values were national guidelines for ancient China, and they share similar importance to their Western counterparts, freedom and democracy. Therefore, people of other civilizations should recognize and support these Chinese universal values and concepts, and join the process of helping Chinese ancient core values become truly universal once again. Confucianism, Daoism and Buddhism all advocate that being humane, benevolent to all living creatures are fundamental values for the flourishing of human society and these values are deeply rooted in our ordinary and familial lives.

Third, like Indian Buddhism and Hinduism, Chinese philosophy helps people's minds become peaceful, thus bringing more inner-peace to every person's life. In the Han Dynasty (206 B.C. – 220 A.D.), under the influence of Indian Buddhism, Chinese Daoist philosophy evolved into the Daoist religion, and the quiet-sitting idea in the *Daodejing* and *Zhuangzi* developed to become a systematic practice in the Daoist religious tradition, remaining influential across the world today. Chinese culture is a culture of great openness. From ancient times to the present, many different thoughts in China have been engaged in peaceful dialogue with each other, especially among China's many different religious groups. In most historical times, Islamic religious groups found no problem living peacefully with China's local communities. The cultural openness and peaceful mind involved in harmonizing various religions is very significant for a contemporary world that is full of conflicts among religions or civilizations. Many different religions have had diverse impacts on China, and Christianity has become more and more influential, especially in the last 400 years, but China remains a peaceful environment for most religions, and very few wars or conflicts have happened among religious groups. This is because Chinese philosophy has played a mediating role among different religions. On the one hand, Chinese philosophy can reduce religious dogmatism, and on the other it can help other religious groups to be more open and less exclusive, so it can help sustain a harmonious and peaceful situation throughout history. Chinese people have strong religious feelings, especially to their ancestors, but their religious feelings did not develop into a religion of worshiping transcendent deities, rather asking people to rely on their own efforts.[3] Thus, Chinese people developed a tradition of systematic harmonious lifestyles which has gone on to influence many neighbouring countries. Ancient Chinese philosophies like Confucianism, Daoism and Buddhism function in common people's everyday lives and their inner minds. Ancient Chinese people documented their wisdom about how human beings should deal with the changing world, and this kind of wisdom is still meaningful and powerful in the contemporary world, not only for Chinese people, but for all humankind. For example, while Confucianism and Daoism are typical examples of Chinese thought, Chinese Buddhism was not only a new version of Indian Buddhism, but full of Chinese wisdom, so these Chinese philosophies would continue to play a significant role in our everyday lives. Just as Indian Buddhism evolved into China Buddhism, and Chinese Chan Buddhism later transmitted to Japan and became Japanese Zen Buddhism, the recreation of cultural traditions is one of the most amazing products of ancient cultural communication, and we have a duty to continue this beautiful becoming of human cultures.

Fourth, Chinese historical experience can bring peace to the world. In a global village like ours, Chinese ancient wisdom is a valuable resource for humans to live together peacefully, to help heal this world and create a better world. Chinese people have a long historical experience of governing an enormous state for over more than 2000 years, and have forged a unique path of sustaining such a great power in harmony and peace. This kind of historical experience is very valuable for the whole world to live and develop together. As Nalin Surie points out, India and China share many social, economic, political and cultural traditions, and problems due to the size of the nation, population and long history of cultures, so the cultural communication between India and China is the most important instance of reviving ancient peaceful cultural relations. As a nation that has been imbalanced for millennia, but remained relatively united throughout most historical times, the "China Model" and Chinese experience are very valuable for the whole world. China is not only the most populous nation, but also a nation with the most detailed documents of governing experience. Chinese thinkers are very anxious to help not only their own nation and people, but also to work hard to make sense of their past experience on terms which can influence the modern world. For example, by borrowing wisdom from Confucianism and Legalism, Chinese people have come up with a system of balancing power, to enhance the stability and prosperity of society, which is now called the "China Model" or "Beijing Consensus", and it can play an extremely important role for the world in a historical moment in which it suffers from economic crisis, political dangers and religious conflicts. The relevance of Chinese thought for today's China and the world is clear: through the process of internationalizing Confucianism, Daoism and other Chinese schools of thought, Chinese people, together with the people of the whole global village, can help people pursue their greater happiness.

In short, Chinese thought can promote justice and universal values, while simultaneously spreading inner peace for every individual and outer peace for the world as a whole. I hope all prominent minds and leaders of the world will take Chinese thought seriously, and promote Chinese thought for the future of humankind. In the Song and Ming dynasties, in responding to the challenges from the Chinese Buddhism, which itself was another version of Indian Buddhist traditions in China, Neo-Confucian philosophers developed their systematic philosophical arguments, and Chinese philosophy reached one of its peaks in history. Today, facing challenges from Western philosophies and civilizations, like their ancient forerunners' responding to Indian thought, Chinese thinkers focusing on Confucianism, Daoism and Buddhism are making efforts to continue the tradition of cultural communication between China and India, and in doing so, they would like to shape world culture into an ever more flourishing and harmonious one.

NOTES

1 Ji Xianlin, "History of Sino-Indian Relations," in Tan Chung, Zhang Minqiu and Ravni Thakur ed. *Across The Himalayan Gap: A Chinese Quest for Understanding India*, New Delhi & Seattle: India International Centre in association with Konark Publishers Pvt Ltd. 2013, p. 100.

2 Poonam Surie, *China: A Search for its Soul, Leaves from a Being Diary*, Konark Publishers Limited, 2010.

3 In light of Syyed Hossein Nasr, we might say that the Chinese cultural tradition is composed of many different traditions, like Confucianism, Daoism and Buddhism, etc., but nearly all of them are not "earthly manifestations of celestial archetypes related to... the Logos or the World...the Universal Logos and the Universal Logos as such." See Syyed Hossein Nasr, "What is Tradition?" in *Knowledge and the Sacred*, p. 74.

Zen, Its Origin and the Future

ATSUSHI IBUKI

PREFACE

Zen is a religion or a thought that was born in China. But it was introduced to the West through Suzuki Daisetsu's (鈴木大拙, 1870-1960) English works; therefore, the Japanese word "Zen" rather than the Chinese word "Ch'an" is generally used to refer to it. If Suzuki was a Chinese, do you think Zen would have spread as "Ch'an"? I don't think so. Because I think one of the most important reasons for the spread of Zen to the West was that the Zen introduced by Suzuki was Japanese Zen. Japanese Zen follows the tradition of the Song and the Yuan dynasty, but in China, Zen changed very much after the Yuan dynasty.

The philosophical viewpoint of the original Zen Buddhism was represented by four slogans:

1. Free yourself from the letters of *sutras* (不立文字)
2. The transmission of the Buddha-mind beyond *sutras* (教外別傳)
3. Become aware of the absolute value of your mind (直指人心)
4. Become one with the Buddha to become the enlightened one (見性成佛)

But, after the Yuan dynasty, Chinese Zen proceeded in the opposite direction, and the thoughts of "the reconciliation of Zen and the studies of sutras" (教禪一致) and "the reintegration of Zen and Pure land practice" (禪淨雙修), which are in conflict with the original Zen thought, became

Suzuki Daisetsu (鈴木大拙)

the mainstream of Zen in China. I recognize that Zen was widely accepted throughout the world because it was Japanese Zen that had maintained the original thought and vigour.

What matters here is why Zen, which was of Chinese origin, was able to have firm roots in Japan. In Suzuki's opinion, the reason is the affinity of Zen thought with the character of the Japanese. But, as we do know, it was Suzuki's effort that contributed to the spread of Zen in Europe and America. We cannot thus help thinking that Zen may not only be compatible with the Japanese, but may be universally compatible.

As Confucianism and Daoism suggest, Chinese thought has its base in the unique nature of Chinese society, therefore it is hard to spread to outside of China. Then, why could Zen get the universality? What is its universality at all? Is the universality still valid in the present time? To answer these questions, we must know the origin of Zen.

1. ORIGIN OF ZEN

The four slogans I just mentioned were established as the manifestation of the philosophical position of the Zen sect in the Song dynasty. These contents can be interpreted as follows:

1. The value of *sutras* is limited, because enlightenment can't be expressed by words.
2. Therefore, we must practise under an enlightened Zen master's directions to attain enlightenment.
3. Enlightenment is not unusual status at all and it should be obtained in ordinary life.

We do know that these points were already in the East Mountain Teaching (東山法), which was the direct origin of Zen, and also in the teachings of Bodhidharma (菩提達摩) and Huike (慧可), who are regarded as the first and the second patriarch of the East Mountain Teaching.

The philosophical position of the Zen sect is definitely different from the other sects. Zen was established by disciplinants of City-Buddhism. They were disappointed with the religion, which overly enjoyed benefits from the state and provided services to them in return. They rejected the academic-centred activities of City-Buddhism and went into mountain forests to exercise their religious beliefs. They pursued enlightenment by ascetic practices (頭陀, Dhuta) and made efforts to guide disciples there. Huike and his disciples were exactly these kind of people.

Afterwards, Daoxin (道信, 580-651) and his disciple Hongren (弘忍, 601-674) became famous among Huike's descendants. They abandoned traditional wandering life and settled down in mountain areas. There, they

Vairocana-stupa (毘盧塔), the tomb of Daoxin (道信), the fourth patriarch of Zen

established a big religious community which had hundreds of members. This was the so-called East Mountain Teaching group. They kept the values of the Dhuta disciplinants as a legacy from Bodhidharma and Huike. It can be said that they established a community whose sole aim was to obtain enlightenment. In this community, rules of everyday life and practices were appropriately put in place based on their experience, in order to achieve enlightenment. Therefore, many disciplinants were able to realize enlightenment in a relatively short period of time. They only aimed to attain enlightenment and took no notice of benefits as official monks, that many of them were called "illegally ordained priests" (私度僧). Moreover, many "illegally ordained priests" were unable to abide by the Hinayana precept because they were required to carry out some activities that were prohibited by it, such as farming, as a part of their ascetic training. So, the rules of community life were based on the Bodhisattva Precepts (菩薩戒) according to the "Sutra of Brahma's Net" (梵網経), because the Bodhisattva Precepts are common to both monks and laymen. In short, those who were defined as "neither monk nor layman" (非僧非俗) aimed to attain enlightenment while engaging in activities that were prohibited by Hinayana, like farming, to maintain their living. That is why laymen played an active part in the Zen sect from very early on.

The Zen sect was established by truly religious people who were unconcerned with status and privilege, and who only sought enlightenment. Therefore, Zen was able to become universal, overcoming values and limitations presented by Chinese society.

2. ESSENCE OF ZEN MEDITATION

As stated above, the universality of Zen resulted from the founders' unorthodox way of life. And then, the enlightenment itself which they pursued also transcended cultural differences.

Now, we must understand what enlightenment is. To understand it, let us look at KUOAN Shiyuan's (廓庵師遠) *Ten Bulls* (Ten Ox Herding Pictures, 十牛圖). This series of artworks shows 10 stages of a Zen practitioner's progression towards enlightenment, likening it to the process of searching for a lost bull. The 10 stages are as follows:

1. Searching for the Bull (尋牛)

2. Finding the Bull's Footprints (見跡)

3. Finding the Bull (見牛)

4. Catching the Bull (得牛)

5. Taming the Bull (牧牛)

6. Riding the Bull Home (騎牛歸家)

7. The Bull Transcended (忘牛存人)

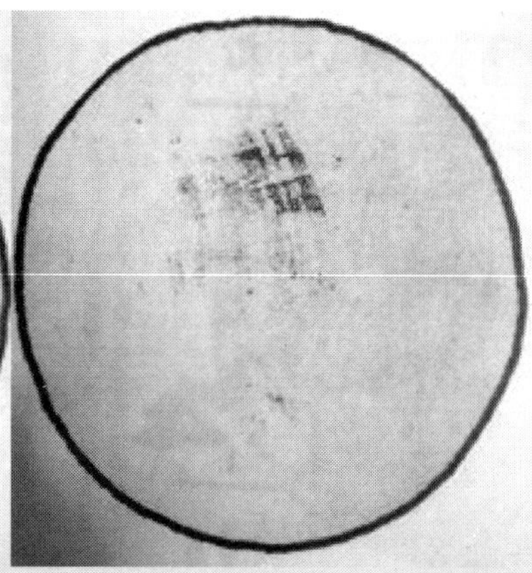

8. Both Bull and Self Transcended (人牛俱忘)

9. Reaching the Source (返本還源)

10. In the World (Return to Society, 入鄽垂手)

These 10 stages can be interpreted by the following four steps:

A. One faces a hard time in daily life and has an identity crisis (No. 1)
B. He learns of salvation through Zen practices, from sufferings, by *sutras* or through the Zen masters' teachings (No. 2)
C. He gets enlightenment through Zen practices and cultivates it by degrees, and at last becomes one with it (Nos. 3-8)
D. He returns to the real world as the enlightened one and utilizes his knowledge for the sake of the others (Nos. 9-10)

On the whole, it shows that Zen practices start from the awareness of the sufferings of life, through the conquest of it through enlightenment, and end in absolute life, which is full of peace of mind. The concept to realize the enlightenment out of the ordinary life has been well kept ever since the establishment of the East Mountain Teaching.

Thus, what is the concept of enlightenment in Zen? In Zen Buddhism, a man is thought to be nothing but the enlightenment itself (in the *Ten Bulls*, the round shapes which surround these paintings indicate it). Nevertheless, we always suffer from various things (A). That is because we have gotten various stereotypes and wrong ideas by living in the society, and were caught up in them, and finally we lost the true self (i.e.

enlightenment itself, in the *Ten Bulls*, the bull represents enlightenment). Therefore, we should get back to the original state by means of Zen practices (C).

Now, we can recognize the reason for the great universality of Zen. From the Zen point of view, the culture or ideas that we learned in society is the main cause of sufferings that they must be denied once. That is to say, Zen sets up the logic of the relief based on human existence which is beyond any cultures and ideas. And, whilst this may sound paradoxical, this is the reason that Zen has been traditionally related to forms such as literature, painting, calligraphy(書道), martial arts (武道), and the Japanese art of tea ceremony (茶道). Because to create something new, it is necessary to break existing cultures and ideas.

3. RE-EVALUATION OF ZEN IN MODERN JAPAN

If the philosophical structure of Zen was what I just mentioned, Zen must be able to surpass not only national and ethnic distinctions, but also time. The prevalence of Zen in modern Japan may prove this notion.

Zen was traditionally the religion of the Samurais. They were always near death because their primary job was to fight in battlefields. So, they wanted to have peace of mind by practising Zen. For the same reason, many military personnel practised Zen meditation in modern Japan. But one thing was different in modern Japan. Because of the introduction of the universal conscription system, ordinary citizens were forced to fight in battles. Besides, the history of modern Japan was filled with wars. That's why the citizens' interest in Zen increased.

Natsume Soseki (夏目漱石)

Apart from this historical fact, intellectuals also became intensively interested in Zen. During rapid modernization (i.e. Westernization), intellectuals accepted the Western concept of "self". However, the western concept of "self" forced Japanese intellectuals to face loneliness and anxiety, which they had never felt before. Zen received remarkable attention from them as a solution to overcome such feelings. In Natsume Soseki's (夏目漱石, 1867-1916) *Mon*, one of his most famous novels, the main character Sosuke is described as a man who is very interested in Zen, but can't practise it thoroughly until the attainment of enlightenment. It is clear that Sosuke was the projection of the author's personality.

Syaku Soen（釋宗演）

Going by the social trends of the era, Zen masters actively promoted Zen. Especially, Syaku Soen (釋宗演, 1860-1919) of Engaku-ji (圓覺寺) Temple had a great influence on intellectuals. It was Syaku who guided Natsume Soseki and Suzuki Daisetsu.

Suzuki's activities can be regarded as one of the movements that emphasized the uniqueness of traditional Japanese cultures in revolt against Westernization. That's why he made a lot of effort to write his works in English to enable Western people to appreciate Zen. Even apart from this, Nishida Kitaro (西田幾多郎, 1870-1945), one of Suzuki's most familiar friends, established a unique philosophy by integrating Western philosophical concepts and Zen experience into a whole.

Zen played a very important role in modern Japan. It proved that Zen can win the hearts and minds of people in a timeless way. Contemporary spread of Zen to the West is the result of it.

4. ZEN TODAY AND ITS FUTURE

The development of science and technology has been very rapid, and has brought significant changes to the world in our time. But the human condition itself never changes. We must face the inevitable four sufferings of life—birth, ageing, sickness and death, just as Buddha had to live through two thousand several hundred years ago. This is why religions are necessary. But, because many religions have their own views which often contradict scientific ideas, many of us living in modern times may find it difficult to understand their concepts and philosophy. However, Zen doesn't need the mythology of universe creation or an unscientific view of the world. It only requires us to look at ourselves and to see the base of our own existence by the practices such as "seated meditation" (坐禅).

Nishida Kitaro（西田幾多郎）

Also, the Zen tradition encourages us to attain enlightenment through ordinary life. Therefore, it is very convenient for us who must work to live. And we may be able to lead the creative life by destroying the existing stereotypes by Zen experience. These aspects of Zen are becoming more attractive according to changes in society. I think that Zen will spread more and more around the world in the future.

I would like to conclude my speech by giving you two examples which show that Zen practices are useful in Japan today. The first example is the Kojilin (居士林) of the Engaku-ji (圓覺寺) Temple. At this institution, everyone can experience a life similar to that of Zen monks on every weekend for a modest cost. No reservations are necessary. If you want

The Kojilin of the Engaku-ji temple（圓覺寺居士林)

to participate, you only need to go there at the designated time. Among the participants, there may be long-disciplined laymen, persons who are overwhelmed by agonies of life, and persons who just come out of mere curiosity. The reason does not matter. The master does nothing other than

Seated meditation as one of the extracurricular activities of a high school

providing directions to all in the same manner. The next morning, each participant goes home with satisfaction.

The next example is the seated meditation experience programme conducted as one of the extracurricular activities of a school or employee training of a company. It is often organized to give participants a chance to reflect on themselves because it gives them the power to face tough tasks, such as school entrance examinations or the competitions among companies. The experience of the self-reflection in a pure and quiet Zen temple inevitably becomes a cherished memory.

Polycentrism as the Core of Global Dialogue

LOKESH CHANDRA

THE 20th CENTURY WAS WRAPPED in gold plundered from a thousand flowers. It was consumerism at its height. It clothed the mind with physicality. This century seeks inner steppes, immense and pristine. We have to work out a journey to values in ever-creating, all irradiating forms. We have to avoid the tragedy of becoming nondescript and monocentric beings, deprived of roots. The poetry of our deeps has to be the presence of the perennial in the present and the ferment of a "Living We" of our futures. No hatred events or blood-stained spikes of dogmas. Romain Rolland, the great French writer, had said, "Teach us to understand all things, Asia, teach us your knowledge of life. And learn of us action, achievement." This is possible only when distinctive spirits are respected. Asian nations have to make the journey together with many nations, sharing and at the same time varying. Substantive voices have to come from our own beyond and within, our own forms and movements, our own dreams and spaces. The raptures of our roots have to live in the kinetics of tomorrows, close to fire without kissing its flames.

The 20th century is done, but its "global universal" is a depersonalizing hegemony, wherein the Creative Consistence and the Autonomy of Cultures are victims. A new morphology of cultural reciprocity, a heart-work of variations, has to be resurrected. The multiple dream-spaces of life and joy are being ripped by the hegemony of globalism and dialogue.

The concepts of globalization and dialogue are contemporary softening up of the triumphalist terms of the 19th and early 20th century when thinkers like Max Weber spoke of the uniqueness and universal importance of the special Western culture and civilization. They saw their direction of development, as of universal importance and validity, and as a chain of factors that led to cultural events in the West. The plurality of cultures was an idealized presentation of the non-European ways and institutions as a critical counter-image, as backward stages of Western development. Plurality was neither owned nor honoured, but merely provided a clarity to the formulation of European culture as the only regular and scientific progress. All foreign cultures were backward as they lacked the socio-historical roots of a dynamic force to bring forth science and technology. Western thinkers posit their cultural value systems of the world. Achievements, destructions and crises were the threefold dynamics of change. Crises were not regressions, but catalytic forces. The traditional non-Western social structures and values have been derogated and brought down so that non-Western thinkers are compelled to channel their ideas in the Western mould. The lack of perceptible human purpose and the threatening ecological crisis introduces a fleeting era of Western self-doubt. Is the Western Faustian man with his eternal striving the carcinogen? "There is a cancer in this world; and it is a man," complain the ecologists. Yet the West cannot accept a diminution of its values, which are the driving forces of its civilization.

Kaneko Masaru, in his book *Anti-globalism*, is outspoken: "Is this greedy, survival-of-the-fittest capitalism really what we want… We must not forget issues like Japanese tradition and cultural identity." The fall of communism was a victory for human rights, and the demise of globalism will be a victory for values. Globalization provides confrontation and hereby new opportunities to assess our traditions. In the words of Emmanuel Todd of Paris, traditions are the heart of a culture. Family system stubbornly resists globalization and thus helps cultures preserve their individuality. Yamazaki Masakazu of University of East Asia's Graduate School has pointed out that "values common to all humanity are an illusion".

Civilization had swept Japan after the Meiji Restoration of 1868 with the slogan "Civilization and Enlightenment". After the Second World War, civilization was replaced by culture, and the phrase "culture nation" (*bunka kokka*) emerged as a national slogan. The "Huntington shock" has led to a further realization that cultures wield power. Asian cultures are aesthetic contemplation, an appreciation of beauty and charm, nobility and fervour. The concept of culture as power has made the Japanese reflect on self-awareness, and to nurture the "search for our roots". Their perception is: "We should accept what we are, namely, a distinctly minor civilization that operates best on a scale commensurate with its own physical size."

As silence gives new voices to historic symbols, the Japanese have noted the importance of "linguistic sovereignty". Takashina Shuji, Director General of the National Museum of Western Art, writes: "Preserving it is absolutely essential not only to safeguard the Japanese language but also to contribute to the world through the Japanese language and Japanese culture." The famed novelist Natsume Soseki taught his students that the correct Japanese translation for "I love you" is *Tsuki ga tottemo aoi naa*—"the moon is so blue tonight". This emotional expression has to work within the Japanese cultural framework.

Kawakastu Heita of the Waseda University says: "Culture emerged from our involvement with the land. The word *culture* comes from a word meaning 'to till the soil', which was eventually applied to cultivation of the spirit... We are suffering from...a cultural crisis. We have to return to the land again."

A new self-awareness is emerging. All the varied cultures cannot be measured by a single yardstick. "Heavyweight" cultures have to acknowledge the existence of "lightweight" cultures that possess a mysterious charm, refinement and unique flavor of belonging. It is the difference between a house and a home, an expression of inner identity, alive within, the cultural flowering of a dwelling. The West seeks to submerge non-European identities into an industrial civilization, that exaggerates the value of human rationality, and repudiates the transcendental which can give life meaning. As humans are not completely comfortable with modern industrial consumerism, the clash becomes internalized and spiritual. It is easy to be nihilistic and pronounce tradition and religion, symbols and significance, history and national identity as dead. To deny them is to deny ourselves. Human society is a system of symbols. Symbolic meaning holds sway in the realm of life. It preserves continuity and unity. Mass culture is being projected as a counterpoint to break up the dignity of higher symbols and their vitality of spontaneous development. Artistic genres, traditional rituals and conventions, i.e. Forms, are suffering from ignorance and contempt. Form is the very foundation and main stay of culture. Today there is a crisis of form, whereby contemporary society demonstrates spiritual and cultural shallowness.

Secularization and cultural denigration undermines the institutions of Asian nations. The stronger this drive becomes, the greater is peoples' identification with their own culture. Kawakatsu speaks of "an encounter between a Japan of beauty and a West of strength... Beauty is not always something that wilts before might." The Meiji government let this spirit and virtue fall by the wayside in its headlong dash to build a wealthy state and strong army, with disastrous results. In his policy speech on August 7, 1998 Prime Minister Obuchi Keizo spoke of *fukoku yutoku* "a country of wealth and virtue". Nakanishi Terumasa elaborates the Japanese sense of values, along with accomplishing economic vitality, under three national goals: "freedom and vitality, revival of history and tradition, and independence." Nishibe Susumu has been forthright in his comments: "the spread of globalism" is nothing more or less than the Americanization of the world... Let us make the 21st century the century of de-Americanization."

We will have to move away from glorifying consumerism, sex and violence through the omnipresent and omnipotent electronic media. The West cannot stain the mind of humanity. The sky looks blue but does not leave its stains on the wings of a bird. To avoid tensions and reprisals, clashes and crushings, the disinherited of the earth will have to be respected and owned. The roots of humanity as a whole, and of the West in particular, must go deep down into the universal and infinite. The Upanishadic seers, having become men-in-the-universe, were inspired by the mighty living cathedrals of nature, and felt that the same serene depths of the mind pulsate in every living being, and called upon us to strive for a profound reverence for life:

Everything has sprung from immortal life
And is vibrating with life.
Life is immense.

Technosphere has to be an auxiliary of the biosphere. It should not intrude into the functions of the biosphere, with all its *sukha* and *duhkha*, its happiness and gloom. High-tech will have to be harmonized with the needs of life. Life includes human life, animal life, and stationary life (plants). Flora, fauna and humanity have to co-exist. Spiritualization of the image of the future in its creativity through pure science and applied technology provides a new structure for the continuing process of human development. In a world where science has become cannibalistic and humanity has become edible, will technology devour the significance of human existence? As the Isha-Upanishad says: "You should therefore only take what is really necessary for yourself, which is set aside for you. You should not take anything else, because you know to whom it belongs." The world will have to be "the land of duty, not the land of enjoyment," as Mahatma Gandhi said.

The real fulfillment of the human spirit is the values of the inner life to mitigate the acid rain of unbridled pursuit of material wealth. The mad cow disease, for instance, has been a warning. Continued industrial exploitation will invite massive retaliation by nature. Man is to give up the illusion of being the supreme creation, whose mission is a struggle against the forces of nature. He is to be a gentle disciple of life, for the stiff and unbending is the disciple of death. He is to celebrate the green plants that are tender and filled with sap. As Lao-tze wisely put it:

A man is born gentle and meek
At his death he is hard and stiff.

Dialogue was between teachers and their disciples, and the neophyte occupied a position of submission to the teacher. In the 19th century when Western countries were dominant, both politically and economically, dialogue involved Christians and non-Christians. Dialogue is seldom between equal partners. The new emphasis on dialogue is a subtler and more insidious form of missionary apologetics. Dialogue has become a prerogative of Western thought. To quote Wilhelm Halbfass of the University of Pennsylvania: "The medium, the framework of any 'dialogue' seems to be irreducibly a Western one… the global openness of modernity is still a parochially Western, European horizon". Further on he says: "The meeting and 'dialogue' of the cultures and religions of this world coincides with their trivialization…." Halbfass is again blunt: "The Europeanization of the earth continues to be inescapable and irreversible."

We have to redefine dialogue as the emergence of a catalyst that breaks through its territorial, civilizational and cultural entrapments. It has to free us to function in a universal ambience. It is the opening up of constantly emerging "illusions" that go on fading out so that the future lives in cultural autonomy, and scientific freedom.

SOME ASIAN PARADIGMS

1. The European theory of cultures and civilizations is a structuring of a mind that has seen phenomenal advances during the last millennium. The Western mind is seeking room to move meaningfully in a pluralistic universe, while it is rooted in the meaning and being of its own thinking and understanding. It has to seek a revaluation of transvaluation of its *bodhicitta* in the rich structures of consciousness of Buddhism, Hinduism, Islam, Taoism, Confucianism, Shintoism and nature-religions.
2. A uni-dimensional norm of humanity is against the deep reality of existence. We have to discover freedom to acknowledge variousness. All the centuries, climates, lands, languages cannot be articulated according to a single symbol system. The "new science" is bringing in indeterminism, plural logical systems, quarks without substance, irrational numbers, and so on. They compel us to a polycentric world, to a new sensibility of multi-centric consciousness. The new paradigms will have to be many-splendoured, with a liveliness of sharing. Values do not exist in a vacuum. They have a history of centuries, exegeses of hundreds of minds, the faith of millions, and now the dreadful power of technology. So concepts like "cultural

commonality" and "universalism" are counter-productive rather than creative. Asians have to accept and respect differences, the beauty of many forms, the eternality of various values. We have to mesh the many in the harmony of divergence rather than in that of convergence.

3. Universalistic hegemony, "standards of life", promiscuity, the glorification of violence, the denial of roots in an unprincipled universalism, the destruction of nature and the mad race for consumerism, have to be replaced. For normalization of life, for the renewal of our inner space, and to avoid deracination in multipolar societies, we need to give up unnecessary acquisitions, to inculcate a vision of values as the supreme quest of life, to bring about a world wherein the state of Being overrides the plenty of possessions. This has to be a Century of Life that will preserve the inside against the outside. Creative Coexistence and Autonomy of Will have to become the absorption of the human mind and action. "Spiritual ideals of reciprocity" have to shape the heart of culture.
4. From a focus on politics and economics to an emphasis on civilization and culture.
5. The ability to unite people culturally will be as important as political, military and economic might.
6. A new paradigm of globalism, to bring together globalism and localism.
7. Confucianism teaches that we are not born human but become human.
8. People are part of nature, not its rulers. In former times Japanese farmers used to plant three beans in one hole: one to be eaten by the insects in the ground, another by birds in the sky, and the last sprouts to be eaten by the people.
9. Kawachi Takashi of the Mainichi Shimbun points out the core Asian values as: "restraint of individual desires and ambitions, harmony with nature, and concert between the group and individual." Freedom and fairness have to go together.
10. The vocabulary of post-structuralism, with words prefixed by inter (internet, interactive, intersexuality) is a paradigm shift to relationality. The Chinese ideogram ren l= combines the elements

for 1 "person" and = "two". It focuses on the individual and his surrounds acting in unison.

11. Re-valourization of the distinguishing features of Asian cultures, which are neither fixed nor absolute. In the domestic architecture of Japan and Korea, the interior and exterior are separated by a single thin sheet of paper. The *shoji* or "paper homes" are to welcome the sounds and breezes, the lovely chirping of birds and insects. It is an open culture as contradistinguished from West's culture of walls. It encourages openness.
12. The wave of modernization is being replaced in Japan by a new but opposite wave of datsu-O nyu-A: "get away from Europe (O) and unite with Asia (A)".
13. Respect for the cultures, civilizations and religions of each other, and no interference or conversions by a subtle psychological agenda, should be the values of our century.
14. True universality can only be rich diversity, with no single meaning. The various lines, the many realities will be lived in everyone's deepest feelings. Religions, in the plural, will be global in the sense that they will be rooted in human consciousness as the vision and faith of fellow beings, whatsoever their demographic numbers. Universality of culture and civilization, rather than a universal culture and civilization, will seek civil behaviour in the affirmation of diversity. Such a culture and civilization will be multiple and their centres will be everywhere.
15. Love of one's land is to value the rights of humans to be sculptors of themselves. Some mysterious flow of energy and resolve invests territory. The Territorial Imperative is a genetically determined form of behaviour, as amply attested by the biological sciences.
16. Love of history. Millenia of time are the subtle and profound "living space" of men. History is the deeper ground of our existence.
17. Sacredness of all life, and the divinity of nature. Awakened awareness, no ideology but ideas, so that tiny pebbles gathered on the shoreline of life become fine like pears. When we carry these pebbles back home to our hearts, intertwined with them will be the Sea of Consciousness in our sleeves.

18. Human values of divergence are the deepest core of the humanum. We will have to inhabit the spiritual universe as a continuing relationship between "inside" and "outside". There is no "inside" without an "outside". It has to be a continuing realization in the dream-space of humans. Without diminution of religious autonomies, we will have to own the "other". Alterity or otherness will be integral to humanity. No universal mission as a management of the world, but the acceptance of pluralism as well as respect for multiplicity.

We have to pass from de facto plurality to pluralism. It has to be an authentic human plenitude of various strands, held together by mutual respect.

Lee O-Young, a former Minister of Culture and Sports of the Republic of Korea, says: "At length we will hear, wafting in from the once-forgotten Asian steppe, a song that transcends the spiritual, emotional discord."

Relevance of Traditional Cultures for the Present and the Future: A Case Study in Safeguarding the Intangible Cultural Heritage of Vietnam

LE THI MINH LY

LIKE SOME COUNTRIES IN AFRICA, South America and Asia, the history of Vietnamese culture has existed for about 4,000 years. It has been extremely sustainable in spite of the ups and downs undergone by the country and its turbulent trajectories, and the dependence on different political regimes, economies and sufferings. The hundred-year wars, the poor and not very good living standards during that difficult time in Vietnam could not prevent Vietnamese scientists from doing their research. The diverse cultural pictures of the 54 ethnic groups have been drawn up more and more clearly through the rich and profound research work of the Vietnamese scholars and several foreign researchers. However, these works have had limited purposes, aiming at documenting and publishing books or to exploit the composition of music and dance, plays and cinemas, and so on.

Yet, the core value of Vietnam's culture and civilization has been preserved and continued from one generation to another so that today when looking back they can still be found in harmony with the culture and civilization of humanity.

Culture is the sum of values created by humans in their interaction with their living environment and their surrounding natural world.

Those values have been handed down, preserved and acknowledged as an inseparable part of human life. That is cultural heritage. Safeguarding cultural heritage is closely connected to sustainable development, i.e. linkages for creating "the relevance of traditional cultures for the present and the future".

However, the greatest challenge to cultural development is the fading away of intangible culture—the heritage that exists in everyday life. This is really hard to see and measure. Each city or rural village is a centre gathering cultural expressions and traditions. There, local cultural traditions and other cultural traditions are integrated into the local culture. The media always promotes tourist and typical heritage sites. Many people do not know the heritage that exists in their surrounding environment, in their families and their own lives. Thus, they do not know the values and economic and cultural potentials of their own heritage. The more modern the life is, the more the heritage fades away and the less opportunities the people have to turn heritage into their driving force for development.

The safeguarding of the intangible cultural heritage (ICH) in a sustainable way of ensuring its continuous transmission and inheritance is still very limited because we have not got in place strategic orientation and policies in several decades. However, after having access to several UNESCO recommendations and the 2003 Convention, the ICH awareness process and safeguarding activities are being quickly and strongly implemented and have brought about much positive outcome. This resulted from the reform in thinking, beginning in 1996. The strategy has changed the awareness and practical work in various aspects of life, including culture.

Established in 2007, the Centre for Research and Promotion of the Value of the Cultural Heritage (CCH) is a non-governmental organization under the Vietnam Association of Cultural Heritage. The goal of CCH is to apply latest study achievements on tangible and intangible cultural heritage to promote and strengthen sustainable development of the cultures of local communities in rural and urban areas. CCH aims to closely coordinate with local authorities, policy-makers, cultural practitioners, educators, private organizations, media agencies and communities to promote public awareness on the importance of local knowledge and traditional culture. CCH's activities are to build capacity for local people and local groups, particularly young adults and children.

As a non-governmental organization, which has clear principles and objectives, concentrating on studies for the safeguarding of cultural heritage to serve human needs, CCH has an on-going commitment to the development and application of new and effective methodologies of approaching cultural heritage education, based on ideas that are conceived of as more practical and with the potential to be particularly effective in their effects as a basis for a wide and ever-growing range of educational and information projects.

CCH is deeply aware that heritage education is one of the most important measures for safeguarding cultural heritage. The use of the values of cultural and natural heritage—tangible and intangible—for teaching and self-learning to improve knowledge and for life-long learning is not different from that in developed countries worldwide. However, the question of access to heritage, identifying heritage as a resource of culture and sciences for teaching and learning has not yet been recognized by civil society organizations and people in Vietnam, and has not received proper investment in both strategy and approach. Vietnam is a country that has many heritage potentials. The country is developing rapidly and has many opportunities in the use and implementation of heritage as an effective tool for life-long learning. The question is how this invaluable knowledge source is to be studied and how it can be used effectively for learning in Vietnam at the present and in the future. There are four aspects to be considered:

- No comprehensive and overview vision on heritage is available. Attention is paid more to tangible values than to intangible values; and more to the tangible and material values than to information and archives; to past heritage more than living (human) heritage and intangible heritage and related cultural spaces.
- No good approach is available for identifying fully and deeply the values of all heritages in order to define information sources, data, opportunities and conditions for heritage education.

- No method is available for coordination between educational institutions and cultural institutions in achieving a common strategic goal initiated by UNESCO, i.e. heritage education.
- No professional institution, policy and strategic plan are available for this goal.

Thoroughly grasping the perception on the four development pillars (Culture, Information, Education and Science) being developed by UNESCO, CCH is aware that cultural heritage is an endless resource for teaching and life-long learning, and has a relevant approach for developing heritage education programmes. Over the past five years, CCH has carried out some activities on heritage education, attached intangible heritage to schools and used intangible cultural heritage for teaching.

In 2010, as a means of tackling the problem of inadequate collaboration between educational and cultural institutions in the exploitation and use of cultural heritage resources for educational purposes, CCH submitted a proposal for linking with schools for ICH education development in museums, historic spaces and historical and cultural heritage sites in Hanoi on the occasion of Thang Long-Hanoi's 1,000-year anniversary celebration, which was received and approved by UNESCO. A major objective of this pilot study was to build a set of guidelines on cultural heritage education for teachers, museum and historic heritage site staff at certain schools in Hanoi. The underlying aim of this initiative was thus to create a wholly new methodology for schools and the education sector more widely in making productive use of the information and knowledge emanating from museums, historic spaces, artefact collections and historic-cultural sites in their local neighbourhoods for educational purposes. At the same time, this initiative was conceived as a novel contribution to the work of museums, historic spaces and historic-cultural institutions as a way of approaching a new and diverse range of public audiences by reaching out to school children and students. Those projects paid special attention to the identification and documentation of significant spaces and sites of local cultural heritage in the vicinity of schools that could be suitably made a feature of everyday curriculum-based school teaching. The set of guide documents on cultural heritage education is expected to be a sample reference document for a wide

The Face of Traditional Culture Today and in the Future (The Life of Javanese Shadow Puppet Theatre as an Analogy)

SRI HASTANTO

I AGREE COMPLETELY WITH THE India International Centre's note which states: "There is now an overall consensus that a shift is taking place in the structure of power from the West to the East; not simply to Asia but also via select parts of South America and Africa." Nevertheless, we should be aware that the process of a shift in power is highly dependent upon the ability of communities to use their traditional cultures to oversee the changes that take place from one era to another. The topic to be addressed in this international conference is a changing era which is of a historical nature rather than simply a change in government. The latter can be measured in a period of days, months, or years, whereas the time measurement for history is no longer days, months, or years, but rather decades and centuries. Therefore, the phrase "that a shift is taking place" contains hundreds or even thousands of phenomena that could occur, depending upon the situation of the community which lives inside the circle of a particular traditional culture, since the duration of this change may take several decades or even centuries.

I believe that a shift will indeed take place in the structure of power from the West to the East. This means that Eastern cultures will become the reference for world cultures although this necessitates a number of difficult requirements. Today, a number of Western people are beginning to search for enlightenment in their lives by engaging in Eastern cultural practices (learning to practise yoga, meditation, gamelan, shadow puppet theatre, or Wayang, and so on). In this instance, we must look closely to see who is taking the initiative, the people from the East or the Western people themselves. Since if the Westerners feel that their own works of culture (technology, science, philosophy, and so on) are unable to satisfy their physical and spiritual existence, and consequently look to the East for spiritual enlightenment, this means that the initiative is still in the hands of the people from the West. On the contrary, if people from the East are active in introducing the greatness of Eastern culture in managing human life, only then can it be said that the East is playing a part in this shift of power. However, in accordance with human nature, which is not always made up of black and white, it is not possible that what I have described above will take 100 per cent place; a degree of 60 per cent to 70 per cent is sufficient to represent this shift in power.

In order to concretize the thoughts and ideas presented above, I will use a case study about the role of Surakarta-style shadow puppet theatre, or Wayang Gaya Surakarta during the changing times over the last few centuries, and also a predication of its role in the future. I have chosen Surakarta style Wayang for the following reasons:

1. This performing art genre is more widespread than other performing arts, and even exists among other ethnic groups outside the Surakarta Javanese community;
2. This art form has been in existence for several centuries and has very close ties with its surrounding or supporting community;
3. It has gained international recognition from UNESCO as a World Masterpiece of Oral and Intangible Heritage of Humanity.

However, from decade to decade, the close ties between this art form and the community have begun to decrease and may even be said to have been broken. This is due to the changes in the community's structure, which have led to changes in people's daily lives and behaviour. I hope than an analogy of the existence of Surakarta style Wayang in the past, present, and future will provide an explanation of my own personal thoughts on the idea "that a shift is taking place in the structure of power from the West to the East".

THE WAYANG CULTURE IN THE JAVANESE COMMUNITY

Wayang first entered Javanese culture in the form of the well-known literary works from India, namely the Ramayana and Mahabharata. The Ramayana, written by Valmiki, and the Mahabharata, written by Vyasa, fascinated Javanese literary scholars, who adopted the two works as literary adaptations as a means of conveying Javanese philosophy in order to increase the wisdom of the Javanese knights or nobility. The Ramayana was rewritten in Old Javanese, in the form of classical Javanese poetry, or *kakawin*, during the reign of King Dyah Balitung (the ruler of the Mataram Hindu kingdom from 820-823 AD). It is believed that this *kakawin* version of the Ramayana was an adaptation of the Sanskrit book *Rawanawandha*, written by Bhattikawya during the 6th or 7th century in India. A version of this story, which was given the title *Serat Rama*, was subsequently written using the new Javanese language by Yasadipura I, during the era of the Kasunan Court in Surakarta (in the reign of Susuhunan IV and V). In *Serta Rama*, the writer presents a number of teachings about how a knight or nobleman can attain a perfect existence. One of the most famous of these teachings is *Astabrata* (eight characteristics), which essentially states that the life of a nobleman must contain eight characteristics of nature, viz. water, cloud, sun, moon, wind, earth, sea and fire. Another equally important teaching contained in Ramawijaya's words is that when sending out Hanuman to find where Sita was being hidden: "*Yen wania ing gampang wedia ing ewuh sebarang nora tumeka*" (If a person only has courage to face that which is easy but is afraid to face that which is difficult, he will never achieve anything).

The development of the Mahabharata as a literary work in Java focused on the plot of the Bharatayuda (the battle between the Bharata blood relatives as a symbol of the battle between good and evil). This story was written in the form of *kakawin* in Old Javanese by Mpu Sedah during the reign of King Jayabaya in Kediri in 1157 AD. Prior to this, there already existed *Kakawin Arjunawiwaha*, which was a fragment of the

Mahabharata, written by Mpu Kanwa during the reign of King Erlangga in approximately 1030 AD. In this work, there is one particular stanza that is often quoted to provide information about shadow puppet theatre (verse 9):

> "hanânonton ringgit manangis asekel mûda hidepan
> huwus wruh towin yan walulang inukir molah angucap
> haturning wwang tresnêng wisaya malahâ tar wihikana
> ri tatwanyân mâyâ sahana-hananing bhâwa siluman"
>
> (Arjuna Wiwaha, 1030:Verse 9)

> There is a person watching a performance of shadow puppet theatre,
> Crying, sad, his heart filled with sorrow.
> He knows that it is carved skin that is moving and speaking.
> That is how a person looks when fixed to the target of his senses, simply bemused and not knowing
> That in truth, it is only a hallucination, only an illusion.

The book of *Bharatayuda* was subsequently rewritten using the modern Javanese language by Yasadipura I with the title *Serat Baratayuda*. There are many other literary works with roots in the Mahabharata and Ramayana. Due to their popular content and humanitarian teachings, the Javanese community transformed these works into a performing art form so that their philosophical content could be more widely dispersed. This performing art form was Wayang, which means shadow or imagination. Wayang includes performances using two-dimensional puppets (Wayang *kulit*), three-dimensional puppets (Wayang *golek*), and also human actors and actresses (Wayang *wong*). The stories presented in Wayang performances were subsequently developed further to include local stories, such as the Panji legend (which is well-known as far as Thailand, Cambodia and Laos) and other local stories, in addition to stories based on the Ramayana and Mahabharata.

Religious institutions, Islam in particular, have frequently used Wayang to spread the Islamic religion (despite the fact that the stories are based on the Hindu religion). One famous Muslim leader who was well known for using Javanese culture, and especially Wayang, to promote the Islamic religion, was Sunan Kalijaga. Today there are many Moslem leaders who use Wayang for this same purpose. In more recent times, the Catholic and Protestant churches in Java have also used Wayang as a way to spread the Gospel, using stories from the Ramayana and Mahabharata, as well as stories from the Bible.

WAYANG IN THE JAVANESE COMMUNITY

At a Time When the Community was Still Relatively Homogenous

Scholars, both from the West and Indonesia, usually begin a discussion on the history of Wayang by quoting the 9th stanza of Kakawin Arjuna Wiwaha, as quoted on the previous page. From this, it can be understood that Wayang was used to communicate something to other people and as such, it can be assumed that this was in the form of a performance. If a person could cry while watching a Wayang *kulit* performance, this means that the function of Wayang was to influence people, perhaps in an educational sense (to provide moral education), or simply to tell them about something. Since this stanza describes a person crying when watching a Wayang performance, this means that one of the functions of Wayang at that time was to form the character of a person as a member of the community. It may be said that the traditional culture of Wayang at that time was an out-and-out lifestyle reference for the people of the Javanese community.

The Pre-Independence Era in Indonesia

During this period, there was a strong current of nationalist issues throughout Indonesia, and as such, regional affairs, including Wayang, were of secondary importance. From this time on, members of the Javanese community who were more concerned about political matters began to have weaker associations with the traditional Wayang culture. At this time, Indonesia was more important and Java was only a small part of Indonesia. The situation in Javanese society changed as people were swept along by a strong political current. At this time, there was a polemic which has been recorded as the largest polemic throughout Indonesian history and given the title of a "Cultural Polemic".

This polemic began with an idea proposed by Sutan Takdir Alisyahbana (a writer from Minangkabau) entitled "*Menudju Masjarakat dan Kebudajaan Baru: Indonesia-Pra-Indonesia*" or "Towards a New Society and Culture: Indonesia-Pre-Indonesia"*(Pudjangga Baru,* August 2, 1935) which describes:

> A New Indonesia, which should not at all be considered an extension or continuation of the joint generation of Mataram, Minangkabau or Melayu, Banjarmasin or Sunda. Therefore the time has arrived for us to direct our eyes towards the West.

These words received a strong response from Sanusi Pane and Purbotjaroko. Sanusi Pane (a Batak writer) attests that:

> The current era is a continuation of the previous era... The perfect course is to unite *Faust and Arjuna,* to form close bonds between materialism, intellectualism and individualism, with spiritualism, sentiment and collectivism.

Purbotjaroko (a Javanese writer), along the same lines as Sanusi Pane, states that:

> It is my feeling that what is beneficial for our land and our nation is to know the course of history from the past until the present day. With this knowledge, we can, to the best of our ability, endeavour to organize the future. In short, do not become intoxicated with ancient cultures but do not become intoxicated either with the West; know about them both so that we can use them safely in the days to come.

This polemic spread to all corners of the Indonesian nation. The Javanese community was divided. Although only a small number of people agreed with Sutan Takdir Alisyahbana's ideas, it was enough to put a distance between this minority of the Javanese community and mainstream Javanese culture, including Wayang. At that time, even the poorly educated adhered to Sutan Takdir Alisyahbana's belief that Javanese culture was ancient, old-fashioned, or outdated, and this included the Wayang tradition. From this time on, some members of the Javanese community no longer wanted to follow the Wayang philosophy, as they considered it to be out of date.

At this time, it became evident that proponents of the traditional Wayang culture were weak, since there was no apparent effort to promote an understanding that the philosophy contained in the traditional Wayang culture was the best for mankind. They were, in fact still in the majority but they were uneasy or reluctant to speak out and, as a result, a small section of the community defected to the West following Sutan Takdir Alisyahbana.

The Independence and Post-Independence Era in Indonesia

This period witnessed the continuation of the spirit of Indonesian nationalism that had first appeared several decades prior to the proclamation of independence (1945). One of the famous markers of this time was the oath made by the young people of Indonesia to support Indonesian independence, known as the Youth Pledge (1928):

> First, we, the young generation of Indonesia, acknowledge one motherland, Indonesia.
>
> Second, we, the young generation of Indonesia, acknowledge one nation, the nation of Indonesia.
>
> Third, we, the young generation of Indonesia, uphold the language of unity, Indonesian.

This Youth Pledge still reverberates today. In the pledge, there is no Java, no Bali, Sunda, or Minangkabau; there is only Indonesia. In the reference to language, although the pledge only states "to uphold the language of unity, Indonesia", which does not mean eliminating regional languages, those who did not have a strong will to be Javanese began to stop using the Javanese language, whereas the traditional art of Wayang uses the Javanese language as a means of expression and aesthetics. This meant that some of the Javanese community no longer had the wish to understand Wayang.

During the era of the first President of the Republic of Indonesia, Sukarno (1945-1965), the philosophy of Wayang was constantly voiced by the leader of the nation, as he was a great admirer of Wayang. Once every month the Presidential Palace in Jakarta held a Wayang *kulit* performance. Although some people criticized Sukarno's government for running the country in a Java-centric manner, this did not stop Sukarno from promoting the philosophy of Wayang as a way of life for the Indonesian people. At that time, many, or even the majority of, Javanese people were still very attached to Wayang. Nevertheless, it should be noted that the traditional Wayang culture at that time was not as strong as perhaps we might suppose.

In 1956, when I was only 10 years old, I started to learn about Wayang *kulit* from the well-known puppeteer, or *dalang*, Ki Redi Suta, from Sragen, Central Java. I was apparently his youngest student as most of his other students were between the ages of 30 and 45. This is proof that the interest of the younger generation in the Wayang tradition was declining. It also meant that I was exclusive in my role as a child *dalang*. However, the Wayang tradition still held strong since in the families of Javanese *dalang* who performed Wayang in Surakarta style, the sons and daughters would automatically become skilled *dalang*, both in terms of their technical ability and also in their understanding of the Wayang philosophy. Many young people, despite not studying Wayang in any great depth, still idolized certain Wayang characters, especially the Pandawa knights (the good characters in the Mahabharata story). As such, the Wayang philosophy was still believed to be a good reference for people's lives.

During the New Order Era

During this era, a wave of consumerism struck Indonesia (and has continued until the present time). Material goods controlled people's lives. They were conditioned to believe that economic welfare was more important than anything else in their lives, and the government encouraged all efforts to make money, including in the field of education. Even culture was abused because it was steered in such a way as to produce material gain. Wayang, as a cultural product, did not escape these government policies.

At one point, Wayang performances almost disappeared completely. Though cultural figures in the government became busy looking for ways to revive the art of Wayang, perhaps they took the wrong steps because the reason given for the decline in the popularity of Wayang was that its performances were no longer attractive or its *dalangs* were no longer creative. For this reason, a movement was established to educate *dalangs* so that they could make their performances more attractive and more popular among the community. The government was wrong, however, in that it focused only on the *dalangs* themselves, whereas in fact, the audience also played, and continues to play, a large part in the continued existence or decline in the popularity of Wayang. Ultimately, this meant that the artistic and philosophical aspects of Wayang were defeated. *Dalangs* wished to survive by catering towards the desires of the audience, and there followed a large-scale movement in which Wayang was severely abused, and was then revived with its new image.

Many *dalangs* competed with each other to prove that their performances could attract audiences and provide material gain, which was good for the welfare of their crew. Many *dalangs* dishonoured their profession simply for money, and the philosophy that they had inherited was omitted from their performances in which entertainment dominated. Nevertheless, not all *dalangs* followed this trend. There were at least still a number of *dalangs* who allocated 40 per cent or 50 per cent of their performances to Wayang philosophy, and the other 50 per cent or 60 per cent to entertainment, and as such, there was still hope that the Javanese community would absorb the Wayang philosophy as a reference point for living their daily lives.

One strange phenomenon is that the existence of the Wayang tradition at the centre of its origin, Surakarta and the surrounding region, was not as strong as in other areas to which it had spread, especially Jakarta and various transmigration regions where Javanese communities were living outside their native Java (such as Sumatra, Kalimantan, Sulawesi, and even Papua). In these areas, the philosophical values of Wayang could still be heard even if they were becoming dominated by the entertainment aspect of the performance. The quality of performances in and around Surakarta was lower in terms of the philosophical substance that was conveyed to the audience. Most of the content was political propaganda, or promotion of commodities that were packaged as entertainment in the form of Wayang scenes.

Once again, proponents of the Wayang culture showed their weakness and inability to preserve and explain to the community that the philosophy contained in Wayang was a good point of reference for their daily lives. Here, we also see the wisdom of members of the Western cultural community who reaped the Wayang philosophy more intensely through their academic studies in Indonesia. With great apologies, I have to say that all the Wayang experts and traditional Wayang artists were simply "milked" for their knowledge by Western scholars who came to study with them. This was because most Indonesian scholars still felt that it was more necessary to seek Western knowledge, and regarded Eastern culture (or their own culture, including the Wayang culture) as ancient or outdated.

Nowadays, these people—who are cynical about their own culture—are the majority in Indonesia. I would describe them as a group of people who deserve to be labelled the "cultural homeless". They view their own culture as ancient and out of date, while Western culture is seen to sparkle with charm, including in its material aspects. However, unfortunately for them, they are unable to enter into the Western culture, as there are a number of requirements that they fail to meet, such as discipline and work ethic! Since they have left their own home, namely that of Javanese culture, but failed to completely become a person of Western culture, they have no cultural home, or in other words are culturally homeless.

It is this kind of people who often become an obstacle for traditional culture to play a part in the development of each new era, since they are found in all layers of society, including the officials who are responsible for making public policies. There is a proverb which describes this group of people who idolize Western culture as being "more Catholic than a priest". Once again, proponents of traditional culture have not shown the courage to speak out about the importance of traditional Wayang culture for people's lives. It is more important now than ever, since at this time, proponents of the traditional Wayang culture no longer belong to the majority.

Intellectuals who have an understanding of traditional Wayang culture often speak out but without significant reverberations. In certain situations, those in power, who are no longer familiar with traditional Wayang culture, have responded to the outspokenness of these traditional cultural intellectuals. The results of this have been quite positive. They say quite honestly, "I don't understand about traditional culture, but it would be good to give it a try and see what the outcome is," in response to every request for a traditional cultural activity. Although there is a positive side to this, it is still painful for proponents of traditional Wayang culture to hear such a response.

Although examples are few and far between, we can still find a few instances of Wayang philosophy being practised in Indonesian government institutions, such as not being selfish, taking into consideration other people's opinions, avoiding actions that may be seen as greedy, showing concern for those who are really in need and being just in all their actions, being transparent and accountable so that their honesty is visible. It turns out that the leaders of these institutions follow the teaching of Astabrata that is contained in *Serat Rama*, the work by Yasadipura I, as described in previous pages.

This is a picture of the face of traditional culture, or in this case of Wayang culture, as it has appeared from one era to the next in the Javanese community. The wisdom contained in Wayang is evident, at times clearly and at times only vaguely, from early times until the present day, with various gradations. Hence, it can be concluded that when there is a leader who understands traditional culture and is willing to speak out and set an example through his or her actions, this is clear proof that Wayang culture is always relevant and has a role to play in the lives of the people from one era to the next. Now what will the face of traditional Wayang culture be like in the future? Below are a few of my thoughts.

THE FACE OF TRADITIONAL WAYANG CULTURE IN THE FUTURE

Independent human beings have the freedom to choose their own path in life without anyone else interfering. I have explained that the number of "cultural homeless" people in Java is greater than those who have an understanding of the traditional Wayang culture. In order to know what the situation will be like in the future, we must first answer the question: Do we still need an identity in this global era? Broadly speaking, based on the exploits of the Indonesian community in their daily lives, we can divide them into three categories: First, those who no longer feel they need an identity; Second, those who still believe it is important to have an identity; Third, those who do not know and have never given any thought to this matter.

The first group believes that in our global existence, where there are no boundaries, all people are the same, and differences in skin colour, language, and so on, are merely physical differences. People are free to work, free to do whatever they please, to make as much money as they like as long as they do not break the law. This type of people will go with the flow of the changing era and will continue to survive.

The second group believes that as human beings we must have an identity. Without identity, human beings are no more than biological creatures. In the world community, a human being is like a tiny screw in a huge machine. But if a person has an identity, has pride in himself as a human being, he will be considered to be a man with prestige and dignity, he will have self-respect, and this self-respect will be recognized by his fellow human beings. This kind of person makes the world alive and diverse. If we compare it to a forest, the globalized world will become a beautiful, lush heterogeneous forest, not a forest that is boring and homogenous.

The third group consists of people whose existence will depend on which of the two other groups is stronger. This group also has the potential to strengthen either the first group or the second group, depending on how each of these groups performs in day-to-day life.

Nationally speaking, Indonesia has already signalled that its society wishes to have a particular identity. The identity that is often mentioned and sought after is that of a multicultural nation. This can be interpreted as meaning that Indonesia will preserve the identity of each ethnic group that makes up the nation. The clearest kind of identity is the traditional culture of each ethnic group. The Wayang tradition is one of the identities of the Javanese people. If Indonesia wishes to become a multicultural nation, every ethnic group must bring its own traditional culture to a level that is on a par with the other cultures in all areas of life. Only by presenting a traditional culture in a modern way, in accordance with the demands of the modern lifestyle of the community, will a traditional culture continue to be relevant to the present day and to the future

In this instance, it is not appropriate for us to position the traditional and the modern head, to head as two opposing cultures. In my opinion, the most important aspect of tradition is the wisdom it contains, which has withstood the test of time for centuries and has continued to hold firm, enabling its community or the owners of the tradition to preserve their identity up to the present time. Needless to say, in tradition there are also certain cultural habits or customs that are no longer relevant to the present age, such as the customs that are at odds with humanity. This kind of custom must indeed be abandoned so that the content of traditional culture becomes increasingly filtered. The selected content that is found in traditional culture—viz, its wisdom—must be preserved as a point of reference for the life of its community both now and in the future. The way in which this wisdom can be carried to the present and the future is by means of a modern attitude—showing respect for time, for practicality, for appearance, and so on. This is what is meant by a modern traditional culture.

AN ATTEMPT TO REVITALIZE TRADITIONAL CULTURES IN THE PRESENT AND IN THE FUTURE

The attitude of the proponents of traditional Wayang culture from age to age has, as mentioned earlier, shown weakness. This is also the case with other cultural traditions. This weakness has resulted in the appearance of a group of "cultural homeless", people who regard traditional culture as an outdated or antique commodity. Therefore, if all the ethnic communities living in Indonesia wish to become a component of the multicultural

Indonesian nation, they need to have an identity, viz. their own culture. Hence, they must not just sit back and allow the development of their own traditional culture to continue as it has done in the past. They must make amends for the mistakes of their ancestors. Proponents of traditional culture, including academics or intellectuals, need to take responsibility for promoting once again the wisdom contained in traditional culture as the "staple diet" for their own communities in the present day and in the future.

The "cultural homeless" are a group of people who are already damaged. It would take a great deal of time and energy to "correct" their cultural attitude, and as such, they are better left alone, since in another two to three decades they will no longer be around. However, their children cannot be simply left to follow in the footsteps of their parents and become culturally homeless. Together with the young generation of proponents of traditional culture, these children must be raised to become a group that has an understanding of the wisdom contained in their own traditional culture. The rest of the lives of these proponents of traditional culture, along with the intellectuals who have only two or three more decades to live, must be spent working hard to create an education system for these children.

This is a very simple idea and although creating this kind of cultural education system from an early age is rather complex, it is quite feasible, especially to educate a community that is relatively homogenous in nature, namely a single ethnic group. Indonesia has over a thousand different traditional cultures, each with its own cultural wisdom. The cultural experts and intellectuals of each ethnic group need to look at the steps that have been taken in the past, from one era to another, and to reflect on and correct the mistakes that have been made so that their traditional cultures can once again become a reference point for the lives of the community today and in the future by developing the right education system.

In my opinion, therefore, the key to answering the problem of whether or not traditional culture will continue to remain relevant both today and in the future is in cultural education beginning at an early age. One difficulty that will surely arise is the problem of how to convince the government to support this endeavour. This is becoming a new and quite important problem since, as I have explained, the cultural homeless now makes up the majority of the government, the members of which are becoming intoxicated with technology and consumerism. Hence, in the development of cultural education, it is essential to involve expert advocacy in order that the government will support this endeavour. The support of the government should not always be associated with funding. What is rather more important is the political will of the government. In this way, the steps towards developing this kind of cultural education will be lighter, including the steps necessary for fund raising.

BIBLIOGRAPHY

Amir, Hazim.*Nilai-nilai Etis dalam* Wayang. Jakarta: Pustaka Sinar Harapan, 1991.

Guritno, Pandam. Wayang, *Kebudayaan Indonesia dan Pancasila*, Jakarkta: UI Press, 1988.

Hastanto, Sri. "Wayang *Kulit: Keadiluhungannya, Profesionalisme, dan Prospek Masa Depan*". Jakarta: Seminar Wayang Indonesia Senawangi, 2012.

Kats, J. Wayang *PurwaVol. I – VI.* (transl.KRT Kartaningrat). Dordrecht: Foris Publications, 1984.

O'Connor, Garry.*The Mahabharata*. London: Hoder & Stoughton, 1988.

Rustopo (ed). *Seni Pe*Wayang*an Kita, Dulu, Kini, dan Esok, Surakarta*: ISI Press Slolo, 2012.

Sarwanto, *Pertunjukan Wayan Kulit Purwa Dalam Rirual Bersih Desa, Kajian Fungsi dan Makna,* Surakarta: Pascasarjana, ISI Press, dan C.V. Cendrawasih, 2008.

Sudjarwo, Heru S. Sumari, Undung *Wiyono, Rupa dan Karakter* Wayang *Purwa: Dewa, Ramayana,* Mahabharata Jakarta: Kakilangit Kencana, 2010.

Suparno, Slamet. *Seni Pedalangan Gagrak Surakarta: Butir-butir Kearifan local sebagai Solusi Problematik Mutakhir*, Surakarta: ISI Press Solo, 2007.

Sutarno, Sunardi, Sudarsono. *Estetika Pedalangan*: Surakarta: ISI Press Solo, dac CV Aji Surakarta, 2007.

Navigating the Asian Future by Asian Thought

SUSANTHA GOONATILAKE

THE RETHINKING REQUIRED FOR A post-European intellectual world where Asia once again becomes dominant, requires removing the cobwebs of Eurocentric history manufactured on the basis of facts invented during the last 300 years. This covers the intellectual movements of the Renaissance and the Enlightenment, as Europe emerged from the thousand-year Dark Age of Christian dogma and the Inquisition. Since the early 19th century in particular, Eurocentric historians singled out Greece—essentially for the ideological requirements of Empire—as the fountainhead of science and knowledge (Martin Bernal, 1987). Today, this is being re-imagined.

The Renaissance itself is partly associated with the so-called Voyages of Discovery of the barbarous Iberians. Essentially, they relied on the trails pioneered over a thousand years earlier by Asians who had criss-crossed the Indian Ocean to guide them in their venture. The Iberian search was not for knowledge but for plunder and riches and for conversion by the sword, as instructed through the Papal Bulls issued by a number of obnoxious popes, particularly Alexander VI—a model for Machiavelli. In Asia, this brutality was most evident in the destruction carried out by the Portuguese in Goa, and far more significantly in the destruction of structures in Sri Lanka relating to universities. Comparisons of the knowledge base of Portugal of that era and what was destroyed in Sri Lanka indicate the huge gap between Asian knowledge on the one hand, and that of backward Europe of that period. Examining Asian sources before and after the Renaissance indicates the European debt to Asia. If

Florence was a centre of the Renaissance, it was due to trade contacts further afield, as far as South and East Asia. This trade was facilitated by the adoption of what was called the New Arithmetic, the South Asian system transmitted to Europe by Arabs. As illustrative of the differences, 12th century texts meant for the instruction of the common people of Sri Lanka regularly used numbers such as 10^{133} (Jayawardana, 2011) , which was a contrast to the cumbersome and limited arithmetic then practised using Roman numerals. Further, the more specialized texts dealt with far larger numbers than their European equivalents.

Illustrative of the many other external input were inflows from the more advanced Islamic cultures, especially those derived from The House of Wisdom of Baghdad founded in the 8th century. Advanced Islamic knowledge also poured into Europe from another direction—Andalusia in Spain. And the "inventions" of da Vinci, the ultimate Renaissance Man, is now hypothesized through recent discoveries of earlier Chinese drawings to be a partial technology transfer from China (Menzies, 2008).

The plunder brought back by the Iberians also included "curiosities", which spread through the Habsburg imperial network to princely collections which were the precursors of museums. Europe under the Dark Ages had been subjected to Sumptuary Laws, which denied jewellery to common folk. The inflow of luxury items from the East through the Iberians helped change the aesthetic structure of Europe (Jaffer, 2002).

As Europe began discovering what had existed elsewhere, and combining this new awareness with its own new curiosity, figures such as Newton helped transform European understanding. The dead hand of Christianity lay heavily on figures such as Galileo and later, Darwin. But philosophers like Descartes helped Europe evade the challenge to Christianity by inventing a non-existent mind/body dichotomy. Leibniz, the co-discoverer of the calculus, was an admirer of China, and it has been hypothesized that his central theme of Monadology could well have come from Buddhist elements in neo-Confucianism (Needham). In addition, new evidence has been emerging, that ideas related to the calculus were transmitted from Kerala to Europe, during the era of the Portuguese presence in Asia (Raju, 2007). In a similar manner, d'Orta using knowledge from Goa helped transform the false biology of Aristotle (Boxer, 1963).

The new scientific ideas were also to influence the economic and political ideas of their time, creating a climate of scepticism—epitomized in the Enlightenment—which challenged the given order of society.

There was at that time a near fanatical infatuation with all things Chinese (Davis, 1983; Billington, 1995). Voltaire believed that Western religion was derived from South Asia and that secular learning and worldly culture came first in India (Halbfass, 1988). Notably, he asked for toleration towards Buddhists (Edward, 2005), describing the [alleged] king of Sri Lanka as one of the best Asian rulers. Diderot mentioned that according to Sinhalese laws, the King himself could be executed for violation of the law (Dewaraja, 1989). These imagined constructs were very probably derived from Buddhist ideas of kingship. David Hume (1711-1776) who made the Church's teachings unacceptable, saying "Commit … them to the flames," developed a theory of the non-self, very similar to the Buddhist position, due probably to input from Buddhist Thailand (Gopnik, 2009).

When the Newtonian world collapsed and was replaced by Einsteinian and quantum views, they too had resonances with Asian philosophies. Einstein admitted that his ideas were derived from that of Mach and Hume, both of whom had identical positions to the Buddhist non-self. Schroedinger plainly declared that he was a Vedantist (Goonatilake, *Nature* 2000).

Hobson (2004) has given evidence that the rise of the West was a product of Western interactions with more technically advanced Asian societies. In a parallel vein, Bala (2006) has argued that the evolution of modern science was a dialogue between civilizations. The various "mind cultures" of Asia had attempted to construct psychologies, long before the emergence of formal psychologies at the end of the 19th century. And today, therapeutic treatments like Mindfulness-based Cognitive Therapy have secured greater medical recognition than the fanciful mental creations of a Freud, Adler or a Jung. These trends are a counter to Bernal's description of the false enthroning of Greece in the early Imperial age, and are to be seen as a geopolitical reflection of the re-emergence of Asia. For a rapidly transforming post-European future, the civilizations of Asia could be a great resource.

Ongoing scientific developments are changing the very basis of our physical and mental being. For example: mental activities are being projected onto computing artefacts; artefacts themselves at times outperform humans as mental processors, and human senses are artificially projected outward and extended beyond human boundaries; Marx's dichotomy of "brain and hand" is now being erased, as the brain is rapidly transferred into an environment, which is increasingly one of information-processing devices located within and outside us. Estimates of this processing sea of the "Internet of Things" suggest that by 2020 there will be 50 billion items around us through which we will be communicating (Danova, 2013) and further, that there would be far more computers communicating with each other than humans with each other, and humans interacting more through computing devices, than directly with fellow humans; the "other" in social theorising, which meant another human, is being enlarged to encompass a realm beyond humans to include computing artefacts. "Synthetic Biology" could well redesign existing genomes and create new life forms; the Human Connectome Project would give a picture of the neural structure of the human brain, opening the door to changes in the very apparatus through which we perceive the world; we could, in theory, change the windows for our physical perceptions; we could introject brainstem cells and rewire ourselves, so that we could switch from one frame of perceiving the world to another; brain cells in Petri dishes have been connected to robotic devices to do some human-like tasks with "some sense of what is going in themselves"; mind reading technology is creating consumer goods controlled by the mind and is making it possible, in principle, to remotely access the visual content of mental processes.

The product of 3 billion years of evolution as crystallized in the formation of the human body and mind has to be re-thought, as indeed, does the manner in which the environment of the human mind and body is being re-made. Profound questions that challenge existing ethical systems are also being raised.

The currently dominant Western ethical systems in which these new technologies are developing are derived from presumably secular roots, or from Christianity, Judaism or Islam (the Abrahamic religions). Western secular ethics are ultimately derived from the idea of humanity, a Eurocentric concept of humans as sacred, which probably derives from the ideas of the Humanists as Europe emerged from the late Middle Ages, in particular the Dark Age, and the era of Christianity. But in an increasingly non-human and post-human world, humanity has to be transcended in search of ethics. The ethical system of the Abrahamic religions is presumed to be "revealed" and to be "God's word"—and idea which is difficult to use in an era when both humans and artefacts do "play God", creating new entities. As in the coming decades the creative bases of the world increasingly shift to Asia, there has to be Asian thought on these culture-impregnated issues.

A major trans-Asian cultural approach, Buddhism is not in the category of revealed truth, and shorn of the unobservable (rebirth, etc.), it has both a strong core of observation and philosophy. Buddhist observation and philosophy has change and process as its core. Some core Buddhist approaches have direct relevance to a future where both the human and his/her environment are constructed and reconstructed. This paper describes the central Buddhist position on both the human person, including his body and mind, as well as the environment in which he or she operates, as not "given" or "sacred", but constructed and constantly changing. A cultural orientation derived from this core Buddhist perspective of no permanent self and continuous change, i.e. of man and nature being subject to constant reinvention and reconstruction, would be a better guide for examining and living us a future world. This also suggests that Buddhist ethics derived from such a perspective (which, unlike the revealed Abrahamic religions, is not absolute but contingent and situational) may be better suited to help navigate the coming interconnected world of the clone, the robot and the cyborg.

Cultural Fluidity and Continuity: Experiments in Theatre

ABHI SUBEDI

I BEGIN MY BRIEF DISCUSSION with three attributes of culture—its traditional form, its fluidity and its perpetuity. The semantic collocation of these three terms is self-explanatory—traditional cultures continue to exist and become functional. This very theory constitutes the principal mode of discussion about traditional culture that we want to introduce here. I have used traditional culture, not in the "traditional" sense, as such, with conservative and elitist connotations, but as the trope of a creative heritage. I have used it for its aesthetic value, and its unique strength of being with us through the performative arts and aesthetics.

In discussions of culture, people frequently parade topics such as cultural studies, high culture and popular culture, reading and writing culture, political culture and literary culture, religious culture and folk culture, and very recently, cyber culture. At the same time, we perpetually seek to establish a rapport with the underlying concept of culture that has shaped our shared values and purposes, a concept that always surrounds our lives like a halo, like the wind, sky, soil, trails, heterotopic spaces, roofs and structures, murals, canvases, poetry and epics. The list is long and such a quest is not without its challenges. The first challenge is that the concept of culture that we understand through the above attributes is getting diffused. But this paradox is also a reality; despite the multifarious interpretations and perceptions of culture, people have continued to live with it. In other words, culture has remained with us, because we have maintained the continuum. That is why the statement: Where we see the continuity is also the source of our anxiety.

Though this statement sounds simple, it raises some serious points for discussion. Cognition of culture varies from one part of the world to the other. Despite the crosscurrents, claims and counterclaims, cultural cognition has remained an important issue and practice.

We have maintained cultural traditions in this part of the world for reasons that are different from those that apply to the West. However, there are commonalities. The most outstanding character of traditional culture, for that matter, is continuity and its impact on our lives. Equally, we should also not forget that culture has various levels of meaning. Traditional culture foregrounds something and makes something invisible. One important way of studying traditional culture therefore is to open up the sensitive and creative, as well as the social aspects. Discussions today focus on the purity of culture, especially of the traditional mode of culture. But we should also look at the new intervention in discussions on culture. How culture is interpreted today is summed up in ideas such as the following:

> I argue that culture is best thought of not as a bounded 'unit' but as a set of overlapping 'performative flows' with no clear limits or determinations (chaos culture). Culture can be thought of as the continual hybridization of meaningful practices or performances in a global context. Thus, culture is a matter, less of locations with roots, than of hybrid and creolized cultural routes in a global space. Cultures are not pure, authentic and locally bounded; rather, they are syncretic and hybridized products of interactions across space.[1]

The above perception has become commonplace today. But we are not talking about the phenomenon of mixing and losing character but of seeking to understand the force with which our traditional culture still affects our ways of thinking. Therefore, a discussion of high and low culture, the Arnoldian, Leavisian concept of an unalloyed area called pure culture, and the antinomies of what is called hybrid or popular culture, are important here. Without going too much into the details of what is termed the Foucauldian concept of power discourse and knowledge production, I would like to address this theme directly. My perceptions are shaped by the modes of traditional cultures that are maintained by the strong social practices, or, very importantly, in the cultures maintained by several sections of society, significantly, the marginalized groups.

Traditional culture is not free from all forms of debates about the concept of continuity and change. We see contradiction, a form of dialectic, as one form of cultural interpretation that reminds us of issues raised by Raymond Williams.[2] But this discussion may lead towards cultural studies, to questions of social equality, justice and discovery of the muted cultures. Gyanendra Pandey, seeing the continuation of the contradiction, asks, "How does one write a history of unacknowledged prejudice, of simultaneous belief in the promise of freedom and the necessity of continued deferral."[3] But given the fact that no subject of cultural study is free from sociological or historical interpretation, I would like to introduce an argument that is related to a secular, non-oppressive, performative culture. It may sound naïve to speak of an all-encompassing contemporary culture. I do not believe in the common argument that draws an absolute distinction between Asian and European culture, positing the former as being uniquely holistic and logical. It is equally fallacious to say that Europeans are more logical than the Asians; the very cognitive processes of the two are different, making their cultural perspectives different. But as discussed in the beginning, what is true is that culture is among the most widely used words today. It is bandied about by ideological pragmatists, and also used constructively by those who have seen its relevance to present life. Others have seen it as a mantra for restoring lost confidence in countries and regions where great cultural traditions once prevailed. My hypothesis is that such traditions do still prevail, but many people do not see how they are operating, because all the aesthetic forms of culture are performative.

However, when we speak about traditional cultures, we also have a tendency to speak in borrowed terminologies from the West, which propagate the argument that tradition in non-Western countries is another name for obscurantism, conservatism and backwardness. This idea has made inroads into our curricula, into the canons of educated people and of literature. In other words, the entire gamut of Western cultural logic has been tacitly accepted as the basis for education in this part of the world. People who were created by the West for this purpose from the non-Western regions did play a very important role to spread their views. As shown by Edward Said in his book *Orientalism,* and in his other writings, such readymade views were shaped with a conspiracy of silence, and by the creation of hegemony that architected consciousness in our own regions and which was spread with success. In return, such scholars received a socially manufactured and exclusive identity, and the privilege of foregrounding their mimic avatars as all-knowing people, who loved that surrogate status.

I would see, therefore, a need not only to identify the nature of the Western scholarship that is studying South Asian traditional culture, but also to develop a strong scholarship built on the traditional epistemology which can be juxtaposed with those created by Western philosophy and the educational system that has been blindly inherited. The major need is to identify the nature of the traditional culture of South Asia and to create an awareness of the fluidity, as against the cliché of rigidity, inherent in the traditional culture. As a theatre person and a dramatist, I have chosen the genre of drama and theatre to foreground the fluidity of culture through the medium of performative art. I have turned to the heritage of the performative culture of the Nepal Mandala, the Kathmandu Valley and a little beyond, as well as the concepts of South Asian scholars and artists. I have worked with theatre persons and students on this subject. UNESCO, in its definition of the cultural heritage adopted in 2003 in Geneva, says of intangible cultural heritage, that it should be kinesthetic in nature; it should be "transmitted from generation to generation", and should be "constantly recreated by communities and groups in response to their environment, their interaction with nature and their history", and should provide them "with a sense of identity and continuity, thus promoting respect for cultural diversity and human creativity."[4] To cite from my earlier work: "I entered that liminoid part of the performativity through third text, a drama—a textual repertoire that could be dismissed or accepted, and which by virtue of being an exteriority in the cultural discourse of an ancient Newar town called Bhaktapur in the Kathmandu Valley, was more of an interpretation of the intangibility, rather than a meticulous study, of culture".[5] I argue that the fluidity of culture is architected through a combination of continuity and relevance. My experiments on stage have shown me how traditional culture has always been relevant, useful and liberating with us in Nepal, and, indeed, in all of South Asia.

Peter Burke has shown even "historical studies" taking a performative turn. His method "traces the rise of the notion of performance of the dramaturgical model of the 1940s and 1950s" mainly to the methods of Ervin Goffman, Victor Turner and John Austin. Burke sees in "recent studies of ritual, festivals, identity, gender, and even emotions, architecture and knowledge", and notes "the shift from the assumption of social or cultural fixity to that of fluidity, from scripts to improvisations, from mentalities to the habitus".[6] Very importantly, he introduces the discussion of the postmodernist method of fluidity which "goes with a sense of freedom from social determinism or even social constraints, expressed in academic language as the 'invention' of traditions, the 'construction' of culture or the 'politics' of identity," which marks a new emphasis on "doing".[7]

My concept of fluidity has a somewhat different meaning here. The fluidity that Burke describes makes freedom the locus. There has to be innovation in all exercises of fluidity, but fluidity in traditional culture has to be explained in terms of shifts. The important measure of the continuity of tradition in South Asia can be seen in the shift of genres and canons of arts and cultural forms. The concept of fluidity in culture that I have been discussing certainly had its origin in a desire for freedom to experiment, and to be alive to the reality of everydayness. Performing or "doing" was the most import thrust. It is this very thrust that has kept the traditional culture in Nepal Mandala and everywhere else going. There is another question that arises here: Is such continuity, this spirit of doing, susceptible to the postmodernist mode of fluidity? I would think that the traditional cultural fluidity utilizes the spirit of the postmodernist departure from deterministic ideas, but does not go all the way in this direction. Therefore, the challenges of traditional culture in Nepal can be met by recognizing it as the "double-reed flute", to use Kapila Vatsyayan's term.[8]

Scholars in South Asia have been writing about this phenomenon, which is that folk forms have assumed classical avatars, and some classical forms have slipped into folk forms. Such a shift creates energy for the forms to support each other mutually. Some temple dances have become standard semi-classical theatre forms, and classical epic forms have long been adapted and used in folk forms. We can see that happening in almost all genres. Yet another dynamic of cultural continuity can be seen in this recurrence of dialectics between rebellion and the establishment. In poetic form, we have seen this in the work of Kabir (d. 1518), to use just one example. We have other examples from all over South Asia. Such tensions have recurred between what Sheldon Pollock calls vernacular and cosmopolitanism in history.[9] He calls that period beginning with the second millennium the "vernacular millennium".[10] We should also mention Dalit aesthetics here. A class of people who are marginalized in a society known by this nomenclature, has maintained a tradition of culture that opens up discussion in a new light. Tartakov, in one interpretation of traditional aesthetics and culture, draws attention to the fact that our interpretation of the great volume of "the literature of Hindu temple", is made "through the bourgeois perspective of its visual aesthetics…as opposed to any interest in their social significance."[11] This also requires a detailed discussion, and important studies have been made in this area.

As a theatre person, I find it more convenient and relevant to write about some of my own experiences. I see the greatest strength of fluidity in the phenomenon of kinaesthesia in culture, and in performativity. The kinaesthetic concept comes from the sense of "ritual and theatre" says Loxley, by citing Victor Turner's theory of "liminal and liminoid performances".[12] Our method of working with the strength of traditional culture in the ancient metropolis comes from what my fellow theatre worker and young academic Shiva Rijal says regarding the longevity of arts and cultures. He concludes, the "myriads of images that we see in Kathmandu, pull us back to its past, to the physical and metaphysical trails that this metropolis has marched so far. Such images have always remained here under multiple threats.[13] All our efforts are geared towards enlivening that cultural power. A character from my play, which we have performed in different countries, says of culture when challenged with its awe and fluidity:

Culture like this wooden cosmos
Is to wait
For the myriad eyes
To fall like the gliding times
From here to eternity
On these jolts of lives in times
So dear to my heart![14]

We identified the nature of the fluidity of culture in the performativity of culture and put that on stage. This subject is not exclusive to our limited experience.[15] We followed a method for doing this. The first step is to get close to the very essence of kinaesthesia in culture, and to become familiar with the nature of the energy inherent in the liminal modes of the rituals. Being a participant may appear to be an easy process. But participation is a challenging process. It is not an anthropological study, nor a sociologically informed repertoire of knowledge, nor the Foucauldian discourse on production of knowledge. It is a process of being part of the fluidity of the ritual or of the folkloristics. That is where our performative part begins. Writing a play by capturing this fluidity is the next step. The major question that has to be answered is: How are we to represent the fluidity in the dramatic text?

First, my own method is to break the very descriptive and reiterative modes of ritual description. Use of poetic language for some personas, recreation of characters who are lost, representation of joy and pain that are petrified and archived in dramatic forms, and linking the overall drama to the ongoing modes of performative rituals are some of the methods that I use for the play, or others, who are experimenting with it, have been making use of. The other part is performativity, the very dramaturgy that involves the efforts of the stage director/s and the personas' identification with the spirit of the fluidity. There are again two challenges here, as discussed earlier. Use of exuberant and digitalized techniques would not always facilitate the smooth process of foregrounding the cultural fluidity. In our theatre experiment, we have taken the space, the architectural locations of ritual performativity, and trail where the performativity moved/moves.[16]

Our experience has shown us that the most important part of cultural fluidity and maintaining its spirit is performativity that can either work in tandem with the custodians of the rituals, or other forms of traditional culture, wherever it is possible, and where it is not, and participate in important ongoing discussions on the preservation of heritage sites, especially of a theatrical nature. In Kathmandu, there is a shift to a strong focus on the discussion on the architectural sites of the Nepal Mandala. Some foreign scholars have carried out some significant studies on these aspects and these have been published. Native architects, too, have done important work in this area. Our concern here is very modest. Recently, an architect who has been restoring traditional houses and architectural sites has designed a theatre in that style for the Shilpee theatre groups in Kathmandu.[17]

Traditional culture and its continuity are significantly related to the question of management. Traditional cultural forms have always been supported by systems created by societies at different moments in history. This is a big and productive subject. Because it is a socially managed phenomenon, the management of supporting system for culture, especially of the performative character, is related to a strong concept of *communitas*, which invokes meanings such as mutual support and continuity of cultural practices by the joint work of the community. Victor Turner who brought *communitas* into use, borrowing from anthropology, explains it in these words:

> *Communitas* is a non-structured relationship, or, better, a spontaneously structured relationship which often develops among luminaries, individuals in passage between social statuses and cultural states that have been cognitively defined, logically articulated, and endowed with jural rights and obligations.[18]

A kind of guild named *guthi* funded the maintenance and continuity of traditional cultural practices in the Nepal Mandala. That was related to a land system. The income from the land registered in the name of cultural structures would enable the performances of the rituals and other forms of worships, as also artistic practices, continue. But the loss of such land

and encroachment by the people in connivance with state management is the single most serious cause of the decline of the traditional performance culture of the Nepal Mandal. This situation can be seen in other areas as well. The purpose of my submission here is not to discuss the subject in detail but to indicate that the traditional cultural practices are not only philosophically or epistemologically defined, but are also maintained by two factors as far as the performance culture is concerned—the performative dynamic and management structures.

The phenomenon of fluidity and connectivity of cultures is manifested "among luminaries, individuals in passage between social statuses and cultural states." But very importantly, the connectivity and fluidity, as discussed earlier, happen because of the very nature of traditional culture. Any discussion of traditional culture therefore is a very valid and very urgent exercise that should be taken up earnestly with greater openness and seriousness, with a focus on performative creativity.

NOTES

1 Chris Barker Barker, *Making Sense of Cultural Studies* (London: Sage, 2002) p. 16.

2 I am especially referring to the topics Raymond Williams has covered from literature to sociology and theatre to environment in his book *Culture and Materialism* (London: Verso, 1980, 2005).

3 Gyanendra Pandey, *A History of Prejudice* (Cambridge, Delhi: Cambridge University Press, 2013) p. 29.

4 Article 2, paragraph 1 of the definition adopted by the Convention.

5 Abhi Subedi, "Walking, seeing and performing: a playwright's perception of the dynamics of intangible culture" Paper presented at the SAARC Festival of Folklore and Intangible Heritage in Agra on September 30 and October 1, 2, 3, 2011.

6 Peter Burke, "Performing History: The Importance of Occasions", *Rethinking History*, Vol. 9, No. 1, March 2005, pp. 35–52.

7 Peter Burke, ibid 39.

8 Kapila Vatsyayan, "From interior landscape into cyberspace: fluidity and dynamics of tradition", *Culture and the Making of Identity in*

Contemporary India, Kamala Ganesh and Usha Thakkar (eds) (New Delhi: Sage Publications, 2005) pp. 39–50.

9 Sheldon Pollock, "Cosmopolitan and Vernacular in History", *Public Culture* 12(3): 591–625.

10 Pollock discusses this phenomenon in his famous tome *The Language of the Gods in the World of Men: Sanskrit, Culture, and Power in Premodern India*. Berkeley: University of California Press, 2006.

11 Gary Michael Tartakov, "The Hindu temple as a representation and instrument of case traditional India", in Gary Michael Tartakov (ed) *Dalit Art and Visual Imagery* (Oxford, Delhi: Oxford University Press, 2012), p. 64.

12 James Loxley, *Performativity* (London: Routledge, 2007), p. 157.

13 Shiva Rijal, *Performing for Tourists* (New Delhi: D. K. Printworld (P) Ltd. 2010), p. 154.

14 Abhi Subedi, *Dreams of Peach Blossoms* (Kathmandu: Across Publication, 2001) p. 80.

15 See for more discussions, Kapila Vatsyayan, "Knowledge: Fluid Cultures, Frozen Structures", S. Radhakrishnan Memorial Lecture March 19, 2010, under the auspices of Indian Institute of Advanced Study, Shimla.

16 Here I am referring to the work of the talented Nepali theatre director of the erstwhile Gurukul theatre Sunil Pokharel. We have partnered as playwright and theatre director in this process of highlighting the fluidity of culture and foregrounding the performativity. The other young directors are Shiva Rijal and Ghimire Yubaraj, with whom I worked from the writing stage to the moment of staging the play.

17 The name of the young architect is Rabindra Puri, who is an erstwhile associate of the German aid group GTZ and an active participant in the constructions inside Patan Museum. He has restored a 150-year-old house in the heart of Bhaktapur, and won the UNESCO Heritage Award. He is also engaged in several other similar large-scale restoration works.

18 Victor Turner, *Revelation and Divination In Ndembu Ritual* (Ithaca, London: Cornell University Press, 1975) p. 22.

Harmonizing Traditional Cultures with Development: A More Sustainable Alternative

TULASI DIWASA AND MAHESH PAUDYAL

VERY OFTEN, TRADITIONAL CULTURE IS misunderstood as the antithesis of modernization. Most of the stock understanding of traditional culture as something of the past and therefore an anachronistic body of knowledge and behaviour is invalid; traditional culture holds in itself an inherent potential to revise itself, evolve, adapt and dynamically address the shifting needs of our changing times.

Traditionalists often have the tendency of overlooking this dynamism, and very often, they mistake the modern conception of development as anti-traditionalist. This is a misleading approach. Traditionalists have a strong point in their view that "ethical and political reasoning is a creation of tradition, and that it crucially depends on the acquisition of such virtues as practical wisdom and justice," but they are wrong in the belief that modern democracy is the "antithesis of tradition, as an inherently destructive, atomizing social force" (Stout 12).

Modern democracy, as a vehicle of development, can work in tandem with certain nuances of traditional culture, and out of that amalgamation, a newer approach to sustainable development can be imagined. But this requires us to accept the fact that tradition has a dynamic character, and it dispenses with those practices that do not evolve with time and changing needs.

This dynamic character of such cultures, if tied with the nuances of modernization and physical development, can solve some of the discrepancies engendered by the monolithic trajectory of development that has divorced itself from its humane and cultural counterpart.

As power equations in the world are shifting rapidly, there is a serious movement of revisionism which has been set in motion in the existing models of development. In order to guarantee the safety of the earth, so that it remains conducive to life, the dire need to incorporate humane and ecological elements in development agendas is being stressed everywhere. Harmonizing traditional cultural knowledge and assumptions of development with the modern, physical and mechanical counterparts of the process can, arguably, rescue the earth from the current impasse it faces. However, this harmonizing needs a readiness to accept the fact that traditional culture moves in tandem with modern development, and there is a need for us to foreground the points where the two can converge and complement one another, so as to give development a sustainability, and a cultural endorsement from the people it brings benefit to.

Though the technocratic world has apparently excelled in the development process, the very process is recoiling on us, owing to the vehement criticism of the harm such development models have caused, when one considers their ramifications for human values and ecological security. However, an element that hampers this issue being taken up for global discussion is the mutual exclusion of the two models represented on one side, by the exact sciences, and on the other, by the traditional cultures of the world; as summed up by Sutton and Anderson: "Few traditional cultures adhere to the rigorous requirements of Western science, and many Western scientists consider the scientific practices and knowledge of traditional cultures to be inferior" (104).

In the wake of the fast-changing power dynamics in the world, one sees a global trend, of serious contemplation directed at finding alternative models of development that would ultimately revise and replace the monolithic, culture-insensitive and discursively oppressive models of the present, gathering force. This is because the Western model is informed by the vested interest of domination. As Sorenson asserts, First World ideologies underlying development are linked to "domination—a relic of colonialism—and carried out by international lending institutions like the International Monetary Fund (IMF) and the World Bank" (7).

A certain type of self-awareness about the coercive nature of such development pervades the globe today. Even in Africa, the European development model has been vehemently criticized lately, for its failure to address the real needs of the continent. Franz Fanon declares, "Europe is best left to Europeans" (quoted in Chachage, 27). Goran Heyden argues, the Western models of development tried in Africa "fail to account for the historical uniqueness of Africa notably the pre-capitalist, pre-colonial, social relations represented by the uncaptured peasantry" (qtd. in Nnaemeka, 39). What is true for Africa, when it comes to its experience with the Western development model, is equally true for Nepal, India and other such non-Western cultural spaces that are homes to innumerable traditional cultures.

It seems therefore that the time is ripe for a serious quest for alternatives to such models. The alternative models are expected to tackle the serious, coercive ramifications of the models in use. A different cultural counterpart of developmental strategy that integrates the benevolent and ethical considerations promised by traditional cultures could be an apt alternative. There are several reasons why such a model is both possible and viable.

In the first place, Eastern traditional societies, including those of Nepal, have always been ready to absorb healthy influences from outside, and therefore, Western and scientific nuances of development that are compatible with our cultural spaces can easily be imbibed. In the context of Nepali culture, folklorist Tulasi Diwasa, in an oral interview opines: "Nepali culture has always had the eclectic quality of absorbing healthy influences from outside and casting them in the Nepali mould. This is to be seen in our art objects, for example, in the Japanese print that are made on Nepali rice paper, and foreign raw materials designed into local art pieces—a union or blend of the unique and the universal."

The dynamic natures of our traditions enable them to be revised and remodelled to address the changing requirements of the evolving times. However, one must be cautious while introducing new elements because traditional cultures are most often very resistant to imposed categories; characteristically, they imbibe those tenets that organically evolve from within the original schematic of that particular culture. This guarantees the dynamic functionalism of traditional culture, and makes them move in tandem with development, in the meantime preserving their uniqueness, which is their most important asset.

The reason why development is so akin to the dynamic functionalism of traditional cultures is that they belong to traditional communities, where the most valuable assets of the community are its lands and its culture. If taken as an integral whole, the traditional cultures of practically any society in the world, rooted in their belief systems and the structures of these societies themselves—including their conception of land and other elements of nature—have the potential to amalgamate development with human values and ethics. There are also other aspects of knowledge rooted in traditional cultures that can benefit humanity in the long run.

This more sustainable counterpart of development, if taken into consideration while framing development policies, can guide humanity towards a more sustainable model of development. Traditional ecological knowledge, for example, is important, not just for its own sake, but also for its potential to help design more effective conservation programmes for biodiversity and for ecological systems in general. Such an amalgamation, if pragmatically adopted, holds the capacity to inspire a corresponding trajectory of material development that will be more enduring and sustainable. But it is imperative that such cultures should be characterized by an evolutionary and dynamic nature, a modern perspective in their outlook, thus removing all possibilities of their being shrunk to a residual culture that could not only become non-functional, but could also be prone to extinction.

It could be claimed that dynamic and evolutionary traditional cultures inspire a non-coercive participation of the practitioners by multiple cultures in development projects because in such an endeavour, they envision not just material attainments, but also an accompanying spiritual and aesthetic accomplishment. This idea is summed up by Janusz Ziolkowski thus: "If culture brings self-awareness and determines the individual's choices and actions, it also fulfills his aspiration to dignity, perceived at the level of States as national dignity, this being a fundamental prerequisite for any collective effort on behalf of development (21)". This allows each participant to envision the outcome as a product of his or her direct involvement, and therefore, the chance of its being cared for is high. Additionally, since every development project necessarily connects with a vision of spiritual accomplishment, it categorically discourages coercion and a narrow profit motive. This will help summarily revise the focus of the Western development agenda, and shift it to traditional cultures, which will uphold their core values.

This direct participation of diverse people from multiple cultural roots and practices in the development project, enables a democratic exercise to take shape, and can prove to be a step forward towards perfectionism in democracy. As John Rawls argues convincingly, this is directed at arranging political institutions "so as to maximize the achievement of human excellence in art, science, and culture" (325). At a time when modern democratic practices based on more liberal secularism are being criticized for being empty of the "moral and spiritual core of our society" because "the ethical substance of the predecessor culture has been drained away", as Jeffery Stout observes (1), he asserts that democracy is itself a tradition that evolves out of certain patterns of conduct that can be understood in totality as culture:

Democracy, I shall argue, is a tradition. It inculcates certain habits of reasoning, certain attitudes towards deference and authority in political discussion, and love for certain goods and virtues, as well as disposition to respond to certain types of actions, events or persons with admiration pity or horror. The tradition is anything but empty. Its ethical substance, however, is a matter of enduring attitudes, concerns, dispositions and patterns of conduct than it is a matter of agreement on a conception of justice. The notions of state neutrality and the reason-tradition dichotomy should not be seen as its defining marks(3).

Stout's stress on the need to discard the "reason-tradition" dichotomy is the crux of our argument. For a true democratic practice to function, the need for ending the reason-tradition dichotomy is even more imperative, and this can come up only when people, who are the real carriers of traditional culture, are integrated into modern democratic practices, including development, and are given an opportunity to articulate the traditional knowledge of development they have inherited from the vast lineage of their diverse cultural origin. Such an approach would lead to an alternative mode of development, which would address most of the discrepancies associated with existing modes of development. This is in consonance with the contention of Tulasi Diwasa, in the interview cited earlier, regarding the need for harmonizing development and culture: "I believe that it is high time to put some cultural elements in the process of the development and modernization of a nation."

This consideration calls for an alternative model of development based on traditional cultures—sometimes alternatively understood as ingredients of ancient civilizations—and such a call has been internationally accepted even at institutional levels. The 2010 report of the UN Secretary General Ban Ki-Moon in the 65th session of the General Assembly echoes this universal acceptance: "Around the world, ancient civilizations have a rich history of understanding the symbiotic connection between human beings and nature." This understanding, archived in oral traditions and cultural practices of the people, needs to be evoked for universal benefit today.

The proposed scheme calls for traditional cultural legacies and practices based on the shared sensibilities of nations with their uniquely identifiable and multiple cultural traits meeting at an ethical point. Such a scheme takes into account the regional cultural and ecological dynamics, as well as nature and religion, along with a variety of non-coercive variations and diversities, connecting development with ecological and spiritual aspects. This scheme should fundamentally accommodate a few basic assumptions. It should consider traditional culture as dynamic and capable of evolving with changing times, but keeping its inherited uniqueness intact. Secondly, it should accept the idea that in the conservation agenda, it would not be enough to instruct the stakeholders on conservation models; they should rather be taught how their association with a conservation scheme can guarantee them subsistence, and how they can harness this new knowhow in managing their life, without necessarily jeopardizing ecological balance and cultural uniqueness. One should also consider the fact that it will operate not on the basis of the conflict growing out of the West-East binary, or modern-traditional binary; rather, it would incorporate "healthy influences" from outside, and add to it the strengths of the local culture and prepare a composite mechanism, informed intimately by traditional cultural knowledge.

Models detached from cultural baggage have been tried and tested. The alternative model proposed herewith imagines a larger inter-cultural conglomeration guided by traditional cultural legacies and practices that regard development not only from a materialistic and entirely anthropocentric worldview, but also from a more eco-friendly, spiritual and empathetic worldview. The idea refutes all binaries between the rural and the urban, the primitive and the modern, or the traditional and the technocratic. It incorporates the entire human subject as one, and any knowledge, belief and practice the subject inherits from the past as an evolving category of episteme as "traditional culture". There are ample examples in "primitive" societies—in China, South Asia, Africa, Latin America and the Caribbean world—that promise a sustainable, eco-friendly form of development. Observations around the world suggest that traditional culture and indigenous knowledge are maintained by cultural heirs and ordinary households, and those development models that do not ensure the stake and participation of such households are not internally compatible.

Such an incompatibility of a development strategy with the cultural texture of a particular region is one of the main reasons why many technocratic and culture-insensitive development schemes have become counterproductive. Unless and until development is integrated with the cultural realities of a region and informed by its traditional knowledge, its sustainability will always be in question. With time, such a development model becomes obsolete and non-functional in relation to that cultural space. Or else, it will be highly coercive and therefore prone to vehement criticism and rejection by the potential beneficiaries.

One methodology to devise such a development model is to reach out directly to the beneficiaries—who are the heirs and practitioners of traditional culture—and take their knowledge and experience right at the time of framing the policy and development scheme. The consultation should continue through the very process of giving development a shape, and once it has taken place, the same people should be handed over the responsibility to maintain it, and make it sustainable. If that happens, they will feel a greater responsibility and ownership towards it, and the chance that it will survive will be high.

There are so many nuances of traditional culture that function in a close relationship with nature, but such nuances reveal themselves to development agents only if they converse with the people who practice them. This is made possible by the very fact that traditional culture, as S.C. Dube underscores, "is a vast reservoir," and can offer "sustenance to a radical reconstruction of society" (15). About tradition, he argues: "A happy convergence of tradition and modernity is not impossible; it can be witnessed in many Asian countries in several sectors of life, or at least in some segments of society" (15).

A relevant example is the tradition of tree worship in Asia which checks indiscriminate deforestation in the name of development. Historical records on tree worshipping in the region date back to many centuries.

Tree worship in India has been common since ancient times. In Mohenjodaro, there is one depicting a stylized Pipli tree with two heads or unicorns emerging from its stem. In ancient India, tree worship was a regular feature in both Hinduism and Buddhism, a fact that is well borne out in notable places like Besnagar, Bharhut, Bodh Gaya, Ellora, Sanchi, Bhaja, Mathura, Amarabati, Nagarjunakonda, and others. Gradually, people began to feel that the trees were sensitive and animate. This awareness further modified peoples' attitude towards trees. (Choudhury, 55).

According to Shakti M. Gupta, there are several trees, especially Bodhi trees, associated with the name of sages who received enlightenment under them, which gives them sacred status. For instance, Aswattha (*Ficus religiosa*) is the bodhi tree of Sakya Muni or Buddha; Nyagrodha (*Ficus bengalensis*) of Kasyapa; Udumbara (*Ficus glomerata)* of Kanaka muni; Sirisa (*Albizzia labbek*) of Krakuchhanda; Asoka (*Saraca indica*) of Vipaswi; Pundarika (*Nelumbium speciosum*) of Sikhi. ("*Plant Myths and Traditions in India*" 3).

Tree worship in Nepal has been a traditional practice since time immemorial. There are several trees like peepal, banyan, amala, holy basil, bel and others that are either directly worshipped as incarnation of gods, or its parts used during rituals. The practice of performing the nuptial ceremony of trees such as peepal and banyan, too is common. Tulsi—holy basil—is also ritually wedded, which confirms the belief that it is regarded as the incarnation of Lord Vishnu, and the weed, owing largely to its significance in human life, is bestowed high cultural worth. The ecological and medical significance of these plants, too, is a proven fact. They are either very good sources of oxygen, or have medicinal values. This consideration inspires people to preserve such plants and highlight the need to identify more such plants from the archive of traditional knowledge. Foregrounding their relevance in people's cultural life can help us check the development trajectory so that such plants are conserved for all times.

A few more instances can be cited from Nepal's unique cultural and spiritual relationship with various landforms, which can guarantee their safe and sustainable use. Rivers, in most cultures of Nepal, are sacred manifestations of the divine will, and most people, unless otherwise motivated, refrain from deliberately and publicly polluting a river. Revoking this cultural reverence, and educating newer generations on this value-laden conception of rivers can help check pollution. Most mountains are considered abodes of deities, and many Nepali cultures worship the mountain gods annually. As for other geographical features, many lakes—Taudaha, Nag Pokhari and Siddha Pokhari, for instance—are considered homes to Nāg Rāja, the snake god, and such places are culturally protected and preserved. Existence of many shrines and centres of pilgrimage across various forests and slopes of Nepal can, if properly emphasized and foregrounded, can guarantee voluntary protection of these places.

If researched extensively, many primitive and traditional cultures of the world have in their belief systems certain concepts and worldviews that can secure our world from the malice of the present-day trend of development that has divorced itself from its ethical counterpart. Certain geographical spaces, including rivers, lakes, mounds and water spouts, are identified with a certain divine power, or certain incidents in mythology. This accords them a divine significance, and people often do not tamper with such places during their day-to-day activities. There are many more beliefs of this kind in the different traditional cultures of the East. There is a dire need to identify, foreground and reassert such traditions and the practices they promise at the community level. Such traditional practices, taken up as methodological tools for development, can potentially impart insights on the optimum use of natural resources and minimum harm to the balance of nature.

Nepal's unique cultural experiences over the years can be taken as points of departure, and can be kept open to expansion, integrating similar tenets of other cultures until the proposition takes shape as a pragmatic developmental alternative for the entire world. This is being argued for, because Nepal has a huge corpus of traditional knowledge originating in its diverse linguistic and cultural repository. For example, communities living at different altitudes along the extensive plains, hills and mountains of Nepal follow diverse practices, beliefs and explanations of the man-nature relationship, and records confirm that such a relationship has never given rise to any coercive development model. Their settlement habits, food habits and other cultural practices resonate with nature's cycle and geographical reality, and yet, they have accommodated themselves to global development trends, carefully negotiating between modern and traditional development, and maintaining their traditional nuances of development. If such practices are taken together and a new model of development is theorized and put into practice, the benefit it can bring to humankind will be of paramount significance.

Cultural groups that have been living and developing in close harmony with all elements of nature have a huge archive of knowledge that not only ensures dynamic development, but also inspires human beings to make development sustainable. The spiritual aspect of their relationship with nature binds them with values that inspire man to refrain from blind adherence to anthropocentric and coercive development methods. Reaching out to such groups and making them direct stake-holders in any development project could, perhaps, help suggest to the present world a wonderful alternative model of sustainable development.

BIBLIOGRAPHY

Berkes, Fikret, Carl Folke and Madhav Gadgil. "Traditional Ecological Knowledge, Biodiversity, Resilience and Sustainability. *Biodiversity Conservation*. Ed. C.A. Perrings et. al. Netherlands: Kluwer Academic Publishers, 1995. pp. 281–299.

Chachage, C.S.L. "Towards a Critique of Development Theories in Africa." *UTAFITI*- Vol. 9 No J /987. pp. 5–30.

Choudhury Janmejay. "Tree Worship Tradition in India and Origin of Jagannath Cult." *Odissa Review* (June 2012). pp. 55–57.

Diwasa, Tulasi. "The Question of Modernization Coupled with Conserving Cultural Values with Special Reference to Nepal." An oral interview with Mahesh Paudyal.

Dube, SC. Tradition and Development. New Delhi: Vikas Publishing House, 1990.

Gupta, Shakti M. *Plant Myths and Traditions in India*. February 24, 2014. www.arvindguptatoys.com/arvindgupta/shaktigupta.pdf>

Kupchan, Charles A. *No One's World. The West, the Rising Rest, and the Coming Global Turn*, Oxford and New York, Oxford University Press, 2012.

Nnaemeka, Abonyi Nichodemus. "Towards an Alternative Development Paradigm for Africa."*J Soc Sci*, 21(1): (2009). pp. 39–48.

Rawls, John. *A Theory of Justice*. Cambridge: Harvard University Press, 1971.

Sorenson, J. S. (Ed.). (2010). *Challenging the Aid Paradigm: Western Currents and Asian Alternatives*. London, United Kingdom: Palgrave Macmillan.

Stout, Jeffery. *Democracy and Tradition*. Princeton and Oxford: Princeton University Press, 2004.

Taylor, Bron (Ed). *Encyclopedia of Religion and Nature*. London and New York: Continuum, 2005.

Ziolkowski, Janusz. "Cultural Dimension of Development." *Cultures* 6.1 (1979). pp. 17–29.

Articulations of Being: Reflections on the Crisis of Modern Civilization[1]

ADITYA MALIK

If they see breasts and long hair coming,
They call it woman,
If beard and whiskers,
They call it man:
But, look,
The self that hovers in-between is neither man
Nor woman,
O Ramanatha!
Devara Dasimayya (10th century CE)[2]

THE COMPOSER OF THIS SHORT verse belonged to a community of poet-saints from southern India called the *Lingayats* or *Virashaivas*. Between the 10th and 12th centuries these poets—both women and men—composed collections of short, inspirational poems that expressed a personal, intimate relationship to a deity that they had chosen to devote themselves to. In doing so, they radically questioned several entrenched beliefs and practices of the society in which they lived: the inequalities and hierarchies of caste and gender, the imbalance of wealth and power, the blind adherence to scripture and ritual, and the mediation of religious experience through organized priesthood. Religious experience as the unmediated, direct union of the human and divine, was obtainable—they asserted—by anyone, regardless of their social status, education, gender or age. While the movement these poet-saints initiated had a strong religious component, it was, at the same time, a revolutionary basis for social change that was uncompromisingly critical of our assumptions—whether personal or social—with regard to what we in modern parlance call "identity." For example, in the poem above, the poet speaks of a "self" that "hovers in-between," being neither male nor female; a self that is not contained by the obvious categories of "man" and "woman" that are so familiar to us in our everyday transactions. Similarly, other poems point to a "self" that is not limited by social representations and modes of operation whether given by religious practice or social status. The poet-saints criticized our habitual and customary ways of identifying ourselves through our professional affiliations, social roles, family lineage, religious rituals, and so on. These ways of identifying and representing ourselves, the poets claimed, were restrictive, constraining and limiting, resulting in deadening positions that created unnecessary boundaries between human beings, but also between human beings and God.

II

What is the "crisis of modern civilization"? Clearly, one of the manifestations of this crisis is the increasing alienation and fragmentation that we are encountering in societies and environments all over the world. The condition of modernity in which we find ourselves has crystallized through a series of acts that distance the individual from community, community from cosmos, culture from nature, mind from body, and so on. These acts of distancing are grounded in sets of binary, oppositional categories beginning with modern vs traditional. In its political manifestations, "modernity" continuously creates and perpetuates the existence of antagonistic dualities without which it loses legitimacy as an intellectual and political ideology. To be modern then is to both live and fervently believe in a society that values and, indeed, sustains divisions between public-private, human-divine, human-non-human/animal, secular-religious, individual-community, mind-body, and a bounded-permeable personhood. While these dichotomous categories may seem neutral on paper, in practice they are far from being so. Thus these oppositional categories involve a suppression in many instances of one of the pairings: the secular is clearly valued over the religious which may continue to exist, but only in the private sphere; humans are valourized over non-humans, "specially animals" such that human survival can take place at the cost of the extinction of several thousand other species; the mental (mind) is valued over the biological (body) that it can presumably control, understand and analyse; the individual is given precedence over the community in his or her quest for personal success, and so on. Moreover, it also involves living in a political state that administers and rewards fixed, impermeable, singular categories of identity over porous, flexible, shifting, permeable and multiple notions of personal and social identity.

The consequence of this dichotomization, fragmentation and division of human beings into nationalities, ethnicities, religions, cultures, regions, languages and other collectivities including human and non-human, is such that we can no longer be certain whether, or for how long, the human species along with thousands of other animals and plants that are going extinct because of an anthropocentric worldview will survive—perhaps not even beyond this century. What is the source of this fragmentation? Is there indeed a single source? Is the crisis of modern civilization traceable to a pervasive inner violence that we experience and engender? A violence that goes beyond and yet underlies the commonplace notion of physical conflict and abuse? Is "identity" itself a source of this fragmentation? What if one looked at violence from the perspective of "identity" drawing a distinction between "identity" and "self"? 'Identity' as defined in terms of particular signifiers such as ethnicity, religious affiliation, nationality, profession, gender, etc., and "self" in terms of that which can be considered to be beyond particular signifiers, as the *being* of human being that is neither definable nor limited to particulars. Could the source of fragmentation and violence lie in a mistaken understanding of human subjectivity solely in terms of particular signifiers that are ultimately limiting and exclusionary rather than with "self" that is not limited but is inclusive in scope providing a common ground for humanity?

III

What is this notion of "selfhood" that goes beyond our everyday, commonplace representations of self that are informed by our ethnicity, religious affiliation, nationality, occupation, and even gender? Moreover, is it possible that the very notion of identity informed (and constrained) by various modes of social representation is the source of violence and conflict? Following from the poem composed by the *Virashaiva* poet-saint *Devara Dasimayya*, could we consider that conflict and violence come into existence because of pervasive, yet mistaken notions of "self" as being clearly definable, fixed and contained by what we regard to be our identity? Pursuing this idea, we can draw a distinction, as mentioned earlier, between "self" and "identity". Whereas "self,"[3] in the sense being used here, is not limited by identifiable features given by the general parameters of space, time and society, "identity" is specific to space, time and society. Broadly speaking then, identity is *identifiable* through the signifiers of particular social and historical conditions; "self" on the other hand, can be described through the metaphor of context, i.e., a framework within or inside of which the specific expressions of identity are created, manifested, formed and played out. While a context may provide meaning to its content, it is not the same as the latter. Along the lines of the poem cited above, the "self" is not identifiable, quantifiable or definable. It is "in-between", neither here nor there, neither this nor that, neither man nor woman, neither East nor West and so on. It transcends specificity. Any definition of "self" would therefore be limiting. Nevertheless, this "unidentifiable," "unquantifiable," "intangible" context is an essential aspect of being human. In fact, it is what constitutes the *being* of human being. Yet, in our discussions of social, religious, national, ethnic and other forms of identity and the array of social and political issues we face, there is rarely any reference to what it means to be a human *being*. What is the *being* of human being? If we claim that all people across cultural, political, economic and other boundaries are human *beings* regardless of their identification with those particular formations, then surely we need to understand what this means! The question facing humanity today is whether there can be articulations of *being* (traditional or modern) that gain primacy over the many exclusive articulations of identity. If we claim that all people are human *beings*, we are also stating that there is a common ground that is not limited in its potential to be socially and politically inclusive.

NOTES

1 Sections of this response were published in *The Journal of the Te Awate Violence Research Centre* of the University of Canterbury in 2013.

2 Translated by A.K. Ramanujan, 1973, p. 92.

3 It needs to be noted that there are multiple uses of term "self" depending on academic discipline. I am using "self" in a philosophical sense as co-terminus with the ontological category of *being*.

Time and Space in Mayan Culture

MARÍA DEL CARMEN VALVERDE VALDÉS

IN THE MAYA WORLDVIEW, THE concepts of time and space are understood as a unity. Thus, the cosmos is regarded as the result of constant movements in an endless series of movements of creation and destruction. In other words, the Maya universe is subject to immutable and cyclical laws of death and birth. Such laws are ordered and coherent, and can be observed everywhere in nature (from microcosm to macrocosm).

In the last five centuries, such a worldview has been constantly confronted by opposing considerations in regard to time and space, mostly related to Western thought. This conflict embodies the fight between individualistic and pragmatic motivations, and a sense of full integration with the surrounding world and its cycles. In spite of such conflicting views, Mesoamerican communalism has survived from ancient times and can be found, even today, in the way the Maya people organize themselves, in their sense of relatedness to the earth, in their celebrations, and in many other areas of their everyday life.

These ideas regarding the concept of time in Mesoamerica are usually focused on the pre-Hispanic era and on conceptions that depict a cyclical time, inextricably linked to space.

Likewise, in the Maya world vision, the concepts of time and space cannot be separated from each other. In this system of thought, temporality is precisely the dynamism of space. Nothing that exists is ever a static reality, but rather is in constant movement and change (De la Garza, 1978). Thus, as in the rest of Mesoamerica, speaking of time-space in the Mayan world opens up the possibility of entering an incredibly rich universe. This universe is perceived by the Mayan people as profoundly sacred, and is therefore revealed to the individual or to communities in various forms, which are generally hierophanies.

But what became of this substantial part of the Mesoamerican world vision, particularly that of the Maya, following the arrival of new ideas regarding destiny? These ideas are largely based on a linear, tangible and measurable conception of time, contrasting with the apparently eternal series of cycles, in which Mesoamerican temporality develops. What happened to the universe in which human communities and their circumstances were part of repetitive cosmic cycles, rather than cosmic time being conceived in the image of a human being, an individual, with a single principle and an ultimate goal? In other words: what happened to the infinite time of indigenous peoples when they were confronted with the Western concept of time, determined by human measurements and proportions?

In the process of developing these concepts, it should be said that the Mesoamerican peoples' conception of time, cosmic rhythms and the role of humans differs substantially from the Judeo-Christian view. The latter possesses a predominantly individualistic vision of destiny, which is, arguably, personified so to speak, since man somehow transfers the image of his own existence, of a unique, unrepeatable human life, to universal time. This means that within this linear, finite world vision, in which man's individual being is projected onto the entire universe, fashioning it in his image and likeness, the world had a beginning and will have an end, like the life of a person. Thus, the cosmogonic myth narrates the origin of the world, and assumes that it will have a definitive conclusion, thus giving existence clear and, to a certain extent, measurable dimensions. Obviously, this certainty that, the universe will have the same fate as an individual, provides man on the one hand, with great security in the face of the immensity of the cosmos (clearly, immeasurable and infinite), but, on the other, demonstrates the perishable nature of existence. This underlying unease and sense of continuous urgency imposes, therefore, a very particular rhythm and stamp on the Western world. Likewise, here, convinced that the cosmos and his life have parallel fates, man faces his future directly and walks forward with the confident step provided for by the present, leaving the past behind, as it will never return.

Conversely, Mesoamerican societies in general, and the Maya in particular, conceived of the existence of the cosmos as the result of a constant movement of a never-ending sequence of creation and destruction; in other words, governed by a cyclical law of death and rebirth, like the laws of Nature, which are ordered and coherent and manifest themselves in the primary evidence man has before him, such as plants or stars. Within this conception, the idea of an absolute beginning becomes unclear and the future is presented as a constant chain of formations and catastrophes (De la Garza, 1987: 7). This is why the immediate image of the universe as something that is infinite, involving the contemplation of the cosmos and its natural cycles, is accepted. Unlike the Judeo-Christian tradition, in the Maya worldview, man's life itself is part of cosmic cycles, and acquires a cosmic dimension (instead of the cosmos acquiring a human dimension) and ultimately, this cyclical time of the universe is what lends meaning to everything. Thus, though humans have a beginning and an end, the community, and existence itself, does not. Consequently, this perishable human life acquires meaning and transcends time and space, and becomes part of cosmic destiny, and becomes another link in the interminable chain of cycles.

These two different conceptions of destiny translate into a contrast between two life systems and two positions towards the world. These are, to a certain extent, the Western (Judeo-Christian) individualistic and pragmatic spirit, on the one hand, and on the other, the Mesoamerican community, which has survived since ancient times and is primarily reflected in the organization of peoples, their relationship with the earth, their celebrations—in fact, virtually all spheres of everyday life.

It is true that there is a whole symbolic universe, made richer and more complex by the contact between two different world visions. The contradictory aspects of two cultures are reincorporated, reinterpreted and assumed. Thus ideas, symbols and customs were gradually integrated over time, some quickly and others more slowly, to create new structures and ways that help to explain existence.

Be that as it may, these processes always involve a break with reality as it is experienced and interiorized, constructed and reconstructed throughout pre-Hispanic history, and which, until that moment, reflected a specific way of living and understanding the world. Thus each of the Mesoamerican populations has had to develop different methods of responding and adapting to the numerous changes brought about by the Europeans. All of these involved a certain degree or form of resistance.

The various resistance movements and mechanisms that arose in the Maya sphere after their territory was conquered and colonized had their own logic and were part of this specific conception of time and space, which had little in common with Western culture's vision of temporality and destiny.

Thus—and this is the thesis of this paper—I believe that after the arrival of the Europeans, the ancient Mayas' particular manner of conceiving temporal spaces, or time in space, became one of their most important resistance strategies. Indeed, their determination to maintain traditions, by telling stories embedded in time cycles within the context of communal spaces, and the constant, overt struggle against authority through insurgencies and armed uprisings, has formed part of the everyday lives of these men and women for almost 500 years.

We are, therefore, faced with two pathways, and two intelligent survival strategies developed by the Maya people.

First, tradition, recreated through oral stories, and experienced through the populations' rituals and celebrations—candles and aromatic resins, music and stories, ceremonies and customs—which bring sacred times and spaces to life in a kind of mosaic, reflect the richness and complexity of this universe.

But whether by the warmth of a fireplace or in the feverish activity of a fiesta, I believe that the various kinds of stories that are still told today, which include complex cosmogonic or founding myths depicting the richness of Mesoamerican cyclical time, are often symbols of the resistance of contemporary Maya communities.

These ideas maintain a meaning and relevance in celebrations of patron saints, pilgrimages, mutual visits from one virgin to another and stories told by the elderly, in which the different conceptions of time are apparent in so far as they contain prophetic elements, which acquire meaning in the updating of myths.

Moreover, as sacred stories, these myths were recorded in sacred books, community books written in several Mayan languages, throughout the centuries of colonial domination (or even after Mexico's independence) and gradually acquired new meanings. Their characteristics place them firmly in the category of sacred texts. This corpus is famously complex and heterogeneous, one of the best known being the collection of texts written in Yucatán Mayan, the *Chilam Balam*.

The word Chilam means "he who is the mouth," i.e., he who prophesizes. The chilames were the prophet priests who interpreted the ancient books and, through the storytelling process, created prophecies. Consequently, the object of the divining practices was not only to know the future, but also understand the present and past, an essential part of this cyclical conception of time. In short, it is a tool for understanding the cosmos. The use of sacred language and the presence of a ritual specialist following precise laws were fundamental to achieving this.

Recording events is a priority within this conception of time, in which history and prophecy are inevitably intertwined. Codices—prophetic almanacs that the priests or *chilames* had to interpret—are sacred because they contain lines of action, reveal divine actions and provide certainty about the future. In light of this idea and the Maya world vision, events such as those mentioned by Father Diego de Landa, take on tragic dimensions. The monk said, "We found many of their writings, and as they all contained demonic superstition and falsehoods, we burned them all, which was a source of terrible grief among them." (Landa, 1982: 105). Through this action, the Spanish were not only burning the Mayas' books but also their possibilities of existing in the future. Moreover, these events occurred during the Maní *Auto de fe* in 1562, which, according to Bricker, acquired an enormous symbolic meaning, as it coincided with ill-omened dates in the Mayan calendar, the *uayeb* (Bricker, 1993: 46).

In this distant era, the 16th century, when the Yucatán Maya saw "their books of paintings burned" and with them their future, they appropriated and used, as a complement to their orally transmitted culture, one of the main tools for evangelization: the Roman alphabet, as a means of preserving in writing what they considered worthy of being stored in people's memory.

The legitimacy of this tradition, linking writing to the oral tradition, lay in the fact that the history of the community, despite dating back to the earliest time, was still relevant at the time of those who preserved it, since it was a reality that acted on the present and therefore explained and lent meaning to existence. These written stories contained the events and ideas that should be preserved and were part of the world vision of Maya people. Combined with the powerful strength of oral tradition, which was constantly recreated over the course of five centuries, they remained present in ritual actions and eventually emerged through their presence in several armed movements.

Thus, both books and ritual or military actions preserve the past yet are principally oriented towards the future.

The second resistance strategy is clearer and more obvious. It consists of active manifestations of rebellion in response to the new order, overt expressions of disobedience, riots and local disturbances, sometimes culminating in violent confrontations with the dominant regime.

In general, the underlying feature in the genesis of these rebellions comprises attempts to reinstate a new era with new indigenous governors, which would also involve returning to ancient times with the old Maya leaders.

Regardless of the armed movement itself, the uprisings usually involved a series of religious symbols accompanied by ritual processes as an inherent part of the insurrections. These processes are ritualistic because as the struggle begins, sacred time is reinterpreted, breaking continuity and abolishing profane time, at least momentarily. Man is torn from his individual, chronological and historical temporality, and is projected on sacred time, the timeless moment of divine order.

Consequently, these armed movements imply a particular way of constructing space and instating sacred time, based on a mythical story.

The rebels' aim of taking over territory symbolically implied recovering control of spaces. At the same time, the structure of the mythical tale became tangible, in which there was an initial time, before the War (which involved the oppression of the indigenous populations), before a divine, supernatural event destroyed the "established order". The divinity (whether a cross, a virgin or an oracle) spoke and called for rebellion. A liminal time was then established, that of the War, the time of myths, the achievements of men and sacred entities. This time and this story have not ended, they have merely been interrupted, and it is through pilgrimages, community celebrations and the activation of sanctuaries, that the "new time" is reinstated, that of the "now", of men and women narrating the myth, which creates a legitimating discourse as a means of relating the origin.

Time, seen in this manner, is inseparable from the various processes of cognitive processing through which group memories are constructed. It is therefore polytheistic, polyvalent and multi-faceted, insofar as it is the result of several factors interacting among themselves. It is also a social construct. Therefore, in order to understand how time is produced and organized, we must know about the social relations of the people who experience, produce, reinvent and recreate it on a daily basis. However, we should be aware that this time is not the context in which social relations develop, but rather the product of these social relations. It is constructed by the persons moving in it, who "activate" positions inside it.

The Maya have usually taken up arms because they consider that they have completed a cycle, and it is time to free themselves from the yoke of the oppressor. In this regard, the phrases from *Chilam Balam de Chumayel*, quoted almost directly in the speeches of the rebellion led by Jacinto Canek, are revealing, and warn that other times will come and that the power of the ancient Maya people will return. Other phrases warn, "The moment has arrived, sending them superstitious messages, prophecies telling them that the time has come to free them and live out their ancient rites." (Bricker, 1993).

Moreover, it is no coincidence that the Canek uprising took place in the region where, according to the texts that have survived, the tradition of the *Chilam Balam* books was particularly strong.

This story, despite its short duration (just a fortnight) and apparent defeat, is still alive and present, preserved in the collective memory and armed struggles as heroic deeds defending the Maya identity. It is also maintained in a series of religious practices that take up the tradition of armed movements yet also reinterpret the ritual in a modern context, from points of view that use religious emblems and sacred allegories linking the time of "before" and "after". This world vision is recreated and remembered from a past that the modern-day Maya appropriate and reconstruct every day.

This "remembering" involves the notion of restoring an earlier time, based on a clearly mythical discourse; recreating collective history to achieve a legitimacy of identity, consolidated through ritual experiences that traverse and reoccupy space. In this process of reoccupation, as in other moments of the cyclical destiny, such as the written tradition of the Yucatan Maya in the accounts of the *Chilam Balam*, when the Itzá re-appropriated the territory, when "land management" (*tsol peten*) occurred, present-day Mayas traverse, occupy and appropriate it. Along with the territory, these tales relate to those other eras. Therefore, as these paths are travelled, various aspects of the spatio-temporal conceptions of the Maya become tangible; there is a specific means of constructing space and instating time. Thus nowadays, village churches and, in the case of Quintana Roo, each of the Maya ceremonial centres, exert ritual and political control, which is in evidence during pilgrimages and celebrations, all of which are related to the Catholic liturgy and crop cycles.

To conclude, the resistance movements that defend and demand a geographical and ritualistic space are long-term; in other words, they are historical realities that are slow to form, develop and disintegrate. These elements remain effective at all levels of the history of communities, and will be a determining factor in them, since they are part of a complex ritual discourse. In this regard, they are a means of keeping these sacred experiences alive, an attempt to reconstitute these spatio-temporal spaces destroyed during the Conquest.

In the light of the Maya concept of destiny, the symbols linked to Maya resistance movements, like the most important aspects of existence, were part of the life cycles of the community. When these symbols emerge, they show that the collective identity and memory of a people remain alive and demand their place in history.

BIBLOGRAPHY

Bricker,Victoria R. 1993. *El Cristo indígena, el rey nativo. El sustrato histórico de la mitología del ritual de los mayas,* México: Fondo de Cultura Económica.

Garza de la, Mercedes. 1978. *El hombre en el pensamiento religioso náhuatl y maya.* México: Universidad Nacional Autónoma de México, Centro de Estudios Mayas (Serie Cuadernos, 14).

1987. "Mitos cosmogónicos mayas" en Monjarás Ruíz, Jesús (coord.) *Mitos cosmogónicos del México indígena.* México: Instituto Nacional de Antropología e Historia. (Colección Biblioteca del INAH).

Landa, Diego de. 1982 *Relación de las cosas de Yucatán,* Ángel María Garibay (introd.) México: Editorial Porrúa (Biblioteca Porrúa, 13).

Valverde Valdés, María del Carmen. 1999. "El hombre mesoamericano y su conciencia ante el devenir" en *Intersticios Filosofía/Arte/Religión. Los avatares del hombre: Preguntar para no callar de nosotros,* México, Escuela de Filosofía de la Universidad Intercontinental, año 5, no. 11, pp. 143-151.

2002. "De vírgenes, profecías, cruces y oráculos: religión y rebelión en el área maya" en *Enciclopedia Iberoamericana de Religiones* (Mercedes de la Garza, Martha Ilia Nájera Eds.), España, Trotta, (EIR, 02) pp. 283-319.

A New Spiritual Horizon for Humankind

HUGO NOVOTNY

THE US, JAPAN AND THE nations of the European Union are gradually losing their dominant positions in the world. At the same time, powerful countries like Brazil, India, Russia and China do not seek to impose their political and cultural values on less developed countries, but to base their relations on a structure of mutually beneficial cooperation. Thus, the new system of international relations taking shape due to the growth of Asian, Latin American and African nations is erasing the fragile dependency and colonial servility inherited from the last few centuries, through the power of common agreements as well as the convergence of interests. There is hope that this will turn the current global crisis into a true opportunity for global change.

For international affairs, the new paradigm that is being configured could be defined as the power of agreement, reciprocity and convergence in diversity, as opposed to the failure of hegemonies and homogenization. The success of this model depends on whether the participants in the game seek to impose their will—economically or culturally—on others, or desist from doing so.

The global crisis we are going through requires a deep change in the model of growth. Asia, Africa and Latin America cannot follow the path trodden by the US and the EU, with its promotion of false freedom at the cost of social fractures, consumption for all, indebtedness for the majority, but accumulation by only a few. A radically different vision must be defined. In other words, the crisis of global change must generate an entirely new social paradigm in which the idea of development does not only mean economic growth as it is the case nowadays from the standpoint of central powers, but it also includes the integral growth of all human beings grounded on the essential understanding that "progress for a few ends up being progress for nobody" (Silo, 2004).

In the Latin American continent, the rise to power of Evo Morales of Bolivia as the first President of native origins marked a watershed moment in the history of the Americas, doubtless a sign of the beginning of a new era for the whole continent. The creation of the Union of South American Nations (UNASUR) and the Community of Latin American and Caribbean Countries (CELAC) demonstrates a resolute determination to move towards a real integration of the continent, and points to the decisive departure of Latin America from the orbit of the political, economic and military influence of the US.

In my opinion, this phenomenon is closely related to the spiritual renewal of native cultures throughout Latin America, with particular strength in Bolivia, Ecuador, Guatemala and Mexico (in the last country, this process is developing in an open confrontation with the government and US interests in the region). In the case of Brazil, we can also appreciate the renewal of a highly diverse native spirituality with Afro-American roots, despite suffering persecución by the Christian churches, who are strongly engaged with economic leaders and the media of the country.

This crucible of cultures is immersed in a common spiritual atmosphere, in a sensibility that highly values the bond with the ground (the PachaMama), the ecologically harmonic and reciprocal coexistence between human beings and nature; the convergence in the diversity of cultures (interculturalism); the right of ethnic and social communities to self-determination; provision of official health and education for everybody, with an intercultural approach; the integrality of body, soul and spirit for everyone's well-being (Suma Qamaña—Buen Vivir) of individuals and communities.

We find a strong resonance between this Latin American sensibility and Asia's millenary cultures and spiritualties, especially with the spiritual currents that led to the development of great philosophical schools and highly inspiring mystical practices, like the multiple branches of Shaivism,

Buddhism and Taoism. Our hyphen or dash schools that also promote the harmonic and reciprocal coexistence between human beings and nature; the wholeness of body, soul and spirit for our well-being and the self-development of each individual, access to the experience of the Absolute. These are schools that have spread through the ages in the entire Asian continent and beyond, and nowadays are renewing and attempting to open new ways in the critical transition of the 21st century towards a new evolutionary spiral of human being.

The rich and mightily diverse cultural traditions of Africa—the cradle of humankind—are also called upon to be relevant to the effort to overcome the global crisis, contributing to the necessary transition process, with progressive elements that will be a basis for the next evolutionary stage. This involves the Ubuntu concept—the belief in a universal bond of sharing that connects all humanity—as well as many other components of the African ancestral sensibility.

At this point, the global community should realize that the expansion of one country or culture at the expense of others must come to an end. Horizontal expansion will not work anymore. We should take the vertical way—to develop the depth of space and the oceans through joint efforts directed towards common benefits. And it is only by using the same approach, instead of competition, can we solve the problems of poverty, starvation, illnesses, providing all the people of the world with healthcare and education at a worthy level for all. This approach envisages not only new international agreements concentrated on disarmament, but a real change of mentality from the habitual philosophy of violence and confrontation, to a new culture of nonviolence; from the "clash of civilizations" concept to the dialogue of civilizations, the unity in diversity of cultures and interests.

One more question specially deserves our attention. As soon as the human being went outside the limits of the Earth and saw through his own eyes our fragile world wandering among billions of stars and galaxies, he has woken to the vision that there are no real frontiers separating people; he felt, deeply in his heart, an ineffable love for human life and for every creature existing in the Universe. This feeling is capable of inspiring people to work towards a real change of worldview and behaviour, for deep changes that will lead to the humanization of the Earth (The Overview Effect).

In the same sense, human conscience is at this very moment striving to get rid of the corset of linear temporality and of discovering simultaneity, resonance, synchrony, new laws and phenomena relating to nonlinear complex systems and quantum physics, which are radically modifying the way of structuring reality.

It is fundamental to think about the consequences of the human conscience breaking free from the ties imposed by natural, spatial and temporal determinations of its physical prosthesis. We are speaking not only of the experience of living in weightlessness, or of some undeniable and subtle technological accomplishments such as virtual reality or telepresence[1]. We are talking also about the real possibility that, through a brave and deliberate act, human conscience would decide to break with its internal contradictions, to yield its heart to love and mercy towards all living kind and liberate itself so as to gain the inner unity that would allow it to project itself beyond the body and time.

In our opinion, a new spirituality that would enable the inclusion of the most progressive of the extremely diverse cultures and traditions worldwide, without limiting, but highlighting the identity of each nation; a spirituality that, at the same time, includes technological language and the experiences of a human being flying across cosmic space may be the most adequate incubator of this new human civilization. Unrestricted access to the experience of the Profound, contact with the fountain of the Sacred from the interiority of everyone without intermediation; the possibility of sharing this fundamental experience among people belonging to different cultures and confessions, may be meaningful elements for the spirituality of a new human nation worldwide.

Latin American (Argentine) philosopher and writer Silo (Mario Rodríguez Cobos, 1938-2010), founder of the current of thought of Universalistic Humanism, tells us in his message about the need for a spirituality where "the non-meaning of life can be converted into meaning and fulfilment" for everyone without external limitations or conditions; a spirituality that emphasizes "joy, love of the body, of nature, of humanity, and of the spirit", where "the worldly is not opposed to the eternal". Silo's message speaks about the possibility of "the inner revelation at which all arrive who carefully meditate in humble search" and about "mastering the Force in order to achieve unity and continuity" beyond the physical existence; it speaks about the essential priority of "learning to surpass pain and suffering in yourself, in those close to you, and in human society", "learning to resist the violence that is within you and outside of you", "learning to recognize the signs of the sacred within you and around you". Silo suggests: "Do not imagine that you are alone in your village, in your city, on the Earth, or among the infinite worlds", "do not imagine that you are enchained to this time and this space". [2]

The fully interconnected world where we are living today makes it possible and indeed necessary to move towards a common intercultural civilization. Horizontal and reciprocal interaction between cultures and nations, non-violent methods of social transformation, real participation of people on making key socio-political decisions will allow the integration of diverse communities as the avant-garde of the human nation in development. In our vision, the previously mentioned experience of the Profound is actually capable of opening up a new spiritual horizon, indispensable for the realization of this paradigm.

NOTES

1 Minsky M. – *Telepresence* – OMNI magazine, June 1980.

2 Silo – *Silo's Message* – Amazon, 2010.

Relevance of Traditional Cultures for the Present and the Future: The Case of Brazil

FAUSTO GODOY

> History has numerous instances of old and well-established civilizations fading away or being ended suddenly, and vigorous new cultures taking their place. It is some vital energy, some inner source of strength that give life to a civilization or a people, without which all effort is ineffective, like the vain attempt of an aged person to play the part of the youth.
>
> Jawaharlal Nehru in *The Discovery of India*

IT IS BECOMING INCREASINGLY COMPLEX for the so-called West to accept that the dynamics of the world have changed in the last decades, and that it is necessary to adapt to new and distinct paradigms in international relations: that the so-called countries and civilizations of the South have become a decisive factor in the globalized economy and politics of the 21st century, displacing the geo-economic and geo-politic axes from stratified stances. This irreversible ascension, so it seems, provokes ambiguous feelings: on one side, respect for the awakening of sleeping giants, most of them with ancient history and traditions, and, on the other, fear of its consequences.

The difficulties in dealing with this new reality seem evident. Accustomed to exporting its values and to impose its civilizational concepts over most of the human race, the "West" has not yet fully realized that situations like the Opium Wars of 1842 and 1860, the forced opening of Tokugawa Japan to Western powers in 1853, or, yet, the melancholic withdrawal of the Raj from British India in 1947, and the dramatic consequences it brought about to independent India and Pakistan, are no longer unquestionable. The list is long, and includes, besides the decolonization process of Africa in the early 60s, more recently, Vietnam, and even more recently, the conflicts in Iraq and Afghanistan, which are still unresolved. All of them are proof of how the central powers have been unable to deal with the "different" and to interact with alien values and concepts.

On their side, before they could ascend to their status as a major factor in international relations, the former colonies had to absorb the impact of—and, to resolve—the often traumatic legacies of their colonizers. Most of these related to physical boundaries artificially drawn, showing no respect for human boundaries. The country that would become Laos, for example, is the result of a unilateral demarcation by the French colonizer, and, in the end, most of the Lao ethnic group became part of Thailand. A similar situation occurred between Malaysia and Indonesia: the population of northern Sumatra was split by the Dutch along the Malacca straits, a part becoming Malaysian and another part Indonesian; and India and Pakistan have not yet been able to find a solution to Kashmir, and that has become an argument for Islamic radicalization. At this point, it is important to understand what the authors interpret as the West. The British scholar Niall Ferguson, in his recent book *Civilization, The West and the Rest*, mentions the Latvian-American Professor Adda Bozeman Barkhuus's division of the world's pre-modern civilizations into the West, India, China, Byzantium and Islam. And Samuel Huntington, in *The Clash of Civilizations*, circumscribes the West only to Western Europe (exclusive of the Orthodox East), North America (exclusive of Mexico) and Australasia. For him, Greece, Israel, Romania and Ukraine, or the Caribbean Islands, do not belong to this core group.

According to Ferguson, the West is much more than a geographic expression. It is a set of norms, behaviours, cultures and institutions, however fluid its frontiers might be. For him, what has distinguished it from the East is what he calls the "propellers of the global power", i.e., six systems connected to institutions, ideas and people's response to them: competition; the development of science; the right to property; the improvement of health; the spread of the consumer society; and Protestantism and its labour ethics. According to him, it was the good response to these challenges that propelled the West to the leadership of the world.

This is no longer the case, if it ever was. Globalization and migration on a global scale have blurred these lines. The countries of the "South" are finding their own path to development and prosperity, no matter how complex it may be, and, in many cases, challenging the First World whenever they find room for the "comparative advantages" they may possess. Indeed, today among the countries with the 10 highest GDP (according to 2012 data produced by the International Monetary Fund), four are not considered Western, if we take into account the definition indicated above: China (second), Japan (third), Brazil (seventh) and India (tenth). And Russia, eighth, may not be considered fully Western, either. In the reverse sense, the Western powers have not been able to find an equation to absorb alien immigrants in their own territories. As the Palestinian-American scholar Edward Said pointed out, "Metropolitan Europeans and Americans are confronted now with a numerous 'non-white' population in their territories who demand that their own narratives be heard."

The question that comes to one's mind at this point is: How will traditional cultures survive and adapt to a world that is becoming increasingly blended? I believe each of them will have to search for its own answer, some succumbing more easily to the attractions of mass consumerism, others resisting—barely—and, still others finding a possible balance between tradition and modernity.

A first conclusion that we all may agree upon, I presume, is that the differences between the livelihood and traditions of urban and non-urban populations, worldwide, are becoming increasingly accentuated: the cultural distances that separate New York (USA), Tokyo (Japan), São Paulo (Brazil), Shanghai (China) and Mumbai (India), from each other nowadays, are much smaller than those that set apart Park Rapids (USA),

Kurashiki (Japan), Crato (Brazil), Suzhou (China) and Chamba (India). The "contamination" of cultures, to use a better phrase, the insemination of foreign cultural references into the everyday life of the cosmopolitan urbanite, be it in the West, or in the East/South, forces us to revise our values and perceptions and to assimilate these alien imports—*sushi* in traditional Brazilian grill restaurants *(churrascarias)*, yoga in gym academies, or Pizza Hut and McDonald's all over the world—into our daily lives. We are no longer islands, or, to put it better, the islands are now being drawn back into the global continent. Would this be the birth of a new and global tradition? Welcome to a new Pangea.

This does not mean that we have lost our references and values, I believe, but that we have globalized them, whenever there is communicability among them. Others, however, remain untouched, for they are the pillars of a given culture. For me, these are non-negotiable spaces. One of these is the way the individual finds his place within his society. In the West, he is its core, its *raison dêtre*. The social contract by which he abides in order to participate in the group, as Jean Jacques Rousseau would say, establishes the boundaries of how much he has to concede of his liberty—*son droit naturel*. That is what the *Déclaration des Droits de l'Homme*, the daughter of the French Revolution, states: "Men are born free and remain free and equal in their rights... Freedom consists in being able to do everything that is not detrimental to others." The Declaration of Independence of the United States would stress more or less the same idea: "...We hold these truths to be self-evident, that all men are created equal, that they are endowed by their Creator with certain inalienable Rights, that among these are Life, Liberty and the pursuit of Happiness." Confucius, however, in Zhou China, would say almost the opposite. In the *Analects* he preaches: "...the young man must be a good son at home and an obedient person outside, frugal in his words, but trustworthy in what he says, and he must love his people, in general, but seek to nourish the friendship of his companions... and if there is any energy remaining, he must devote himself to humanity." (*Analects* 1:6)

The inability to relate to other cultures and traditions with a free mind and spirit, devoid of prejudices, is the root of most of the clashes among civilizations. The imposition of politically—or socially—correct patterns of behaviour, as perceived by a given culture, upon another, often thought of as inferior in terms of economic project, but nonetheless consistent in its culture and traditions, is, I believe, one of the reasons why we are living today in such a troubled world. But where does Brazil fit into this scenario? Basically a country of immigrants, how do/did we blend so many cultures in our geographic space? And where are we heading? In order to understand this, one must look back on the process of Brazil's formation. Unlike the families of the Pilgrims who looked at America as a haven for starting a new life, or counter-Reformation Spain, that had the Christianization of the "uncivilized" natives of Latin America as a cardinal point of its colonization thrust, most of the Portuguese men who settled in Brazil in the early 1500s went alone, to exploit the riches of the land and return as quickly as possible to the metropolis. Many, if not most, never did return, and found in Brazil a welcoming native population in whose women they encountered solace and bred children. Therefore, the Brazilian race has been a mixed one from the very beginning of our history.

However, the indigenous inhabitant of the land would not submit to the harsh treatment by the colonizer. So, already in the 16th century, Africans from the western part of that continent began to be taken to Brazil as slaves. This traffic persisted until the end of the 19th century; in fact, it was only on May 13, 1888, that the daughter of Brazilian Emperor D. Pedro II, D. Izabel, acting as regent, abolished slavery. Brazil was the last country in the Americas to do it. So economically important was the system, that in 1825, the Afro-descendant population amounted to 56 percent of its inhabitants. The contribution of Africa to Brazilian culture is enormous, from the traditional cuisine to the splendour of Brazilian baroque churches, and beyond. I firmly believe that, at its core, Brazilian popular culture remains African, blended with the native Indian. The Yoruba/African mysticism—*candomblé*—has impregnated our Christian faith, generating a syncretic Catholicism.

And, above all, our race: inter-racial marriages are not just common in Brazil, they have indeed changed the face of the country. According to a survey done by the Instituto Brasileiro de Geografia e Estatica (IBGE), the government census agency, in 2010, 50.7 percent of Brazilians declared themselves *mulatto* or black. Quite often the frontiers that distinguish the races are blurred, though, as it occurred in 2007, at the University of Brasilia, when two brothers—twins—applied for admission under the quota that was established for Afro-descendants: one was accepted and the other not. Policies are being developed by the government to promote a more racially egalitarian society, but the question remains: "What is it to be white in Brazil?"

As an immigration country for most of its history, Brazil has absorbed peoples and races from all over the world, particularly from Portugal, Spain, Italy, Germany and, in Asia, from Japan and Korea. The contingent of immigrants from the Middle East is also quite substantial. One example: the population of Lebanese living in Brazil—born or *oriundi*—is almost thrice the population of Lebanon: there are around 10 million of them in Brazil, as opposed to 3.5 million in their motherland. Brazil also has the largest concentration of Japanese and their descendants, outside Japan. And, according to a census organized by the Italian Embassy in Brazil, last year, around 30 million children of the immigrants who sought our shores between 1870 and 1960—that, is, 15 percent of our population—are today part of the "Brazilian race". Nobody in Brazil, to my knowledge, would call himself/herself Italian-Brazilian, Japanese-Brazilian, German-Brazilian, and so forth. We call ourselves simply Brazilian. And very few of the children of immigrants can speak the language of their parents. I honestly think that Brazil can be considered a melting pot in the South.

The immigrants have brought with them their own stories, their traditions and their perceptions of the world, which paved the way for the syncretic mix that is Brazilian culture today. It is the result of what we absorbed from these different contributions, adapting them to the cybernetic-Internet world, where frontiers are constantly transposed by the social media and their network. In fact, I wonder if a totally uncontaminated, pure civilization—or untouched culture—could be possible in the today's world. TV, mobile phones and the internet would not allow it, I presume. The idea of the *bon sauvage*, unfortunately belongs to history. Welcome to "Urbania", for better or for worse.

What we need to do is develop new stories in this new context, and transform them into new and extended traditions, involving new and unsuspected supporting content which help in their narration, taking care that the previous stories don't get lost in the cacophonic world of global civilization. This is a challenge for opinion makers and the academia. But, most of all, it is a decision—conscious or unconscious—to be taken by each one of us who are the ancestors of future generations.

Getting Rid of Stereotypes as a Condition for Cultural Dialogue: From the Greek Paradigm to the Idea of a Universal Cultural Contract

YANGOS ANDREADIS

A CONFERENCE ON THE RELEVANCE of the Cultures of Asia, Africa and South America in the contemporary world is of primordial importance because those cultures constitute an immense contribution to what we call the world's cultural heritage, whose teachings are quintessential for the present, as well as the future survival and progress of the planet. In the past, and even in the recent past, as a result of the West's domination, cultural communication in the rest of the world has been largely based on the mediation of Western scholarship, literature, art and media. What each one of the non-Occidental societies knew about the others was what the West could, and/or wished to understand or wanted the others to understand.

The present conference constitutes one more sign that such mediation should be largely replaced by horizontal and direct cultural, political, economic communication among all members of a multi-centred world. To make things clearer, what must be done is not to exclude the very important Western cultures from this dialogue, but to accept the Western contribution in a spirit of real equality, free from any inferiority or superiority complex. Planet Earth being round, the necessary quest beyond the West will lead us again to an encounter with the West. But, as Valmiki in the Ramayana and Homer in *The Odyssey* have taught us, great travels change the travellers, endowing them with a superior force, enabling them to understand, to act and to love.

Greek culture, along with several others geographically situated in Europe, holds a particular position on the matter. In order to appreciate this, one must refer to the past for the sake of the present and the future. For the ancient Greeks, Propheteia, the goddess of prophecy, was the daughter of Mnemosyne, the goddess of memory. Seers had to undergo exercises requiring their remembering long oral texts. For folk poets, this practice of training has remained alive in the Balkans till very recent days. Remembering and engaging continuously in a dynamic dialogue with the past, communicating with origins, is therefore, for Greeks, as for other cultures, a means for foreseeing the future, and acting consequently.

Origins are not, however, a simple matter. Greece, along with Rome, is indeed considered to be a leading source of Western culture. This fact has had an impact that goes far beyond what we usually term culture. For the West, its Greek origins served as a pedigree of superiority versus the non-Occidentals, who were either considered as sub-human, as Sepulveda has argued, born to become and remain slaves, or, at best, as immature children needing a long period of education and, when necessary, rigorous punishment. The enlightened voices of several people who have personally known the cultures in question, such as Father Lafiteau in France and Father Bartolomeo de las Casas in Spain, have declared that the so called savages and barbarians were highly civilized and moral people, superior to their Occidental oppressors; yet this trend of thought, alive till today, did not have any serious influence—at least till the first half of the 20th century—on the behaviour of Western states towards the Americas, Africa, India, China and other regions of the world.

Apart from such crude exploitation of the Greek origins of Western culture, we may state that Greece is geographically European, though not all Greeks are—if, for example, we think of Cyprus belonging instead to the Middle East. The question of the cultural relationship between this country and the West is a complex one. From Roman times, Greece exported cultural elements to Europe and continued to do so during the Middle Ages. This will be clear, especially if we recall that Ukraine and Russia, which are both celebrating their relations with Greece this year, were Christianized during the 10th century, and are inalienable and fundamental parts of the culture, politics and economy of Europe.

The Renaissance and the Enlightenment offer good examples of Greece's bi-directional and ambiguous relationship with the West. No doubt the West has received many elements from Greece, including forms of thought, and, most of all, the famous concept of *logos*—unilaterally interpreted as reason—and art. Yet, the Western world presents a diachronic particularity concerning the way it has dealt with its traditional cultural heritage. Westerners were not, in most cases, what we call the first inventors in the fields of politics, economy, science and even in technology. But, as Bacon has put it in his *New Atlantis*, they converted all those elements into instruments of what Aristotle has termed in his *Politics*, the "useful", namely the non-spiritual field related to wealth and domination. Consequently, they transformed what they had received from Greece and other traditional cultures of the East in a manner that suited such an approach.

This was not an easy task. For example, Greek myths—and one could say the same about Indian myths—although constantly present in Western culture, were deemed to be full of irrational and immoral elements, and in a way, the entire project of Western mythology could be termed as a vain effort to rationalize and to moralize them, forgetting—as Adorno and Horkheimer have put it in their *Dialectic of the Enlightenment*—that such an attack on myths constituted the greatest and the most absurd myth of all. In fact, it was not until Nietzsche and Freud accomplished their attack against what has more recently termed *logocentrism,* that the fundamentals of Western *logos* were challenged, despite the fact that both Nietzsche and Freud imposed several distortions serving their positions. *Logos* (returning to some fundamental meanings it had in ancient and mediaeval times) since then has, at least partly, renewed its relationship with the unconscious part of the self, thus opening up an important path of dialogue between the other cultures of the world and the West.

No doubt Greece was, on the other hand, influenced by the Enlightenment, in the years before the 1821 national revolution as indeed were many other countries, including India and several in Latin America. Romanticism, modernity, political and economic forms and institutions, as well as technological achievements were part of what the country received from Western Europe. Yet—and this is in a way an absolute oxymoron—Greece was deemed by several Westerners to be non-Western or pseudo-Western. This approach dates back particularly from the era of the Greek revolution, but towards the end of the 20th century it has acquired new forms and has come to be based on new arguments. Greece—as well as the Slavs—has been considered by international relations theorists such as Samuel Huntington in his *The Clash of Civilizations* as, an abnormality, a culture foreign to the common heritage of the West. Fausto Godoy, speaking at this conference was quite right when he asserted that countries like Greece, Ukraine, Israel, etc. have, according to Huntington, no European characteristics. This remark acquires a nightmarish dimension when we realize that people like Huntington did not and do not write simple scientific dissertations, but are helping prepare real plans for foreign policy, intended to be instruments of political action for the sole superpower and its allies. The non-European—meaning the non-Western—character of Greek culture, including elements ranging from politics and economy to the arts and cuisine, still serves as an argument for several European Union politicians and media people, who wish either to oust Greece from Europe or to transform it, (along with other countries), into a pool for providing cheap and docile modern-day slaves.

Greece, as well as almost all the countries of Latin America, has suffered more Western occupations or invasions, and indeed, permanent political subjugation and economic exploitation by the West, nowadays routinely disguised under the mask of economic assistance programmes. The story goes back as far as the Crusades, especially the fourth (1204). His Holiness the Pope John Paul Woitila had indeed asked to be pardoned for this occupation, which probably cost Byzantium as much if not more damage than the Turkish occupation. After the war of liberation from the Ottoman Empire, Greece was occupied at least four times by France, England, Italy and Germany, while Cyprus, inhabited mostly by Greeks, was first occupied by Richard the Lionheart and then by the Venetians and the Turks, and was finally bought by the British who made it one of their colonies. After World War II, the mainland itself became a satellite of Great Britain, and thereafter of the United States, which, in 1967, imposed a dictatorship for which Bill Clinton, echoing the Pope's initiative, asked Greece's pardon, when he visited the country in 2000. To cut a long story short, Greece, like so many countries of South America, Africa and Asia, has for a very long time been a neo-colony.

It would be unfair and inaccurate to assert that Greek culture is not linked to that of other Western countries, including the Anglo-Saxon and Germanic world, the countries of the Mediterranean South and Latin America as well as the Slavs. Dostoyevsky, Lorca, as well as Shakespeare, are, in a way, considered and cherished as "Greek" writers, and in modern times they have influenced a long series of eminent artists, like the leading novelist Papadiamantis and the two Nobel laureate poets, Seferis and Elytis, who have both underlined their connection with as well as their difference from the Western creators that have inspired them. On the other hand, elements of difference and discord have traditionally been important: the Oriental Greek and Slav Orthodox Christian religions have long been considered by the Vatican as heresies. Folklore, politics and art, cuisine and elements of everyday life are no doubt influenced by a Western lifestyle, yet they contain several elements linking the country with the Mediterranean, the Slav world, Africa and Asia. Among them, I would underline the field of traditional music—in which *dromoi*, literally, *roads*, are quite close to the Indian *ragas*—as well as shadow theatre, dance and several rituals in which initiates worship a series of protector saints, which, to a considerable extent, represent masks of ancient gods, especially Dionysus, Athena, etc. The analogy with the deities and saints of the Brazilian Condomble and the Cuban Yoruba would, in this sense, be quite instructive. Today, such concepts and modes of behaviour, regarding time, work, hospitality, political engagement, etc., make our friends in the German press and government rather nervous, as they are not compatible with their Protestant idea about what Europe must be.

The question of cultural origins might shed more light on our relationship with the Western world on the one hand, and with the non-European world on the other. To do so, we must realize, once and for all, that the discussion regarding the priority in the discovery of arts, sciences or political systems serves only to disguise ideological intentions under a seemingly scientific mask. It is certain that Greece's cultural, scientific, religious origins have much to do with Egypt—we are the only European country to possess two 4,000-year-old pyramids—as well as with the Phoenicians, Central Asia and India. The Greeks adopted the Phoenician alphabet and shared deities and rituals with Central Asia even before 2000 B.C. They travelled to India long before and after Alexander—at the entrance of New Delhi's Archaeological Museum one can visit the rock on which are inscribed the laws Asoka dedicated to his Yavana subjects. Greek sculptors decorated Darius's palace in Tehran, and Greek sculptors and vase painters borrowed abundantly from Egypt and the East. In more recent times, starting from the beginning of the 19th century, movements of national independence and emancipation from colonialism have brought the Greek people very close to leading figures from Africa, Asia and South America, including the liberators of the peoples in Latin America, and the creators of democracy in Venezuela; the generals Miranda and Bolivar are both fervent admirers of the Greek classics. One recalls that several Latin American nations were the first to recognize the Greek revolution of 1921. In the field of culture, we are still discovering that poetry, theatre and the arts Greece shares, many common elements, and analogies with the material and non-material cultures of India, Egypt, Mexico and many other countries.

I have tried to mention more points that might help liberate us from the stereotypes we have inherited, mostly unconsciously, either from Western domination or from a narrow-minded and fanatical opposition to it. My references to Greece should not be taken to be a narcissistic monologue. They should be seen as constituting a simple paradigm serving to underline that such stereotypes can undermine our efforts at mutual comprehension. Horizontal communication among non-Occidental cultures is more than relevant in the present day, when neo-liberalism tends to undermine traditions, identities and national frontiers.

What I say here does not imply that any constituent of universal culture should be excluded from the dialogue, or that the West/East or the West and the Rest dichotomies are absolutely pertinent. Such dichotomies should not be understood according to purely geographical criteria and, in any case, cannot be conceived in a holistic manner. Purely geographical criteria risk becoming simply irrelevant, and in many cases the position on the map does not constitute a guarantee that the structures of a state, a society, a culture basically differ from what we consider to be the West. We, therefore, must seek dialogue with all cultures if we aspire to construct a better, more harmonious world, animated by the synthesis of opposites at a higher level.

I am perfectly aware of the fact that we, the people participating in this important conference, do not constitute a political forum. Yet, I think that people of culture who are also people of goodwill, should realize that at this very moment, a threat, either cultural, economic, and/or military is menacing more and more societies at a planetary level. This is also the case for several "abnormal" Europeans, like Greeks, Italians, Spaniards, Portuguese and the Slavs. Politics and culture partly belong to different spheres, yet cultural issues always play an important, although not easily visible, role. As a citizen of the universal state of culture, extending beyond frontiers while respecting them, I nourish a deep and sincere interest in participating in initiatives such as the present one, for which I heartily thank Kapila Vatsyayan and the institutions of the IIC and the ICCR, and hope to contribute to the promotion of future events of this kind.

I believe we are all here in order to contribute to the defence of cultures and identities, all over the world, because everywhere they are under a terrible multiform attack: we may praise culture but at the same time, what really deserves to be called culture occupies a less and less central place of the interest for the majority of the people in power, and therefore of the ideas, values and institutions they incarnate and the measures they adopt.

A dialogue of cultures will contribute to the reinvention of democracy at a time, when the democratic system constitutes frequently not more than a façade and decision making becomes the privilege of the few. Such reinvention would be the most essential and the most ambitious of all revolutions.

Our world urgently needs a new global contract among human beings, as well as between mankind and nature. Great efforts have already been dedicated to such an objective. But the fact that in the present moment, neo-liberalist development remains totally connected with more and more wars proves that such efforts are not enough. We must, therefore persist in working in this direction. The improvement of the dialogue among our cultures should be the basis of such efforts.

Relevance of Russian Historical Experience for Other Cultures

SERGEI SEREBRIANY

THE THEME OF THE CONFERENCE was formulated somewhat ambiguously. When I first read the title: "The Relevance of Traditional Cultures for the Present and the Future", I thought it referred to the recent book by Jared Diamond, *The World Until Yesterday: What Can We Learn from Traditional Societies?*[1] According to Wikipedia, this book "explores what people living in the Western world can learn from traditional societies, including differing approaches to conflict resolution, treatment of the elderly, childcare, the benefits of multilingualism and a lower salt intake." In this case, "traditional societies" refers to those human communities that may otherwise be called "primitive societies".

But when I further read the concept note of the conference, which mentioned "a shift... in the structure of power from the West to the East" and opposed "the old civilizations of Asia, Latin America and Africa" to "Western Civilization" (which sounded rather *Toynbeean* or even *Huntingtonian,* though, of course, with a different accent), I realized that "traditional cultures" meant "non-Western" cultures/societies, and the so-called "Western civilization" was opposed to "non-Western" civilizations.

Before going further, I would like to put on record some caveats. First of all, I think that responsible scholars must strictly differentiate between discourses of power and power politics, on the one hand, and discourses of culture(s)/civilization(s) and cultural/civilizational values, on the other.

I am not a political scientist and, perhaps for this very reason, I am afraid of any talk about "shifts of power", "balances of power" and the like. In 2014, when we mourn the centenary of the outbreak of World War I, discourses on power politics sound especially ominous. During the so- called *belle époque* (roughly between 1871 and 1914), many Europeans thought that the balance of power was a guarantee of lasting peace. But all too often this rhetoric was just a smoke screen for great power ambitions. The rivalry between the European Great Powers brought about the ruinous and fratricidal World War I (with World War II as a sequel). Russians must be especially sensitive to all talk about power politics. The excessive power ambitions of the Russian Empire brought it to a collapse in 1917. The Bolsheviks, who restored the Empire (under a different name) by the early 1920s, inherited its love for great power politics and, very much because of this perverted love, ruined the country once again, by the early 1990s. And now, as I am writing this essay (in May 2014), great power politics once again endangers the fragile edifice of civilization (using this word without any adjective and article, I mean humankind as a whole).

Now the words "civilization", "culture", "tradition(al)", "modern(ity)," etc., like many other terms in the social sciences, are used both in scholarly and political (public) discourses. The two usages are quite different. Scholars usually do not forget that the meanings of all terms are fluid, contingent and conditioned by many circumstances, so that, while using them, one must always be on guard against possible misunderstandings and must always define what exactly he or she means by this or that word. On the contrary, in political discourses words are often used as if they have clear-cut meanings, even though these alleged meanings are hardly ever defined. Such political usage aims not at genuine understanding, but rather at making people think and behave in a particular way. Such a discrepancy between the scholarly and political usage of the terms "civilization", "culture", "tradition(al)", and "modern(ity)" is very much in evidence in today's Russia and, probably, in other countries as well.

Perhaps, one of the best known and most dreadful cases when a word, initially introduced as just a scholarly term, a neutral designation of certain languages and peoples, was later used for pernicious political purposes, is the use of the word "aryan". As we know, the English word "aryan" and the corresponding words in other European languages have been derived from the Vedic word "ārya" ("noble"), which was the self-appellation of the people who composed Vedic poetry. Nineteenth-century European linguists and historians used this word for designating particular groups of languages and particular peoples, mostly in historical reconstructions. But in the 20th century, this originally rather innocuous scholarly term became a terrible ideological weapon in the hands of the German Nazis, a means of pitting peoples against each other and even a justification for genocides.

In a similar way, the scholarly terms "civilization", "culture", etc. may be used for sinister political purposes. In fact, already during WWI, German propaganda claimed that Germany fought for Kultur against the "decadent" French and British (Western) civilization. Nowadays some politicians and/or ideologists may claim that their particular civilization (i.e. their country) is superior to other civilizations (countries) and therefore may be permitted to behave in certain ways normally regarded as not being permissible.[2] Of course, the word "civilization" as such is not to blame: other words (religion, nation, people and what not) may be also used for such purposes.

I do believe that the discourses on culture(s)/civilization(s) and cultural/civilizational values, if and when they are undertaken not in order to foster (or hide) some kind of power politics, but in the spirit of genuine scholarly inquiry, may help us understand the real problems of today's world and contribute towards their solutions. And I do not believe (pace Samuel Huntington) that today's world is divided between several (opinions differ as to their number) civilizations, which have got irreconcilable value systems and are destined to fight each other.

The above-mentioned propagandistic opposition between Germany and the "decadent West", incidentally, shows the historical mutability of the terms "West" and "Western civilization". Now, of course, Germany is usually included in "Western civilization", but in the 19th century and probably through most of the first half of the 20th century, many Germans would not agree with such an attribution.

The relations between Russia and the "West" ("Western Europe") have been even more complicated and controversial. The questions similar to those that were offered for discussion at our conference had been discussed in Russia for almost two hundred years.

At this point let me recall that, according to Arnold Toynbee, Russia belongs to "the great non-Western majority of mankind",[3] specifically to what he called "Orthodox Christian civilization". Samuel Huntington used the term "Orthodox Russian Civilization".[4] For today's Russians like me, this term sounds funny, but I have to agree with both Toynbee and Huntington that Russia is, by and large, a non-Western country.

Here again I must make a digression. What has been said above about the contingency and changeability of terms, fully applies to many (if not to all) names of countries, peoples, and, for that matter, civilizations. Thus, the name "Russia" (in Russian "Россия") has had different meanings in different times and has now different meanings for different people. From the early 18th century till 1917, the official name of the country was "Российская Империя" which is usually translated into English as "Russian Empire", but might better be translated as "Empire of Russia".[5] In 1917 this Empire collapsed and was partially restored by the Bolsheviks by the early 1920s. From 1922 up to 1991 the official name of the country was Union of the Soviet Socialist Republics (USSR), though it was often called just Russia by many foreigners. After the collapse and disintegration of the USSR in 1991, the former largest Union Republic, officially called "Российская Советская Федеративная Социалистическая Республика" (RSFSR), became a separate state with two official names: Россия (Russia) and Российская Федерация (Federation of Russia).

Now the question "What is Russia?" has been much discussed, among the inhabitants of the country, by now at least for two or three hundred years, and the question remains as controversial as ever.

In terms of territory, by the middle of the 19th century the Empire of Russia had spread over three continents: Europe, Asia and America. In 1867, Alaska was sold to the USA, and the Empire of Russia remained only on two continents, but in the following decades it expanded considerably in Central Asia, moving rather close to the British Indian Empire.

In Europe, the Empire included Finland (taken from Sweden in 1809) and a large part of today's Poland. Finland became independent in 1917, and Poland was reassembled in 1918 from several parts divided up among Russia, Austria and Prussia in the 18th century.

After the revolution of 1917, three Baltic peoples, the Estonians, Latvians and Lithuanians, got their own respective independent states, and Bessarabia (Moldavia, today's Moldova), taken from the Ottoman Empire by Alexander I in 1812, was taken by Romania (for the reason that the Moldavians and Romanians may be considered "one people").

In 1940, under a secret agreement between Stalin and Hitler, the three Baltic states and Moldavia (together with Northern Bukovina) were reabsorbed into Russia (the USSR). In 1939, under the same agreement, Stalin took some parts of the Polish state (diplomatically called Western Ukraine and Western Byelorussia). After WWII Stalin took Subcarpathian Rus (alias the Transcarpathia) from Czechoslovakia and joined it to the Ukrainian Soviet Socialist Republic. Thus Stalin almost restored the former borders of the Empire (in 1939-40 he tried to reabsorb Finland as well, but failed), and even added some territories (Northern Bukovina and the Transcarpathia) which had never been parts of the Empire.[6]

In the USSR, ethnic Russians lived not only in the RSFSR, but practically in all other Union Republics as well (whose borders had been drawn rather arbitrary, because nobody took them too seriously). After the disintegration of the USSR, the Russians indeed became a "divided people". Those Russians who found themselves in newly independent states outside the Russian Federation faced, in various degrees, a number of problems. A substantial number of such Russians preferred to move to the Russian Federation, but many continue to live in the new states. A special case is Eastern Ukraine where the ethnic identity of many people has been rather blurred. Here it may be a matter of personal choice to consider oneself Russian or Ukrainian. Another special case is Belarus where the dominant language is Russian.

In the USSR, since the 1970s, the official view was, that out of many different peoples of the country, "new historic community, the Soviet people" had emerged. Like most other tenets of the official Soviet ideology, this statement was a kind of myth, but, nevertheless, it did contain a measure of truth. For many Soviet citizens (especially in big cities) belonging to a supranational Soviet whole was at least as important as belonging to their own specific nationality. For many Russians, who were (or were considered to be) the majority of the Soviet people, their being Russian and their being Soviet were rather difficult to separate.

In the post-Soviet Russian Federation, the question "What is Russia?" acquired new dimensions, but remained as controversial as in the earlier historical periods (and probably even more so). Some people still have a kind of nostalgia for the imperial past.[7] For some others, the Russian Empire and the Soviet Union are undoubtedly things of the irrecoverable past, and they strive to give definitions to post-imperial Russia. And this definition must include not only ethnic Russia proper. Today's Russian Federation, like the Soviet Union, is still a multi-ethnic state, even though on a reduced scale. Russians constitute about 80 percent of the whole population, and the remaining 20 percent ismade up of about one hundred peoples and ethnic groups, many of them with a well-developed individual identity. Any realistic definition of Russia must take into account this immense ethnic diversity.

We may say that at present the country is going through a period of transition not just political, social and economic, but also with respect to self-understanding and, to use a fashionable word, self-identification. In all this, Russia is hardly unique: Russia's problems today are problems of transforming an imperial structure into a post-imperial one.

But in this essay I may be allowed to put aside geopolitical problems as well as the multi-ethnicity of the Russian Federation. By "Russia", I will mean, by and large, the *cultural tradition* of Russia proper, of the Russian Russia, so to say.

In the 20th century, after the Bolshevik takeover and the ensuing Civil War, many people emigrated from the country. Exact figures are not yet known, but it was undoubtedly the most massive emigration in Russia's history. Moreover, the "first wave" of emigration (later in the 20th century, there were two or three more "waves") deprived the country of many outstanding people from all walks of life: writers, painters and other artists, composers and musicians, actors, scientists, philosophers, engineers, doctors... For several decades, Russian culture developed as if in two different worlds, with little communication between them. Bridges between these two worlds began to be slowly built after Stalin's death, but it was only in post-Soviet times that the reunification could be effected in earnest.

Now we may come back to the central theme of our conference. This theme is disappointment and discontent with the so-called progress initiated by Western civilization some centuries ago. This progress has proved to have many dark spots. Several speakers at the conference have suggested that various ideas and values from what we call non-Western civilizations might be offered to humankind as correctives and/or remedies. In Russia, during the last two hundred years, many thinkers and political activists were busy with a more or less similar criticism of the West, suggesting various correctives and/or remedies from the Russian side. So, in my essay, I will try to contribute to the general discourse by recalling some of those correctives and/or remedies, though one cannot be sure of their efficacy. By way of compensation, I will shift the emphasis of my essay from the relevance of Russian culture to the relevance of Russian historical experience.

Russia evidently does not belong to the company of ancient civilizations (like Egypt, China or India) discussed in other papers at our conference. Russia as a political and cultural tradition is only about one thousand years old. The political history of Russia is traditionally narrated from the year 862 when, according to a legend, several Slav and Finnish tribes invited the Varangian (Viking, that is Scandinavian) prince Rurik to rule over themselves. Rurik is reported to have ruled from the city of Novgorod, but his successors moved their capital to Kiev (now often spelled Kyiv, according to the Ukrainian pronunciation) on the river Dnieper. The state (now unified, now disintegrated) ruled by the Rurik dynasty (Rurikids) from Kiev later (at the beginning of the 19th century) got the name Kievan Rus.

Kievan Rus was situated along the trade route from the Varangians to the Greeks and was closely connected with European states to the west. At the end of the 10th century, prince Vladimir the Great started Christianizing his people and chose to do it with the help of Greeks (Byzantines). This choice is usually taken as one of the crucial ones in Russia's history. In 1054, the Great Schism between Rome and Constantinople took place, and this schism eventually separated Russia, as Orthodox Christian, from Western Europe. There is a *bonmot*, ascribed to Oscar Wilde, that Britain and the USA are divided only by their common language. Similarly, we may say that Russia and Western Europe are divided by their common Christianity. For many centuries Western Christianity and Eastern Orthodox Christianity were two worlds apart, separated by mutual distrust and even hatred. For Western Christians, Orthodox Russians were "Schismatics", almost as bad as Muslims, and for the Orthodox Russians, Rome was the centre of a hideous heresy. As S. Huntington has put it, "[Western] Europeans universally acknowledge the fundamental significance of the dividing line between Western Christendom, on the one hand, and Orthodoxy and Islam, on the other...".[8]

But before the Great Schism, and even for some time after it, the principality of Kiev kept in close touch with Western Europe. The matrimonial relations between Kiev and royal families of Western Europe are a telling index.

Thus, prince Yaroslav the Wise (r. 1019–1054) was married in 1019, to a Swedish princess by name Ingegerd Olofsdotter (in Kiev she was called Irina), a daughter of the Swedish king Olof Skötkonung, one of the first Christian kings of Sweden, who reigned in 995–1022. Historians call this Yaroslav "the father-in-law of Europe", because his daughters became queens of Hungary, France, and Norway; one of his sons married a daughter of a Polish king, another son married a daughter of a Byzantine emperor. Yaroslav's grandson, the Grand Prince Vadimir II Monomach (ruled from 1113 till 1125) married Gytha of Wessex, the daughter of Harold II, the last Anglo-Saxon king of England, who perished at the Battle of Hastings in 1066.

Vladimir Monomach's sister, by name Eupraxia (1071–1109), married, in 1089, Henry IV, the Emperor of the Holy Roman Empire. To quote Wikipedia: "Eupraxia of Kiev...became notorious all over Europe for her divorce from the Holy Roman Emperor Henry IV on the grounds that he had attempted a black mass on her naked body".[9]

Unfortunately, matrimonial interconnections between Russia and Western Europe were interrupted for several hundred years and were resumed only at the beginning of the 18th century, at the time of Peter I.

In the history of Russia, there was one more event and one more period which are often held responsible for having drastically separated Russia from the rest of Europe. I am talking about the Mongol invasion of the 13th century and the period of more than two hundred years that followed when most of the former Kievan Rus was dominated by an Oriental power, known by the name of the Golden Horde. This period and its significance for our history have been interpreted in various ways, and a consensus will hardly be reached soon. But it was under the Golden Horde's suzerainty (and cultural influence) that the Principality of Moscow grew and strengthened itself, so that by the end of the 15th century it could defy its suzerain and become an independent power.

There was one more consequence of the Golden Horde's rule in Eastern Europe: the division of Eastern Slavs into three different ethnic entities—Russians, Ukrainians and Byelorussians (though the dividing lines between these three entities are often blurred and controversial). The Principality and later the Tsardom of Moscow, with time, assumed the name Russia and yet later grew into the Russian Empire. But the south-western and north-western parts of the former Kievan Rus (including the city of Kiev itself) remained outside the long-time influence of the Golden Horde and were influenced more by Polish (Catholic) and even German culture, though most of the people remained Orthodox Christian. It was only much later, from the middle of the 17th to the middle of the 20th century, that these people were gradually taken inside the borders of the Tsardom of Moscow, then the Russian Empire, and part of the Soviet Union. And now there are three independent states: the Federation of Russia, Ukraine and Belarus.

The contacts between the Principality of Moscow and Western Europe became quite intense as early as the 15th century. Thus, under the Grand Prince Ivan III (aka Ivan the Great, r. 1462–1505), the Moscow Kremlin was designed and built anew by Italian architects. The grandson of Ivan III, Ivan IV the Terrible (r. 1533–1584) assumed the title Tsar (which was derived ultimately from the Roman title Caesar), corresponded with Queen Elizabeth I of England, and, as some historians surmise, once even proposed marriage to her.[10]

However, up to the 18th century, the Russians participated very little, if at all, in the cultural life of Western Europe. Western Europeans developed scholastic philosophy and universities, lived through the Renaissance and the Reformation, then started the Scientific Revolution of the 17th century, but Russia did not take part in these processes. The intellectual expansion of Western Europeans was accompanied by their global expansion, across the seas. Russia in the 16th and 17th centuries undertook a similar territorial expansion across the Eurasian landmass, but without a comparable intellectual and technological expansion. As a result, by the end of the 17th century (if not earlier), Russian elites realized that Russia had to learn and borrow a great deal from its Western neighbours. This process culminated during the reign of the tsar Peter I (r. 1682–1725), who by the end of his rule, in 1721, acquired the Roman title Imperator (i.e. Emperor). The name of the country became Российская Империя (The Empire of Russia).

Under Peter I, Russia became the first non-Western country to launch a radical self-Westernization.[11] Much later, Japanese reformers of the Meiji era (in the second half of the 19th century) explicitly referred to Peter I as an inspiring example, as did Kemal Ataturk when he launched his reforms in Turkey.

But as early as 1835, Thomas Babington Macaulay in his well-known Minute on Education, arguing for the promotion of European education in India, referred to the example of Russia as a country that had progressed a lot due to the introduction of European education.[12]

Indeed, the history of the Russian Empire from the early 18th till the early 20th century, the activity of Peter I and his successors in Russia, may be quite meaningfully compared with the history of the British Indian Empire from the middle of the 18th till the middle of the 20th century.

The history of both Russia and India during the last three hundred years (the 18th–20th centuries) is, to a considerable extent, a story of confrontations with the West, as well as a story of the transfer (transplantation) of many Western cultural products to the non-Western soil. The history of the Russian Empire begins with the reforms of Peter I who tried hard to transfer (transplant) some elements of theWest European civilization onto the non-Western Russian soil. The empire-building activity of Peter I and his successors in Russia is paralleled in India (South Asia) by the empire-building activity of the British who also, during the process, transferred (transplanted)—deliberately or undeliberately—a great many elements of Western civilization onto non-Western Indian soil.

Peter I founded the capital of his new empire, St. Petersburg, in 1703, at the mouth of the Neva river, which connected the mainland with seas and oceans. Around the same time, in the late 1690s, the British in India founded the future capital of their empire in India, Calcutta (now Kolkata), at the mouth of the Ganges, the river that connected, for the British, the seas and oceans with the mainland. Peter I wanted, according to the famous phrase, "to cut through a window to Europe". The British wanted "to cut through a window to India". In both cases the choice of the place for the capital, the choice dictated by political and economic considerations, was not quite fortunate: complaints against the bad climate of St. Petersburg and Calcutta are recurrent themes in Russia and India respectively. There are also some haunting similarities between the architectural images of the two capitals.

By another strange coincidence, the two cities ceased to be the capitals of their respective empires about the same time: Calcutta officially in 1911, but actually by the early 1920s; St. Petersburg (then already Petrograd) in 1918. In both cases, the rulers decided to move the capital back to its former seat at the heart of the mainland: to Delhi in India and to Moscow in Russia. It would be worthwhile to undertake a comparative study of the motives and reasons that caused the British government, on the one hand, and the Bolshevik government, on the other, to make the similar moves.

Usually the stories of these two empires are told in very different ways and terms: the one as the story of Russia's transformation, initiated and carried on by Russians themselves, the other as the story of a foreign power in a colonized and subjugated country. But this difference may not be as absolute as it seems. The transformation of India in the 18th–19th centuries was effected not only by the British, but by many Indians as well who joined and/or supplemented (and sometimes corrected), in one way or another, the efforts of the foreign rulers. The transformation of Russia, on the other hand, was not only inspired by the example of Western Europe, but many Westerners in the 18th and even in the 19th centuries also played very important roles in the process. From the second half of the 18th century, even the monarchs in Russia were ethnically more West European (mostly German) than Russian. Thus, the Empress Catherine II (r. 1762–1796), one of the key figures in the 18th century history of Russia, was a German princess married to a grandson of Peter I, who was himself half-German. After the Westernization introduced by Peter I, the cultural distance between the ruling and educated elite, on the one hand, and the traditional masses in Russia, on the other, was hardly less than the cultural distance between the British (as well as the Europeanized elite) in India, and the rest of the people there. The Slavophile thinkers of 19th century Russia emphasised the "foreignness" of the Russian educated elite and sometimes compared it in precise terms with the British in India.

Comparing the processes of Europeanization/Westernization in Russia and India (South Asia) from the 18th until the 20th century might be a fascinating subject of research in the field of comparative history. As far as I know, such research work has not yet been undertaken to any considerable extent.[13]

In Russia, Peter I and his Westernizing reforms (or a Westernizing revolution carried out from above) remain a very controversial subject. For that matter, almost our entire history is very controversial for us now. We permanently fail to come to terms with our past, as we permanently fail to come to terms with our present as well. Of course, we are not unique in this respect. Here I seek to narrate a version of Russia's history which seems the most plausible to me.[14]

As I have just said, the reforms of Peter I are a very controversial theme. The official view before 1917, confirmed under Stalin, was that Peter I was the great reformer who turned the backward Tsardom of Moscow into the powerful Russian Empire, one of Europe's great powers. Opponents of this idealized image point out that Peter's "reforms" cost the country too much, that too many people fell victim to his great undertakings (so that the population of the country diminished during his reign by about one third) and that, in any case, his Westernization was very one-sided, and not so much beneficial as harmful for the country and the people in the long historical perspective.

Karl Marx, who wrote many unpleasant things about the Russian Empire, once remarked that "...Peter the Great defeated Russian barbarism by barbarity..."[15] Vladimir Lenin, as if quoting Marx, wrote with approval in an article (in May of 1918, several months after the Bolshevik takeover), that Peter I "speeded up the adoption of westernism by the barbarous Rus, not hesitating to use barbarous methods in fighting barbarism".[16] Lenin explicitly summoned his party comrades to emulate Peter I. As for "barbarous methods", Lenin, I believe, was much more advanced than Peter I. I do not know what opinions there are in India today about Lenin, but now many in Russia, including myself, consider Lenin one of the greatest villains, one of the greatest criminals in our history.

In 1924, in the year of Lenin' death, the poet Maximilian Voloshin (1877–1932) wrote in his poem *Russia* (Россия): "The great Peter was the first Bolshevik" (*Великий Петр был первый большевик*). Much earlier Fyodor Dostoevsky called Peter I "a Nihilist" (i.e. a revolutionary).[17] In the 1930s, Nikolai Berdyaev (1874–1948) amplified the comparison between Peter I and Bolsheviks in his book *The Origin of Russian Communism* (first published in 1937, in English). N. Berdyaev wrote: "Peter was a revolutionary from above; and not without reason is he considered a Bolshevik in type. Peter's methods were absolutely Bolshevik. He wanted to destroy the old Muscovite Russia, to tear up by the roots those feelings which lay in the very foundation of its life... The methods adopted by Peter in dealing with the Church and the old religion are very reminiscent of the methods of the Bolsheviks."[18]

And a bit further: "A comparison might be made between Peter and Lenin, between the Petrine and the Bolshevik revolutions. They display the same barbarity, violence, forcible application of certain principles from above downwards, the same rupture of organic development, and repudiation of tradition, the same étatism, hypertrophy of government, the same formation of a privileged bureaucratic class, the same centralization, the same desire sharply and radically to change the type of civilization."[19]

And still further: "Nowhere, apparently, was there such a gulf between the upper and lower classes as in Petrine, imperial Russia, and not another single country lived at the same time in such different centuries, from the 14th to the 19th and even up to the coming 21st century. Russia of the 18th and 19th centuries lived a completely inorganic life... The Empire founded by Peter grew outwardly; it became the largest in the world. It had an outward enforced unity, but there was no inward unity; inwardly it was broken into fragments. Government and people were rent apart, people and intelligentsia, and the nationalities which were gathered together in the Russian Empire were sundered from each other."[20]

In other words, the imperial westernization of Russia failed to work out a viable synthesis between what was borrowed from the West and Russia's own social and cultural traditions. In Huntington's terms, Russia was a "torn country". [21]

Peter I and most of his successors assumed that they could borrow from the technical achievements of the West in order to build a strong army and navy and, in general, a powerful state without borrowing from the West its social and political principles. By the beginning of the 20th century, Russia indeed became one of the world›s great powers, as far as her industrial development and military might went; but Russia›s social structures and political culture remained rather archaic. This, again, was one of the reasons for the collapse of 1917.

At this point, I would draw a comparison-cum-contrast between Russia and India. In India, in spite of the more than century-long colonial rule (or perhaps, on the contrary, because of this rule) pre-colonial cultural and social traditions have been mostly preserved. In fact, some modern Indian historians reproach the British rule for deliberately conserving many archaic (feudal) traditions in India instead of more radically developing the country along the road of progress. Be that as it may, the history of India during the last three centuries looks much more continuous than the history of Russia. Russian history has moved by continuous "negations" of the past. Thus, Peter I and the whole of "St Petersburg period" "negated" the "Muscovite" past.[22]

In other words, the transformations that Peter I and his successors effected in Russia have been much more radical and more ruthless than the transformations effected by the British in India. The British were always but a minority of foreigners in an alien country they happened to rule and, therefore, had to move cautiously. When they became too enthusiastic and arrogant with their reforms by the middle of the 19th century, they got the Mutiny. As for Peter I and the other Romanovs, they were God-given autocrats in their own country and felt much more free than the British in India. Sometimes there were popular uprisings in Imperial Russia as well (e.g. the Pugachev rebellion under Catherine II in the 1770s), but those uprisings were mercilessly crushed. Later the Bolsheviks and Stalin also acted much more resolutely in their own country than the British in India.

As a result, India attained independence as a rather traditional country but with great potential for change and development, whereas Russia, after three centuries of reforms and revolutions (which often differed only in names), has been virtually deprived of most of her pre-18thcentury traditions[23], but has not acquired, in the sphere of social and political life, any stable new ones. Now Russia is neither traditional nor quite developed, but something in between: at the beginning of the 21st century, Russia is an underpopulated and demoralized country with undermined vitality.

It would be particularly interesting to compare the fate of religion(s) in modern India and Russia. As far as I know, the British in India tried hard not to interfere in the religious affairs of the natives. Religious reforms in India in the 19th and 20th centuries were mostly the business of Indians themselves. But in Russia, Peter I radically reformed (some would say emasculated) the Orthodox Church and turned it into a servant of the state machinery. The Bolsheviks and Stalin continued the work of destroying the Orthodox Church (as well as other traditional religious bodies) in Russia. Instead, Marxism-Leninism became a kind of ersatz-religion in the Soviet Union, and Stalin, while he was alive, functioned as the height priest (if not the godhead) of that quasi-religion. After 1953, the high priest was denounced as a great rascal, but the ersatz-religion lingered for more than another three decades. The process of the revival of the Orthodox Church (and other religious organizations) in post-Soviet Russia has been difficult and controversial.

Nevertheless, it was the imperial period (sometimes called the "St. Petersburg period", roughly from 1,700 up to 1917) that has produced modern Russian culture. Actually this is the culture by which most Russians now live by. The traditional culture that was there before Peter I has very little significance for most Russians nowadays. In various spheres of high culture, the syntheses of Western borrowings and the local soil have been quite successful. Russian composers, Russian writers, Russian painters, Russian scientists have contributed considerably to what may be called "world culture" (I will come back to this topic shortly). But in the sphere of social life as a whole and in the sphere of political culture, modern Russia has been, as I have already stressed, much less successful.

In 1917, the Bolsheviks, headed by Lenin and Trotsky, started what they thought to be a "world revolution". The centre of that revolution was to be in the advanced countries of Western Europe. But for the time being, the Bolsheviks tried to transform the backward, traditional Russia on the basis of the Western ideas known as Marxism. The problem was that the Bolsheviks themselves were products of the Russian Empire, and in their minds, as well as in their deeds, Western Marxism became something quite different from what it was in its homeland. Trying to transform the traditional, non-Western society of Russia with their brutal means, the Bolsheviks destroyed more than they managed to create and caused the country and its people considerable harm. The Bolsheviks interpreted their revolution as a great leap forward into the bright future of the whole of humankind. But now we cannot help seeing (and not a few people saw it *then and there*), that the Bolshevik takeover was, in fact, a great leap backward into the darkness of Russia's past. This became especially evident when Stalin came to power.

Stalin, who liked to be compared with Peter I, went along a similar blind alley, but in a much more brutal, even savage manner. Like Peter I, Stalin assumed that a powerful state might be built with Western technology, but rejecting all Western social and political principles. This discrepancy in the end brought about the collapse of the Soviet Union in 1991.

The post-Soviet reformers of the early 1990s in Russia, though posing themselves as anti-Communist and anti-Marxist, have been rightly called neo-Bolshevik. Like the original Bolsheviks, those reformers thought they were armed with the latest achievements of Western economic theory, which they were eager to apply to the backward ex-Soviet society. The results, again, have proved to be unexpected. As far as I understand, those neo-Bolsheviks also destroyed more than they created. As a result, we have got an ugly economy, based essentially on the export of oil and gas, an ugly social structure and an ugly political system.

The present administration of the Russian Federation seems to have moved into the same trap as Peter I and Stalin's. They want to have all the advantages of the latest Western technological achievements, but do not want to develop a Western-type civil society and Western-type political institutions in Russia.

One of the most obvious failures of the post-Soviet period has been precisely the failure to build a civil society, and what in German is called a *Rechtsstaat* (a state based on the rule of law, i.e. a law-abiding state). It would be naïve, of course, to hope that these nice foreign plants will grow in Russia so quickly. But now it seems that the gardeners do not even want to cultivate them in our garden. What we have got so far probably does not deserve the name of *Polizeistaat* (police state), but may be fairly called an *Obrigkeitsstaat* (authoritarian state). It is widely acknowledged that the distance and the degree of alienation between the rulers and the ruled in today's Russia are great and disturbing. The *Obrigkeit* (authorities) are strong and determined to perpetuate themselves, while the society and the people are weak and have practically no means to assert their will.

The Russian sociologist Boris Dubin (1946–2014), told a bitter truth (in an interview): "Our society is incapable of holding itself. There are no social bones, no complex system of nerves, etc."[24] Dmitriy Furman (1943–2011), to my mind, one of the most penetrating political and social analysts of post-Soviet Russia, wrote in 2007: "As far as the political culture is concerned, Russia remains, to a great degree, a 'pre-modern', traditionalist, monarchist society. Such a society cannot possibly rule itself and does not know how to select rulers. A ruler in a traditional society is like a husband in a traditional family: 'given by God', i.e., he might come from anywhere, but not through your free choice, and remain there till death (yours or his)."[25]

We may say that in Russia, from at least the 18th century until now, the high culture has been European (in other words, Russian high culture has been part and parcel of high European culture), but the structure of the society and the nature of power (what is called political culture) always were and still remain very different from European standards.

This disparity, this lack of integrity within Russian life is reflected—in the sphere of intellectual activity—in the form of a rich gamut of various competing ideas and ideologies. But, on the whole, this part of our life is hardly more satisfying than the spheres of politics and economics. There is no lack of very tough evaluation of the contemporary intellectual and moral situation in Russia. Thus, the philosopher Sergei Khoruzhiy (b. 1941), a distinguished mathematician turned Orthodox Christian thinker, said in an interview in 2005: "Russia today is an insane society (социум невменяемый) or, at least [a society] with seriously damaged sanity. What has been damaged and strongly unsettled in the first place is our capacity to see ourselves adequately, the capacity of self-consciousness, self-evaluation, self-account… The root cause is clear enough: it is the presence of a lacuna, a hole in our consciousness, as we have not settled accounts with our nearest past; we lack a thought-out attitude to it. The cause of this cause is also clear: who among the bosses needs the full understanding of the Soviet past and an honest, strict settling of the accounts with it?"[26]

The 19th century Russian thinker Pyotr Chaadayev (1794–1856) in his famous *Philosophical Letter* wrote (in French) in about 1829: "En quelque sorte, on peut dire que nous sommes un peuple d'exception. Nous sommes du nombre de ces nations qui ne semblent pas faire partie intégrante du genre humain mais qui n'existent que pour donner quelque grande leçon au monde. L'enseignement que nous sommes destinés à donner ne sera pas perdu assurément, mais qui sait le jour où nous nous retrouverons au milieu de l'humanité, et que de misères nous éprouverons avant que nos destinées s'accomplissent?"[27] ("We may be said to be an exception among peoples. We are one of those nations which do not appear to be an integral part of the human race, but exist only in order to teach some great lesson to the world. The lesson that we are destined to teach will certainly not be lost, but who knows when we will find ourselves among mankind and how many hardships we will experience before our destinies are fulfilled?"[28])

These bitter words have been often repeated since then by various Russian authors.

Chaadayev did not specify what "great lesson" (or lessons) Russia may teach the rest of the world. Now I suppose we may say that one of the lessons is this: Russia has shown that Western ideas, unwisely applied to a non-Western society, may yield unpleasant results.

But this is of course, not the whole story. In the same *Philosophical Letter*, Chaadayev wrote, as if anticipating the topic of our conference:

"Solitaires dans le monde, nous n'avons rien donné au monde, nous n'avons rien pris au monde; nous n'avons pas versé une seule idée dans la masse des idées humaines; nous n'avons en rien contribué aux progrès de l'esprit humain, et tout ce qui nous est revenu de ce progrès, nous l'avons défiguré. Rien, depuis le premier instant de notre existence sociale, n'a émané de nous pour le bien commun des hommes; pas une pensée utile n'a germé sur le sol stérile de notre patrie, pas une vérité grande ne s'est élancée du milieu de nous; nous ne nous sommes donné la peine de rien imaginer nous-mêmes, et de tout ce que les autres ont imaginé nous n'avons emprunté que des apparences trompeuses et le luxe inutile."[29]

("Alone in the world, we have given nothing to the world, we have taken nothing from the world; we have not added any single idea to the mass of human ideas; we have contributed nothing to the progress of the human mind, and all that we have received from this progress, we have disfigured. Nothing, from the very first moment of our social existence, has emanated from us for the common good of mankind; no useful thought has sprouted on the barren soil of our country, no great truth darted from among us; we have not bothered to imagine anything ourselves, and from what others have imagined we have borrowed only misleading appearances and unnecessary luxury."[30])

Nowadays this jeremiad sounds strange. But it must be taken into account that in the 1820s, when these lines were written (that is about one hundred years after the launch of Peter's reforms), the cultural achievements of preceding periods were either forgotten or despised, and the new (modern) Russian culture was just at the threshold of its "golden (classical) time". Pyotr Chaadayev himself was very much a product of the century of Westernisation. He could speak Russian, of course and even wrote private letters in this language. But, like most people in the educated Russian elite of that time, he could write intellectual prose only in French. He was very much attracted to Roman Catholicism, was influenced by French Catholic thinkers and despised Russian Orthodox Christianity (though, formally, he remained Orthodox till the end of his days).

Among the younger contemporaries of Chaadayev, two groups of thinkers appeared, who argued between themselves about the past and the future of Russia. One group got the name Западники (Westernizers), the other came to be called Славянофилы (Slavophiles). In a nutshell, the Westernizers thought that Russia was merely lagging behind Western Europe (the West) on the common road to progress and the task was to continue and speed up the movement initiated by Peter I. The Slavophiles, on the contrary, having learned a lot from German romantic authors, believed that Russia was a world apart from the West (another civilization, as we would say now) and had its Sonderweg (a special way) from which Peter I unfortunately had led the country away.[31]

The British historian Geoffrey Hoskings writes, obviously bearing in mind the Slavophiles: "Russia offered the first example of what later became known as a developing country, whose elites were attracted by European culture, yet also resented it as a disruption of a traditional way of life... Russia was the first modern nation that reacted against Western-driven modernization to reaffirm the values of inherited communal and religious life."[32]

Indeed, the controversy between the Westernizers and the Slavophiles in 19th century Russia anticipated many similar controversies in other non-Western countries in the 19th and 20th centuries, including, among other things, some of the polemics in India between Rabindranath Tagore (who often played the role of a Westernizer) and M.K. Gandhi (who in many ways was an exemplary Indian counterpart of the Russian Slavophiles).

In Russia the Slavophiles, unlike Chaadayev, not only did not despise Orthodox Christianity, but, on the contrary, valued it very much and considered it Russia's great asset and indeed the basis of Russia's future development and glory. Some of the Slavophile thinkers even claimed that Russia was destined to benefit the whole world with the truth of Orthodox Christianity. A similar kind of messianism may be found in the writings of various Slavophiles, just like authors in many other countries (India, of course, included).

If I were Orthodox Christian, like some of my compatriots today, I might also preach the unique Russian Orthodox spirituality (this word is as popular in Russia as in India), which is destined to heal all the ills of the rotten and over materialistic Western civilization, as well as to show the way to the Truth to all "pagans" like the Chinese, Indians and other Asians who are as yet deprived of the light of the Orthodoxy. But, for better or worse, I am not Orthodox Christian, but, quite to the contrary, a product of the Soviet atheist upbringing and education. For me, and for Russians like me, Orthodox Christianity is almost as alien as any other religion. I am well aware of the importance of Orthodox Christianity in the history of Russia, but am not sure that it may be as important for other peoples and for the Russians themselves in the future.

Nevertheless, most (if not all) traditional religions (including Orthodox Christianity), have some aspects which in modern Western terms, may be called "aesthetic" or "artistic" and which can be greatly appreciated even by those (or particularly by those) who do not confess the corresponding religious creed. Thus, one need not be a Muslim to admire the marvels of Islamic architecture, in India and elsewhere; or one need not be a Hindu to admire the splendour of Hindu temples and the various styles of Hindu sculptural art. In a similar way, one need not be an Orthodox Christian to appreciate the beauty of old Russian churches, or of Orthodox lithurgy, or of old Russian icons. The art (architecture, music and singing, as well as icons) of Orthodox Christianity, and of Russian Orthodox Christianity in particular, in the 20th century has been acknowledged as a great contribution to world culture, to the common cultural legacy of mankind.

I have said above that when Chaadayev wrote his *Philosophical Letter*, the new (modern) Russian culture was just at the threshold of its "golden (classical) time". Indeed, Chaadayev was a close (albeit a somewhat senior) friend of Alexander Pushkin (1799–1837), the great poet. Modern Russian literature began in the 18th century, after the "reforms" of Peter I, when Russians adopted Western European literary forms and ideas (in a similar way, modern Indian literatures began in the 19th and 20th centuries, when Indians adopted Western literary forms and ideas[33]). The work of Alexander Pushkin was a kind of fruition of 18th century Russian literature and the great beginning of what later was called "classical Russian literature". The list of the luminaries of this literature includes such names as (to recall only the most famous ones): Nikolai Gogol (1809–1852), Ivan Turgenev (1818–1883), Fyodor Dostoevsky (1821–1881), Lev Tolstoy (1828–1910), Anton Chekhov (1860–1904), to name a few. The work of these Russian writers (as well as of a number of other Russian writers of the 19th and 20th centuries) has by now become an integral part of world culture.

Besides literature, Russians from the 18th century onwards took from Western Europe other forms of cultural activity, such as music, painting and science. Now names of such Russian composers (again, to recall only the most famous ones), such as Pyotr Chaikovsky (1840–1893), Sergei Rakhmaninoff (1873–1943), Igor Stravinsky (1882–1971), Sergei Prokofiev (1891– 1953), Dmitri Shostakovich (1906–1975) are well known all over the world and, again, have become an integral part of world culture.

In the field of painting, suffice it to recall such names as Vassily Kandinsky (1866–1944), Kazimir Malevich (1879–1935), Marc Chagall (1887–1985), though, of course, many other painters could be added to this list.

In the field of science, we may refer to Nikolai Lobachevsky (1792–1856), the mathematician, who was one of the first to develop a non-Euclidean geometry, sometimes referred to as "Lobachevskian geometry"; toDmitry Mendeleyev (1834–1907) who was one of the first (if not the very first) to construct the Periodic Table of Chemical Elements (in Russia actually called Mendeleevs Table); to Ivan Pavlov (1849–1936), the physiologist and the first Russian Nobel prize winner (1904, Physiology or Medicine); to Ilya Metchnikoff (1845–1916), the biologist, who also got a

Nobel prize (1908, also Physiology or Medicine); to Andrey Kholmogorov (1903–1987), one of the greatest mathematicians of the 20th century, and to many other names.

So, to give one more answer to Chaadayev's question referred to above ("What lessons can Russia teach the world?"), we may say that Russia and Russians have demonstrated that a non-Western country (culture, civilization, and so on) can adopt the products and achievements of the West and then further develop them in such a way as to enrich their original homeland and the rest of mankind.

Various non-Western countries have succeeded in different degrees in adopting various aspects of Western civilization. Thus, India seems to have been much more successful than Russia in adopting such Western institutions (or shall I say traditions?) as parliamentary democracy, party system, free general elections, independent judiciary, the supremacy of law, etc. I suppose Indians would not think now about throwing away these traditions only because they have come from the West.

In Russia, we still have to implant (transplant?) and adopt properly all these Western traditions. Vladimir Lenin wrote, before 1917, that Russia suffered both from the development of capitalism and from its insufficient development. Now we may say that we suffer from both too many borrowings from the West (like excessive consumerism, the horrors of advertising, drug-addiction, etc.), and from the insufficient adoption of many good Western traditions (such as the ones listed above). The example of India (and of some other successful non-Western countries) is indeed very relevant for today's Russia.

NOTES

1 J. Diamond. *The World Until Yesterday: What Can We Learn from Traditional Societies?* New York: Viking, 2012.

2 Cf. the character of Rodion Raskol'nikov in F.M. Dostoevsky's novel *Crime and Punishment* (1866).

Raskol'nilov got the idea that he had the "right" to kill an old woman-usurer and take her money, because he was an "extraordinary" man and could use the expropriated money in better ways. Raskol'nikov, in the novel, explicitly refers to Napoleon as an inspiring example. One of the real prototypes for Dostoevsky, in creating the character of Raskol'nikov, was Napoleon III who in his book *The Life of Caesar* (two volumes published in 1865–66) claimed for "great men" the right of transgressing the norms which common people must keep to.

3 Toynbee, A. *The World and the West.* L. etc, Oxford University Press, 1953, p. 2.

4 Huntington S.P. *The Clash of Civilizations and the Remaking of World Order.* New Delhi: Penguin Books, 1997, p. 362 (Index).

5 Cf. the French translation: "Empire de Russie". In Russian we distinguish between two adjectives: "русский" (which means "belonging to the Russian people") and "российский" (which means "belonging to Russia [as a state or as a community of various peoples]"). Unfortunately, in English both adjectives are translated as "Russian" which translation sometimes may be misleading.

6 Stalin may be considered responsible for the disintegration of the USSR by the end of the century. In the late 1980s the peoples of the three Baltic republics (who could not forget their independent existence between the two World Wars) and of Western Ukraine were the first and the most vociferous in their demands of the independence from the Union. Had Stalin let them remain outside the USSR after WWII, the fate of the USSR might have been different.

7 On April 17, 2014, a TV "straight line" communication between Putin and the people took place. A woman asked the President: "Now that the Crimea has been reunited with Russia, shall we take back Alaska as well?". Putin replied with a joke: "Why do you need Alaska? It is too cold there."

8 Huntington S.P. Op. cit., p. 309.

9 For more details see my paper: "Russian Culture between Europe (the West) and Asia (the East)." In *Building Bridges between India and Russia. A Festschrift for Prof. J.P.Dimri.* Compiler and editor Prof. Ram Das Akella. Kolkata: Power Publishers, 2012, pp. 169–191.

10 Cf. Pryor F. *Elizabeth I: Her Life in Letters.* University of California Press, 2003, pp. 55–57.

11 The Polish historian Andrzej Walicki writes about "the forcible Westernization of Russia" (Walicki A. *A History of Russian Thought from*

the Enlightenment to Marxism. Tr. from the Polish by Hilda Andrews-Rusiecka. Stanford, Stanford University Press, 1979, p. 1.)

12 Cf.: "Within the last hundred and twenty years, a nation which had previously been in a state as barbarous as that in which our ancestors were before the Crusades has gradually emerged from the ignorance in which it was sunk, and has taken its place among civilized communities. I speak of Russia. There is now in that country a large educated class abounding with persons fit to serve the State in the highest functions, and in nowise inferior to the most accomplished men who adorn the best circles of Paris and London... The languages of western Europe civilised Russia. I cannot doubt that they will do for the Hindoo what they have done for the Tartar."

(http://www.columbia.edu/itc/mealac/pritchett/00generallinks/macaulay/txt_minute_education_1835.html)

13 Cf. the three papers of mine in which I try to draw comparisons between the ways Russia and India borrowed various elements of culture from the West: Le roman en Russie et en Inde. Deux cas de transfert d'un objet culturel occidental dans une culture non occidentale. In: *L'horizon anthropologique des transferts culturels.* Paris, PUF, 2004, p. 149–161; The Transfer of Modern Science to Russia and India: Two Parallel Cases. In: *Science and Spirituality in Modern India.* Makarand Paranjape (ed.). New Delhi: Samvad India Foundation, 2006, p. 31–40; Philosophy as a Free Search for Knowledge: the Concept and Its Transfer to Russia and India. In: *Международная востоковедная конференция (Торчиновские чтения). Метаморфозы. 22–25 июня 2011 г. Часть первая.* Санкт-Петербург, 2013, с. 206–221.

14 Unlike Mohamed Salmawy (who, at our conference, presented a panorama of Egyptian history), I cannot say that there has been a wonderful unity in the history of Russia. Quite to the contrary, as Nikolai Berdyaev in his book *The Russian Idea* (1948) has put it, there have been, through the last millennium, at least five different Russias. Cf. "Discontinuity is a characteristic of Russian history... There have been five periods in Russian history and each provides a different picture. They are: [1] the Russia of Kiev; [2] the Russia of the days of the Tartar yoke; [3] the Russia of Moscow; [4] the Russia of Peter the Great; and [5] Soviet Russia. And it is quite possible that there will be yet another new Russia. The development

of Russia has been catastrophic..." (Berdyaev N. *The Russian Idea*.Ch.1, part 1. Cf. the electronic version in the Internet: https://archive.org/details/russianidea017842mbp, p.3).

15 These words are taken from Marx's letter to J. B. Schweizer, written on January 24, 1865, and published in "*Der Social-Demokrat*", No. 16, February 1, 1865.

(http://www.marxists.org/archive/marx/works/1865/letters/65_01_24.htm).

16 Cf. *Ленин В.И.* О «левом» ребячестве и о мелкобуржуазности // Полное собрание сочинений: В 55 т. Москва: Издательство политической литературы, 1958–1970. Т. 36, с. 301. («варварские методы борьбы против варварства).

17 In 1879 Dostoevsky wrote in a private letter to Konstantin Pobedonostsev (1827–1907): "*Культуры* нет у нас..., а нет – через нигилиста Петра Великого. Вырвана она с корнем" ["*Culture* is what we do not have..., and we do not have it because of the nihilist Peter the Great. It has been utterly uprooted."] (Достоевский Ф.М. *Полное собрание сочинений в тридцати томах. Том тридцатый. Книга первая. Письма 1878–1881.* Ленинград, "Наука", 1988, с. 67).

18 Cf. the electronic version of the book: http://www.jesus-for-all.com/fikr/pdf_3189.pdf (p. 13).

19 Ibidem, p. 14.

20 Ibidem, pp. 15–16.

21 Huntington S.P. Op. cit., p. 139.

22 The Bolsheviks in 1917, in a similar way, "negated" all previous history. Stalin later "negated" and to a large extent "liquidated" the Old Guard Bolsheviks. Khrushchev "negated" (though half-heartedly) Stalin. Brezhnev and his people "negated" Khrushchev. Gorbachev, it is true, tried to do something extraordinary: both to "negate" and preserve the Soviet system. He inevitably failed and was "negated" by Yeltsyn... And so on.

23 As Pyotr Chaadayev (see further) wrote in 1836, in his essay *Apologie d'un fou* (*Apology of a madman*), "Il [Peter I] balaya de son souffle puissant toutes nos institutions; il creusa un abîme entre notre passé et notre présent, et il y jeta pêle-mêle toutes nos traditions" ["He [Peter I] swept off with his powerful breath all our institutions; he dug an abyss between

our past and our present, and threw there all our traditions".] (Чаадаев П.Я. *Полное собрание сочинений и избранные письма.* Том 1. Москва, "Наука", 1991, с. 291.)

24 Шаповал С. "Борис Дубин: Наше общество не способно держать само себя» (Интервью номера)". In: *Московские новости*, № 29 (1346), 04-10 августа 2006, с. 40.

25 Фурман Д. "Большие перемены в отсутствие перемен. Или тихое приближение конца эпохи". In: *Независимая газета*, 27.06.2007, с. 10.

26 "Антивозрождение России. С Сергеем Хоружим беседовал Сергей Шаповал". In: *Политический класс*, 2005, №3, с. 29.

27 Чаадаев П.Я. *Полное собрание сочинений и избранные письма.* Том 1. Москва, "Наука", 1991, с. 93.

28 The translation is partly mine, taken from the book: *Russian Intellectual History: An Anthology.* Ed. Marc Raeff.Harcourt, Brace & World, 1966 (Reprint: New Jersey: Humanities Press, 1998).

29 Чаадаев П.Я. Op. cit., p. 96.

30 Translation is mine.

31 Cf. e.g. Walicki A. *The Slavophile Controversy: History of a Conservative Utopia in Nineteenth-Century Russian Thought.* Oxford, Oxford University Press, 1975.

31 Hoskings G. *Russian History. A Very Short Introduction.* Oxford, Oxford University Press, 2012, p. 53, 77.

33 Cf. my paper referred to above: "Le roman en Russie et en Inde. Deux cas de transfert d'un objet culturel occidental dans une culture non occidentale." In: *L'horizon anthropologique des transferts culturels.* Paris, PUF, 2004, pp. 149–161.

Relevance of Traditional Cultures for the Present and the Future

GEZA BETHLENFALVY

In today's world distance is a feature that we consider as being less and less important, as we can take a flight, and arrive at the other end of a faraway continent. We think this is a new situation because people of earlier eras were living in one spot and did not go far away. But this is not true; people of really ancient times travelled as well.

For example, in early prehistoric times, Bushmen from South Africa wandered up through Africa, India, (where the Adivasis are still preserving their old way of life), through China, and then on to Australia, where one still finds the descendants of the first inhabitants. The Normans entered America from the East, and the Asians from the West. Marco Polo discussed matters relating to the Chinese court with the Chief Lama of Tibet. The ancestors of the Hungarian people had pastured their animals somewhere in the Ural mountains, but they already had an idea of which pass could be used for crossing the Carpathian mountain ridges.

The first highly developed culture of India flourished 5,000 years ago. The Indus Valley civilization had a well-designed town structure, with the main roads crossing each other in rectangular form, houses with bathrooms, from which the water flowed to the cisterns under the roads, public baths into which one could descend for performance of rituals and the use of ships for trading with far away countries (like the Akkades and the Sumerians). Besides, they were carving stone clusters and preparing metal statuettes, and were using a writing system (not yet deciphered). The ethnic character of the people who created this high civilization is not clear, but one of the possibilities is that they were akin to Dravidians—the ancestors of people in South India, who were hunted down by the incoming Indo-Europeans. The so-called Proto-Shiva, is still a riddle, who they were and whether it was related to the principal god is still an open question of later times. In Hindu rituals, the most important god Shiva, appears quite late, and is not mentioned in the Vedas. Later, he has been portrayed as equivalent to the Vedic god Rudra.

The Indo-European tribes appearing around 1500 B.C. in India brought with themselves a world of gods (similar to the world of the Greek Homerian hymns), which have been incorporated in the religion of Hinduism. As S. Radhakrishnan writes in the book *The Legacy of India* (1937, 259-260), "India was a thorough 'melting pot'. [...] In spite of attacks, Hellenic, Muslim and European, among others, Hindu culture has maintained its tradition unbroken to the present day from the fourth millennium B.C. The spiritual life of the Hindus at the present time has not precisely the same proportion or orientation, as that of either the Indus people or the Vedic Āryans or even the great teachers: Śamkara or Rāmānuja. [...] The more it changes, the more it remains the same thing."

The main feature of the traditional culture of India is unity in diversity. The followers of the Hindu religion are a loose group of people, but continue to remain together. Even the followers of the Buddha, Jina, Jesus Christ, or even Allah found their place in the world of Hinduism. A simple Indian peasant visits the Christian temple of Goa, and prays there. The Buddhist stūpa of Sārnāth is circumambulated by people of every religion and nation.

The various folk religions have also an immemorial ancient and a still vividly living tradition in many parts of India, and all around the world. The sky, the sun, the moon, the mountains, the rivers, the lakes, the various forms of land, and all the wonders of nature were glorified, deified since early times. In Mongolia, they worship the Sky-God, the Sun-God, and many other nature-places, like passes in the hills, at which *Obo*-s (stone and wood hillocks) are constructed and circumambulated by travellers. The Mongols and Tibetans have the divine world of shamans, who call the gods down to help the common people. Every important realm around us has got some divine feature, and consequently, it is to be worshipped, and various spiritual cults and religious practices were worked out around them in many parts of the world, including India.

To use just one example: The cult of *grāma-devatā* (village goddess) is a living tradition in Andhra Pradesh and in the Dravidian areas, and it has a connection with India's past. As in the new book entitled *Vicissitudes of the Goddess: Reconstructions of the Gramadevata in India's Religious Traditions* (New York: Oxford University Press, 2013), the author, Sree Padma, describes in detail the role of the village goddess, and analyses the various cults attributed to the *grāma-devatās*. She poses the question: Are the ladies represented on Harappan seals shown as simply full-bellied or pregnant women—fertility goddesses with a fecund, reproductive power? The *grāma-devatā* of the village cult can be related to important goddesses, like Durgā and Kālī, or the Buddhist goddess Hārītī. In Andhra, they worship the naked Dravidian fertility goddesses such as Ellamma and Mātaṅgī through terracotta carvings, ivory seals and stone sculptures dating from the 4th century BCE through the 7th century CE. While comparing Indus Valley goddesses and Buddhist and Hindu religious practices with village goddess worship, Sree Padma enriches the findings of pre-existing research on northern *Satī* practices, and on the goddess in Buddhist and Vaiṣhṇava traditions, temple iconography and ritual symbolism.

Indian, i.e. Hindu and Buddhist, religions have a very important feature—synchronism, which means that the helpful demons and gods and the ones that harm are not so clearly differentiated from each other. They are living and are influencing the world in a mixed form; they intermingle from time to time in a "synchronic" way.

Tantra (Skr.; "continuum" "fabric"; Tib. *rgyud*) is part of the *Sanātana-Dharma*, the eternal religion of Hinduism. Its central theme is divine energy (*shakti*) personified as *Devī* or goddess, the female divine aspect represented as the consort of Shiva, taking up various manifestations, peaceful such as Lakshmī, Sarasvatiī, Umā and Gaurī, or wrathful like Kālī and Durgā, and their union with Shiva. In the Tibetan Buddhist traditions, the term Tantra (*rgyud*) is used to define medical and astrological writings and meditation systems, generally defined as Vajrayāna, a system of teaching revealed by the Buddha, i.e. Sākyamuni in his late manifestation as Dharmakāya. It is a system that is strongly based on human experience and describes spiritual development in the categories of base (*gzhi*), path (*lam*) and fruit (*'bras bu*), the base being the practitioner who uses the path for purifying the base in order to achieve the fruit, which is the result of his practice.

The tantric world of gods and goddesses is a wide circle of cults and divinities. The *Shaiva* (*Kaula*) tantric cult developed around the first centuries of our age, and around the 8th Century; the Buddhist *siddhas* (ascetic saints) learnt it, and developed a very rich Buddhist tantric literature and cult. The six main groups of the Buddhist tantras are: *kriyā*, *caryā-*, *yoga-tantras*, the *mahhāyoga*, *yoga-uttara*, and the *yoginī* or *yoginī-niruttara-tantras*. The *kriyā-tantra* cult is mainly based on the use of *dhāranīs*, (spells, mystic energy words), and with the help of them many interesting *siddhi*-s, magic power perfections, can be achieved, like the *khadgā-siddhi* (flying sword in our interest), *rasa-siddhi* (long life) or *pātāla-siddhi* (underworld-visit). In the *yoga-tantra* group, the main text is the *Tattva-samgrahā*, as is the *Guhyasamāja tantra* in the *Mahāyoga-tantra* school. The *Joginī* or *Dākinī* texts appear in the *yogini tantra* group. The *Hevajra tantra* has an important goddess, the *Yoginī-Nairātmyā*, who, as a "without-ego" (*nair* = without *ātma*) expresses a philosophic idea that is basic to later Buddhism. A wide range of the works of monks in monasteries is expressed in the various texts of the cults that are attached to them. The literature of tantrics and cults was translated into Tibetan and also reached Mongolia, China and Japan. These cultures are active today and spread through Khotan and the Tarim basin into northern Tibet, China and Mongolia in early times.

The various items of folk religion derive from even earlier traditions, and are live features of everyday life today. In Mongolian religious practice, one can recognize the so-called spirits and demons, which represent a huge grouping of power. Demons are often represented in painting, in small tablets, which are framed or included in wooden or linen frames, and worn by the people for defence against the harm they cause, while also hoping for the help they may provide.

Indian gods and spirits were taken over by Tibetan Buddhist communities: Vajrapāni, Tārā, Vaishravana, etc. have all their parallels in Tibet and in Mongolia. Here we set out names of some Indian, Tibetan and Mongolian gods and goddesses, so that one see the parallels: Skr. *Vajrapāni* = Mong. *Ochirvani* / Skr. *Vaishravana* = Tib. *Rnam.thos sras* = Mong. *Namsrai*, *Bismantngri* / Skr. *Sitātapatra* (goddess with white umbrella) = Tib. *gDugsdkar* = Mong. *Sūhert* / Skr. *Rahu* (star demon) = Mong. *Rahu*, *Arah*, *Raqu* / Skr. *Manjushri* = Mong. *Manjushri* / Skr. *Guhyasāmaja* = Mong. *Guhazanyanadagi* / Skr. *Maitreya* = Mong. *Maidar* / Skr. Green *TārāGoddess* = Mong. *NogonDari* / Skr. White *Tārā* = Mong. *TsaganDari* / Skr. *Garuda* = Mong. *Hangardi* / Skr. *Ahuramasda* = Mong. *Hormusta*, *Hurmast*.

The Tibetan mountain spirits, adored on the Tibet-Nepal border, (among them the Five Long-life Sisters or *Tseringma*), were subjugated by Guru Padmasambhava in the 8th century, and they became avowed protectors of Buddhism. They travelled to India and received further Buddhist instruction from mahāsiddha Kānha. In the 11th century, wishing to test the resolve of the great yogi Milarepa, they created apparitions for the purpose of distracting him from meditation. Unable to cause any real harm due to the vows made to Guru Rinpoche (Padmasambhava), they failed, and three days later returned and humbled themselves before Milarepa. He bestowed the Enlightenment Thought, and various *Vajrayāna* practices along with the two special practices of the Hevajra Tantra. From the students of Milarepa, many diverse lineages of practice arose, which have permeated through all the schools of Tibetan Buddhism down to the present day.

Visiting Tibet or Mongolia, one will see many monasteries and meet many lamas who are narrating Sanskrit texts translated into Tibetan, for many hours a day. We can visit big libraries, filled with Tibetan holy books. The Buddhist inheritance is alive among young people as well, and will continue to live on through this century.

The Asiatic Society of Calcutta was an important organization of the British Raj, studying the past of India and bringing out important publications, among them works of Alexander Csoma de Körös, who was the founder of Tibetan studies, and was a pioneer of Buddhist studies as well.

Alexander Csoma de Körös (1784–1842) was born in Transylvania in a poor family, belonging to the military nobility called Székely. According to the Székely traditions, they and all the Hungarians were descendants of the Huns, who fought both the Chinese (the Great Wall was built against them), as well as the Roman Empire, under Attila, the great Hun conqueror of the 5th century. According to these legends, the centre of Attila's empire was in Hungary; his body was cremated in the bed of the Tisza river, and after his death, his son Csaba lead a Hun group of people to Transylvania, where they settled for good, and became the ancestors of the Székely.

In the early 19th century, for a nation in the process of awakening, after a crushed revolution, belief in a glorious past was far more important than even bread. Csoma de Körös decided to take upon himself the task of establishing the linguistic and historic facts about the origins of his nation, and of investigating whether those offspring of the Huns, i.e., the Hungarians who remained in Asia, could be the tribes of the Uygurs (Yoghurs). Csoma de Körös started his journey in 1819, and walking on foot through Lebanon, Damascus, Tehran, Kabul and Srinagar, reached Leh, the capital of Ladakh, from where he tried to enter Central Asia by the Karakorum road. He was stopped, however, as Tibet was closed for foreigners.

It was not the worst place for a philologist to be halted. All around were ancient monasteries full of books unknown and inaccessible until then. Their language had not yet been properly deciphered by European learning. When the English agent William Moorcroft offered Csoma de Körös some financial assistance, he happily agreed to stay on, and within a year prepared a grammar and dictionary of the Tibetan language. He found something else—which was no less fascinating. As he got more and more involved in the study of the language, a hidden treasure trove of literary works opened before the eyes of the astonished philologist: hundreds of unknown Sanskrit works, which had been forgotten many centuries before in India, but had been preserved in faithful Tibetan translations.

His first eight years were spent in the windswept and snow-covered monasteries of Ladakh and Kinnaur. Here he had great luck, because Moorcroft has found for him a real guru. As Csoma de Körös reports, Sangye Phuntsog, a red-sect lama of Zanskar, had professional knowledge of the whole of Tibetan literature and learning. Besides teaching him through conveying the oral tradition, he asked other famous lama-scholars of Zanskar, among them Kunga Choleg, the abbot of the Dzong-khul gompa, i.e. monastery, to satisfy the *furungi* (foreign) student. Some of these question-answer books written for Csoma de Körös, are still preserved and used in the monasteries of Ladakh.

By 1831, Csoma de Körös had completed his work, walked to Calcutta and presented the books and papers he had compiled to the Asiatic Society of Bengal. H. Wilson, the secretary of the Society, did not receive him with particular warmth, but after he left for England, in 1834, Csoma's de Körös two most famous books, the *Dictionary*, and the *Grammar of the Tibetan Language* were printed. All later works on Tibetan lexicography and grammar are based on these pioneering works. Both of them remain in use up to now, and have been reprinted several times in India, England and in Hungary as well.

His other two great works are less known, but are of a similar significance for Sanskrit and Buddhist studies. The first is an edition (with English meanings added) of the Sanskrit and Tibetan Buddhist terminological dictionary called *Mahāvyutpatti*, which is a basic book for Buddhist thought, and originates from the 8th–9th centuries A.D. The other work was a catalogue and survey of the Tibetan holy scriptures, the Buddhist Tripitaka. This work was the first to give us an idea of Sanskrit Buddhist literature, which had practically been lost in India after the 12th century.

Lokesh Chandra writes about the importance of the activities of Alexander Csoma de Körös for Indian studies: "He opened up a vast vista of the treasures of art and thought, literature and philosophy, grammar and lexicography, medicine and metallurgy, astronomy and alchemy and other branches of learning of India hidden in the Tibetan language. This dark recess of India's history shone afresh, through the dedicated and pioneering efforts of Csoma."

The Asiatic Society of Bengal elected him an honorary member and the Hungarian Academy of Sciences a member. Csoma de Körös's conduct was determined by the fact that he came to India as a friend looking for "relatives". As Csoma himself puts it in the Preface of his Tibetan Dictionary (page VII) "...and he begs to inform the public, that he had not been sent by any Government to gather political information; neither can he be accounted of the number of those wealthy European gentlemen who travel at their own expense for their pleasure and curiosity, but rather only a poor student, who was very desirous to see the different countries of Asia, as the scene of so many memorable transactions of former ages; to observe the manners of several people, and to learn their languages, of which, he hopes, the world may see hereafter the results; and such a man was he, who during his peregrination, depended for his subsistence on the benevolence of others." His popularity in Hungary has grown ever since his death. The people of Hungary are proud that a son of their country was able to contribute so much to the knowledge of mankind, to the better understanding of the culture and heritage of India and Central Asia. He became a living symbol of friendship, a link between the peoples of India and Hungary.

Later, many more Hungarians visited the East and worked in India, among whom the most important are Sir Aurel Stein, Charles Fabri and Ervin Baktay, who has written a beautiful book on Indian art, which has not yet been translated into English. And we also have the famous artists—Amrita Sher-Gil, who was the daughter of a Hungarian lady, and had many connections with Hungary, and the two Elizabeth Brunner ladies (Elizabeth Sass Brunner and her daughter Elizabeth Brunner), whose work is also an Indian treasure.

Folk art, more precisely folk song, is another very important treasure trove, which has been very seriously studied and used in modern music. Two names must be mentioned immediately: Zoltan Kodály and Bela Bartok. They travelled through the villages, far away from towns, and recorded the simple people's songs. It is on the basis of these recordings, that the early music of the Hungarian, Romanian, Slovakian people was brought back into reality. In the compositions of Bartok, the "relevance of old culture" lives on into the 21st century. There is a so-called dance-house movement in present-day Hungary, which unites folk song and modern rock and roll music, which together preserve and make popular the music of the old times.

A Department for Indian studies was first established in Hungary in 1872, and we now have more universities that offer Sanskrit studies; Budapest houses the only Buddhist university in the Western world.

Preserving unity and keeping together various peoples is a basic and a living tradition of the European Union as well.

What is Traditional Art and Why is it Still Relevant in the World Today?

EMMA CLARK

"THE ROOTS OF THE PAST ARE THE BRANCHES OF THE FUTURE"

FIRST OF ALL, WE NEED to define our terms. No doubt, everyone speaking at this conference will offer his or her own perspective on the term "Traditional Culture", this being the focus of their important gathering here in Delhi. For my talk on Traditional Art, I would like to first look at the word "tradition" and give it some definition on which to base our understanding of Traditional Art. Another vital reason for defining these terms, is that today most of them have come to be misunderstood and debased, and therefore, misused: thus, we are making an attempt at restoring what we believe to be their original, true meaning.

TRADITION

Today, in the West, and possibly here, too in the East, the word "tradition" has been watered down to denote "custom" or even "habit", but its true meaning is far more rigorous and profound. Not only does "tradition" derive from the Latin *tradere* meaning "to hand over", it also means to "tie" or to "bind". Thus, the questions that arise are: first, to hand over from what or where, and, second, to tie or bind us to what or whom? There is but one answer to both questions: Tradition is both "the handing over from" as well as the "binding to" the transcendent or divine reality, the eternal source whence ideas and beliefs originate. Tradition penetrates a whole culture and "has within itself a secret force which is communicated to an entire civilization and determines even arts and crafts, the immediate objects of which include nothing particularly sacred".[1] This "secret force" is essentially divine inspiration, without which sacred and traditional art would not exist. Tradition is thus, as it were, a proof of the original, sacred revelation from heaven. A vital aspect of Tradition is that it is a living reality, every generation discovers anew the divine principles handed down from the previous generation, a chain of transmission reaching back to the supra-human, transcendent source. Every generation may rejuvenate these principles in a "contemporary" way, but never forgetting their timeless wisdom, that wisdom which is sometimes referred to as the *Philosophia Perennis*, the Perennial Philosophy. This clear acknowledgement that there is an absolute transcendent reality, beyond the physical world of the senses, that we may come to know through our highest faculty, the Intellect—or "heart-knowledge" as it may sometimes be referred to—is what is meant by the "traditional perspective".

ART

The second term we need to look is "art". From the definitions of art in the dictionary[2], two principal points emerge: the first is that art demands both skill and knowledge on the part of the practitioner; and the second is the idea that the so-called "fine arts" have greater intellectual (in the modern sense of the word meaning "rational rather than intuitive or emotional")[3] content, and are therefore superior to the crafts or more practical arts. However, in a traditional society—i.e., in brief, a society centred upon the sacred—this distinction between so-called "fine art" and "craft" did not exist, and there was no place for the concept of "art for art's sake". Indeed, in such a society, the arts and crafts were one and the same: they were produced by hand for practical purposes, were pleasing to the eye and were ultimately for the glory of God. Art was beautiful because it was true. True art, as art from this perspective came to be called, is beautifully made, well-informed and integrated into daily life. It is neither an individualistic, subjective experiment, nor is it a luxury solely for the wealthy elite. True, art is not simply aesthetically pleasing but through a serene and contemplative beauty, indeed, a profound mystery in the greatest examples, it is also awe-inspiring and ultimately reminds us of what it means to be human.

Now we come to the two terms in the title of this talk, "Traditional Art".

TRADITIONAL ART

I would say that this is the art of intimate beauty and of daily life. It is always pleasing to the eye while also serving a practical use. It is art made by the harmonious interaction of the head, the heart and the hand. It demands great skill, knowledge, dedication and patience. No one who has watched a true craftsman at work—whether it be ceramics, stone-carving, stained-glass, wood-carving or carpet-weaving—can deny the painstaking work, dexterity, grace and, above all, love, that is demonstrated by his or her practice.

Traditional art is passed on from master to apprentice, from one generation to another, and thus, each craftsman holds centuries-old wisdom in his hands together with his own particular gift and aptitude. The craftsman of the present (and every new generation is the present) renews and revitalizes ancient skills, breathing life into handed-down techniques of old. He is the vehicle of generations of wisdom that may be traced back "from apprentice to Master until one reaches our Lord Seth, the son of Adam".[4] Traditional art is thus not only useful and beautiful, but it also carries a subtle and profound spiritual message: it is like a constant reminder, in the background of our day-to-day lives, that there is a world beyond this world of the senses, that there is, as Hamlet says, "a divinity which shapes our ends, rough-hew them how we will."[5]

Traditional art is thus the art of day-to-day existence, not the sacred art (see later) of the temple; it is the art of the community, not of the individual, the art of humility and not of the ego. More often than not, it is anonymous, the concentration and contemplation required by the rigours of the art or craft practice, demanding an emptying of the heart and soul from subjective desires and preoccupations in order to be open to inspiration from heaven.

After the Flood: Imagination and the Waters of Life

TOM CHEETHAM

The powerful forces of global capitalism and technologies of communication and transportation are rampant everywhere. An uncontrolled deluge of money, ideas and things tends to obliterate traditional knowledge and indigenous culture wherever it flows. But the drive toward a universal monoculture is opposed by forces that act to scatter and disperse this energy and transmute it in the service of local, particular and creative purposes. The contemporary world is the chaotic result of this dynamic. We live poised between the totalitarian forces of monopoly and globalization, which would result in a world-wide unification of language, culture and economics on the one hand, and a vast array of powerful and creative energies of resistance, on the other. A perennial conflict within cultures has been between orthodoxy and heresy: between conservative members of a culture who revere and guard the wisdom and traditions of the past, and those revolutionary and creatively destructive individuals who celebrate the possibilities of the future. Conflicts between cultures can play out in a similar way with the heresies and challenges to tradition coming from outside, rather than from within. These relatively simple dynamics are enormously complicated by the effects of global capitalism and technology, which are simultaneously totalitarian and revolutionary, unifying and destructive, both constructive of Empire as well as empowering the heretical creativities of individuals. To borrow a metaphor from dynamical systems theory, we live poised on the edge of this chaos.

Global markets and modern technologies emerged from a positivist worldview that assumed a secular, uniform and universal time and space in which all things have a knowable location, rendering them subject to imperial domination and control. This is essentially the Newtonian worldview that William Blake critiqued with such ferocity, referring to "Single vision and Newton's sleep". The metaphysics of contemporary science is far more sophisticated, but the dominant ideology of most global technology and commerce remains totalitarian in its unstated, and largely unconscious, goal of the institutionalization and management of all life, human and otherwise, on the planet.

Confrontations between a global economic and technological monoculture and traditional cultures that do not share its metaphysic, highlight the necessary plurality of kinds of knowledge. The best defence against totalitarianisms of all kinds is the recognition of the wild diversity, essential legitimacy and ultimate value of all the world's languages, cultures, religions and forms of life. We could have a fundamentally biological and ecological vision of human culture, which values diversity, adaptability and beauty. In such a vision of things, we would acknowledge the real infinity of God by celebrating the plurality and proliferation of cultures, religions, metaphysics and forms of life, rather than aiming for an impossible and dangerous unification of humanity based upon a single, perfect and ultimate knowledge of Reality. Such a fantasy of a single universal Truth lies at the root of imperial consciousness and totalitarian political ideology.

The dominance of the metaphysics of secular, historical time that supports narratives of universal knowledge, control and imperial dominion can be broken by the eruptive energies of vertical, sacred time that permeate traditional cultures. From the point of view of an ecological vision of the necessary plurality of cultures, the experiences of eschatological sacred time do not imply any monolithic, authoritarian and dogmatic vision of religious experience and doctrine, but rather provide an antidote to the universalism and fundamentalism of secular modernity. Time, and Space as well, can be understood "relativistically" as multiple, complex and heterogeneous. Such heresy opens up possibilities for the creative exercise of human imagination within and among all human cultures.

Thus, the unity of human culture might be found in a cosmology of Imagination that celebrates the poetic basis of mind and a primary human potential that must manifest in a diversity of forms. This fundamentally creative energy permeates the cosmos and provides the unifying principle not only of humanity as a whole, but of all Creation. Thus, as in the evolution of life itself, cultures and individuals are always poised between past and future, order and chaos, tradition and creation—and this perennial tension is not a curse, but a challenge and a blessing. We are condemned to perpetual revolution, a perpetual creation. In the words of the great French Islamicist and theologian Henry Corbin, we must embrace and celebrate a "perpetual hermeneutics" of the Word. The tensions within and among cultures are an essential feature of our world—our very freedom depends upon them. The alternative is monoculture and authoritarian fundamentalism.

In the Qur'an, God says, "Had Allah willed He could have made you one community. But that He may try you by that which He hath given you (He hath made you as ye are). So vie one with another in good works (5:48)." This is the paradox of monotheism: the infinite God can only manifest in a plurality of cultures and religions. The creative power of the infinite is inexhaustible, unpredictable and uncontrollable. We are all called, on this account, to do what is good, create what is beautiful and celebrate the varieties of human potential.

It is in the practice of art and poetry that we can perhaps best find a metaphysics of the moment that releases us from what Blake called the "mind forg'd manacles" imposed by the metaphor of the causal necessity of universal, historical time and opens us to the ever-present and intimate eternities at the root of Creation. It is in the exercise of the creative imagination that the individual person comes closest to the divine energy and light at the heart of things. As Corbin has told us, prayer is the supreme form and the highest act of the creative imagination—but this means as well that human creativity in all its forms is always also prayer. The creative power in each and every one of us is the result of the flow of the Fountain of Life which, in the Islamic tradition, is found "at the meeting place of the two seas" (Qur'an 18:60). It is the deepest and most profound responsibility of each of us to seek our own Fountain, and then the summed power of these countless new creations of goodness and beauty may turn the tide of the Great Flood, which otherwise will overwhelm us all.

Tradition and Progress: A Metaphysical Analysis

COME CARPENTIER DE GOURDON

I

TRADITION AS PRESERVATION THROUGH REPETITION

Most of our thoughts, they say
Must come from others
How high, then, would I fly
Depends on borrowed feathers

Subhash Verma (From the poem *Open Any Page* in the volume *One and All*)

IN HIS *WEST ÖSTLICHE DIWAN*, Goethe tells the story of the Khalif who was invited to two feasts hosted by two magnificent noblemen of his court who had a contest as to who of them would throw the best reception. The second feast was in every respect identical to the first, which had been unanimously hailed as a supreme achievement of taste, luxury, refinement and art. While many of the other guests were disappointed by the apparent lack of imagination and creativity of the second host, the Khalif declared him the winner for his ability to reproduce flawlessly the perfect party of his rival. He thereby reminded all of us the critical importance of tradition in preserving without loss the best things achieved by man. In that perspective, memory took priority over imagination.

An old Latin proverb translated as "the better is the enemy of the good" encapsulates the essence of this conservative wisdom. The optimum is to be sought and when it is reached, trying to improve on it may simply destroy the harmony, contrary to what our current socio-economic philosophy of endless growth and maximization predicates.

In the words of John Keats:

Truth is beauty, beauty is truth
That is all ye know on Earth
And all ye need to know.

It is, of course, impossible, and even paradoxical, to say that tradition does not allow change, since we all witness traditions changing since as far as we can trace them, howbeit gradually and unobtrusively. In this regard, tradition is like the ship of Theseus: the material may be replaced, but the form remains and the story about its origin is preserved for generations to come.

The root of tradition is found in the Latin word *tradere* which means to "give" (and hence to trade, to exchange goods and, also to follow a route, so that trade signified both a journey and a reciprocated gift), and which has among its derivatives, given rise to the words *traductio* (translation, a rendering) and *traditio* (treason: to give away).

As Raimundo Panikkar noted in his *Mantramanjari*: "Every culture starts from somewhere outside itself." The ambiguity of the notion (similar to the ambivalence of *hos, hostis, hostilis*: host, hostle, hostile) is due to its essential significance as something that is a given, or a gift from the ancestors or from the gods. As such, it must be kept like a sacred legacy, whether it consists of rituals, ways of communicating (a language is, after all, also a traditional way of speaking for the community it binds), art forms or more mundane customs in dress, food, habitat and work.

Some traditions are shared across wide areas by entire nations or even federations of peoples, while others are peculiar to small clans or family groups. Even individuals have specific habits and ways of doing things which, if conscious and not strictly utilitarian, can be seen as traditions, such as taking a walk in the morning or reciting a prayer before going to sleep.

II

TRADITION AS AN INEVITABLE FOUNDATION FOR SOCIETY

In a remarkable collection of essays called *The Abolition of Man*, C.S. Lewis, the Cambridge philosopher who became famous for his children's books, produced during the years of the Second World War, a deep and astute analysis of the scientifically inspired endeavour to replace "traditional" notions and principles by purely functional or rational concepts rooted supposedly in instincts or in individual interests.

As a practising Christian but even more so as a powerful thinker, his goal was to ascertain whether a system of "values" devoid of any transcendent, or traditionally inherited wisdom would be tenable or even possible. Through a brilliant logical demonstration, he concluded that it would not be, simply because, as Gödel demonstrated mathematically, any value system or moral code must, ultimately rest on precepts that cannot be strictly proven but which rather, are intuitively felt to be true by all or most people. He observed that it was not possible to explain, and then justify the explanation, without eventually emptying the explanation of its meaning through a deconstructionist *reductio ad absurdum*. He therefore concluded that a spiritually inspired moral education was required for all members of a society if it was to survive and thrive. He took pains to underline that he was not preaching for Christianity, as he recognized that moral teaching is enshrined all religious traditions and wisdom schools, and called it the Tao, to evince its non-sectarian character, after equating it with the Sanskrit *Rita* and with the laws of Nature or the universal law.

The other perceptive and even prophetic conclusion that Lewis draws in his essay is that those who believe that they can conquer nature and make themselves and their fellow men all powerful through the ever greater application of science and technology are, in fact, falling into the Faustian trap of giving up their souls for the sake of omnipotence and immortality.

The destruction of traditional values (such as morality) gradually empties man of his substance, and makes him less and less human. When we think we acquire mastery over matter and living forms, we inevitably are led to manipulate and transform the human physical and psychological being, and end up robbing it of its humanity by turning it into mere clay that our ever more sophisticated machines will control one day. Lewis speculated on the identity and motivation of the demiurgic minority of people who would control the world through their scientific knowledge and power and predicted that they would behave like monsters, whether or not they meant to, since they would have banished the traditional moral laws and replaced them with technical considerations harnessed in the service of their own selfish desires or whims. He makes the almost unavoidable reference to Francis Bacon who, like Faust, saw knowledge as a means to dominate nature and not for its own sake as "natural philosophy", telling his readers that science should be a wife, intended for generating a posterity and not a mistress to be enjoyed. In his eyes, the true scientist is a magician (or a witch), not a gnostic.

The message that Lewis conveys in this concise essay is that there is no alternative to the preservation and cultivation of the sacred ethical and sapiential norms we inherited from our origins. As he puts it, "Man can no more invent the good or new values than he can place a new sun in the sky".

The modern undertaking, promoted by the hegemonic power structures of the world, to replace the aforesaid timeless norms with new and constantly changing concepts rooted in the elusive notion of individual freedom, is doomed to fail and can only lead mankind and its planet to utter destruction.

The implications of that conclusion, which merely reaffirms what thousands of spiritual teachers have said in many different times and places, are too wide-ranging to be enumerated. Nowadays the philosophy that draws its inspiration from it is dubbed conservative, and often dismissed as such, although there is not always much in common between what is now described as politically conservative and the really traditional, in the Guenonian sense of Tradition with a capital T.

The present debate on the matter of "marriage equality" reflects, in a concrete social context, the attempt to reject tradition, or at least modify it to the point of making it the opposite of what it meant: *Daimon est Deus inversus* says the hermetic aphorism. Marriage is a sacrament intended to reflect the cosmological and hence divine significance of the union between the sexes for mutual support and the generation of offspring. The modern anti-traditional approach defines it instead as the association of two individuals of any gender who have a desire for each other and wish to cohabit and presumably have sexual relations. As for everything else, it follows the axiom *sic volo sic jubeo* (what I want I order).

The fact that homosexual relations are fruitless and even physiologically harmful or at least dangerous by definition is ignored by the proponents of gay marriage who hold that there is nothing above individual desire, that sodomy is equal to natural copulation between opposite sexes and that, if children are also desired, they can either be manufactured *in vitro*, procured through a "leased womb" or that one of the two male or female partners can change his/her sex through surgical procedures in order to correct the "mistake" of nature.

The promoters of this increasingly widespread view rarely fail to factor economic considerations in their demonstrations and show that these are indeed the most important, considering that homosexual couples are becoming a very large consumer market and even the medical and surgical care they may require (for HIV or VD treatment, cosmetic or sex change operations) represents another avenue of growth for the economy.

It goes without saying that this imposition of a new concept of equality is held by its enforcers to be indisputable and, that those self-proclaimed apostles of tolerance are quick to ostracize and sanction all those who disagree, dubbing any differing opinion, however cogently argued, as "hate speech", "fascism" and "expressions of homophobia", even when such objections are expressed respectfully and with due regard to the personal dignity of every person. Thus, the so-called free society soon turns more intolerant of and oppressive towards dissent than many conservative dispensations that it seeks to eradicate.

The adoption of gay marriage as well as the celebration of homosexuality in all its variations, along with the normalization of pornography, commercial sex and other traditionally repressed or fringe businesses is a natural effect of the dismissal of morality, described as "backward", "outdated" or "non-democratic", along with virtue and other words of the traditional religious lexicon that have now become irrelevant or even ridiculous, such as humility, chastity, modesty, honour and piety, because they limit the right to individual self-expression and free will. Without the traditional restraints inspired by the natural order on the basis of millenary experiences, it should come as no surprise that anything goes.

Instead, in the name of uninhibited freedom, which implies the liberation of instincts, we notice that modern "values" include aggressiveness, self-assertion, greed, lust, individualism, material ambition, skepticism or even cynicism, all regarded as corollaries of efficiency and personal happiness and success. That is touted as progress, as opposed to the traditional ways of the world. It certainly is, in the sense of a motion towards a different condition, but progress is a value-free neutral term, at least in its objective meaning. There is no indication that progress is a rise towards a better state; indeed it could be a displacement that has not any other goal than its own motion, which implies that it could even be counterproductive or turn out to be meaningless.

As Lewis observed, the sponsors of this total inversion of values in the march towards a "free, democratic and equal society" are often claiming, or even genuinely attempting, to propose an alternative set of values to replace what they want to eradicate. Like the French revolutionaries after 1789, they promulgate a new religion to take the place of the hated old creed. They talk of the need for "ethics", corporate responsibility, transparency, accountability, solidarity or "citizen values", as they are often lamely defined in French, but they cannot really define what those supposedly new concepts are based on, since the system they rely on is materialistic and recognizes only what scientific research appears to prove (although they usually reject scientific data about natural laws when these do not support their demands for the satisfaction of all human cravings and whims). While they believe that they are conquering ultimate freedom, they are giving themselves over to their own instinctive cravings and hence banishing the true freedom that traditional wisdom points to.

Indeed, as Lewis demonstrates beautifully, the values of modernizing social revolutionaries are only disconnected fragments of the venerable edifice of civilization that they are tearing down, which they try to rescue under new colours and names after rebranding them in their image. Yet in practice those attempts at creating a new utilitarian morality are found quite ineffective, judging by the growing corruption and social decay we are witnessing and, as Lewis eloquently pointed out: "We make heartless men and expect from them virtue and bravery. We make fun of honour and are shocked to find traitors among us. We castrate and expect eunuchs to be fecund."

III

THE UNIVERSAL OR PRIMORDIAL TRADITION

Kasminnu bhagavo vijnata sarvamidam vijnatam bhavati
"Sir, what is it by knowing which everything can be known?"

Mundaka Upanishad, 1.1-3

The notion of a primordial or original tradition (*ritam samantah* in the Vedas) that was in early ages, *ab illo tempore* or "once upon a time": *idam agreka evasa,* common to all men, essentially immutable and directly handed down to the "first man" by his creator or creators is widespread amongst ancient cultures, both elementary and sophisticated. It was periodically revived and articulated in such eras as the European Middle Ages and Renaissance, when some scholars gave it the name *prisca philosophia.* In China, as we have already seen, it was usually defined as the Tao or wisdom of the first Emperors and in practically all societies, this higher knowledge was handed down from master to disciple in a line stretching back as far as human memory could go.

It was a transmission and propagation from one generation to another (*sampatti* in Sanskrit) as opposed to today's propaganda, which is spread among the masses by certain influential minorities. It is significant that the *dharma* or law handed down through that tradition was seen as originating in a primordial sacrifice (*kalpa, yajna* in the Vedas) by many archaic civilizations.

We read evocations of such *paramparas* (in Sanskrit) or *silsilas* and *tariqas* (in Arabic and Persian) or chains of initiation. By definition, this transmission from above "from the one to the one" (as in the *Enneads* of Plotinus) and thence to the few, is not democratic although it finds popular expression, generally through myths, fables and allegories. It is that which is to be remembered (*amnaya*).

This primordial tradition, of a cosmological and metaphysical or "mystical" order (*dhaman*, a sacred domain and law in Sanskrit) is the fountainhead of all traditions transmitted within specific cultic, professional and ethno-linguistic communities, whether they are artisanal, technical, socio-political, agricultural or commercial. They provide defining identity and structure to social groups, clans, tribes, *varnas, jatis* and "estates". Thus the political order and ruling system of any traditional society, whether a city, a kingdom or a league of villages or towns is inspired by and related to the community's fundamental metaphysical belief and the related creation myth, defined by A. B. Keith as "righteousness, Nature, the Way, the Path...that the universe follows, the Way on which things eternally, serenely and quietly emerge, to flow into space and time. It is also the Way that every man must follow to invite this cosmic and supra-cosmic progression by making all his actions conform to the great Model". In that progression, cyclically regulated by the seasons (*rita*), we see the traditional notion of progress as opposed to the predominant iconoclastic and rebellious modern concept. Indeed, the etymology of the name Rita itself implies motion, unfoldment and transformation, as the year moves through the zodiacal and solar calendar.

In a way, we may say that the innumerable little traditions that make a community's life and sense of self, whether in rites, art forms or ways of dressing and eating, are manifestations of the transcendent common tradition like the flashes of light on a shimmering sea are reflections of the sun in the sky and they lose their hidden, allegorical (*yaugika*) significance when they are severed from that sustaining source, just as branches lose their life when cut off from their trunk. There is, hence, a coherence and continuity in all aspects of the traditional social order, whatever be its subjective merits or flaws in a critic's eyes, as the major students of tradition, such as René Guenon and Ananda Coomaraswamy have shown in many of their works.

It is easy to see, for instance, in the design and architecture of many modern Christian churches, that they have been built without regard to or understanding of the esoteric theological and cosmological principles that dictated their construction in past centuries. Too often they are now conceived merely as user-friendly spaces for public assembly in a secular, agnostic society and contain no intrinsic reference to spirituality and to the divine order.

IV

PROGRESS VS TRADITION

The notion of progress must be seen primarily as a logical consequence of the belief that ancient societies and institutions are deeply flawed, immature or evil, and must be corrected, renewed and even replaced by radically new institutions based on different concepts of man and the world. This phenomenon of rejection of an existing reality took the name of Enlightenment, *Aufklarung* or *Lumieres*, in Europe of the 18th century and led to the resolve among many to build a new socio-political and intellectual reality based, not on tradition, but on reason and logic, devoid of faith in traditional teachings unless they could be scientifically tested and empirically justified. The Baconian and later Hegelian conviction that the human race increases in knowledge and in power over time led them to conclude that man and the world could be ceaselessly improved and, that just as the present seemed better than the past, the future would always get better and brighter as a result of man's will which could overcome any other factor. This, in a nutshell, is the progressionist view which found its systematic expression in the positivist ideology.

The pioneers of the endeavour to rethink and reorganize mankind as well its environment almost immediately branched off into various competing and contending factions, which can be broadly divided into individualists and collectivists. The former became the liberal capitalists of the last two centuries, and the latter evolved into Marxists. They were both trying to give different answers to the obvious question: "Whose will determines the future and for whose benefit?" While the Marxists posited an unidirectional "march of history" that would bring about the supremacy of the working class seen as the meritorious proletarian majority, the Liberals point to the individual human as the maker of his own destiny through the mechanism of democracy.

The Marxist and Liberal theories, however fail to resolve their inner contradictions. Human will cannot be collective on a permanent, or even a long-term basis, as it is mostly personal, in the absence of a common law accepted by all, and inevitably the will of some more privileged individuals is bound to prevail and impose itself upon the others, as all Marxist regimes have shown, and we have experienced once more the evidence that history does not follow a constant upward course when the socialist systems broke down without reaching the Communist promised land. Conversely, liberals cannot credibly reconcile their focus on individuals with their confidence in democracy, which can hardly function in an anomic assembly of self-centred persons, as the latter are not sufficiently connected to form a coherent majority, let alone reach unanimity. For these reasons, Communist states have always turned into dictatorships, when they have not dissolved themselves whereas highly capitalist societies like the USA are socially atomized and are ruled by plutocratic oligarchies against whom the disorganized mass of ordinary individuals is powerless. This situation accounts for the obsession with gun ownership observed among Americans who can only rely on their own devices to protect their lonely selves in what they tend to perceive as an inimical, exploitative and dangerous environment.

In the contemporary technocratic age, the growing economies of scale, the increasing requirements for occupational specialization, the compulsory emphasis on educational and professional elitism are in contradiction with the abstract principle of universal equality and the rules of democracy, which are relegated to the status of hollow symbols.

The instinctive reaction from the bottom of the social pile is often to demand that remaining traditional institutions be abolished or whittled down into insignificance in order to remove the vestiges of inequality.

Among such vestiges of a "feudal" past, we may include monarchies, albeit in a constitutional system, and religious hierarchies and rituals in their ancient and esoteric forms and we see how, gradually, the last hereditary sovereigns are either removed or are trying to become as un-royal and democratic as possible, unmindful of the fact that a democratic king is a tautology. Likewise, traditional churches in all "advanced" modern societies are in crisis and are turning into, or being replaced by more "populistic" and commercial spiritual businesses that often rely on modern technology and entertainment to win mass support for their feel- good messages and simplified rituals, generally devoid of esotericism and gnosis.

These trends began long ago and were predicted and diagnosed by traditionalists of many schools such as Ralph Waldo Emerson, Donoso Cortes or the earlier mentioned Guenon and Coomaraswamy. The French poet la Tour du Pin put it most succinctly when he wrote that "all countries... devoid of legend are doomed to die of cold".

The loss of the national and religious customs for which mass sport and pop art performances are a poor substitute, analogous to the *panem et circenses* (bread and circuses) of the late Roman period, makes post-modern liberal societies culturally poor, amnesic and divided, in the likeness of today's United States, and it brings about a collapse in public ethics and decency, since the pursuit of material gain and physical enjoyment is the only objective left to the vast majority of people. Concurrently, the geometric progression of technology in many directions reduces human beings, in general, to the category of intellectual resources at best (for a minority) and genetic material at worst (for the others).

As C.S. Lewis had foreseen, this "abolition of man", in effect, translates into the objectification of the masses in the hands of the privileged controllers or puppeteers who own the means of enslaving or eliminating the others depending upon whether they are "useful idiots" or "useless eaters". "If a man, says he, chooses to deal with himself as a raw material, he will indeed be a raw material."

CONCLUSION

Progress, when devoid of any reference to "eternal" traditional values that may be regarded as metatheorems—which cannot be strictly proven but must be seen as axiomatic—cannot be trusted as a guiding principle, contrary to what many rather naive revolutionaries and reformers of the last three centuries have believed on the basis of unsupported articles of faith. Tradition, however, cannot be blindly relied upon either in its visible incidental and local forms as the latter are often decadent and have lost their direct connection to the wisdom that inspired their inception.

While progress, to be desirable, must be instilled with, and guided by, the ancestral gnosis that all civilizations inherited in one way or another, tradition evolves and periodically requires a reform in the etymological sense of returning it to its pristine form, as is said in the Veda: "Put me together again" (*tvam ma samdhehi*). However, it is difficult, if not impossible, to reform tradition from outside, without being aware of its inner meaning and context.

C.S. Lewis makes an apt comparison in the aforesaid book between the reform of a language imposed by foreign legislators or by a committee of philology experts and the transformation effected by a gifted poet writing in that same language and spontaneously inspired by it. It is, he says, the difference between "the organic and the surgical". Likewise, it is from the Tao and its practitioners that necessary and desirable changes arise, not from those who ignore it and reject its very existence. Overturning tradition from outside by decree is dangerous, often counterproductive, and can lead to the destruction of the culture that is submitted to this intervention, leaving a sociological vacuum in its place.

Lewis, in the last chapter of his book, was already envisioning scientific research as a means of validating tradition by uncovering its essential meaning. Since then, many of the prodigious advances made in various disciplines are proving him right. Quantum physics reveals a subatomic universe infused and regulated by laws that are as subtle and comprehensive as the Tao or Rita. Molecular biology uncovers the structure of genes, chromosomes and the DNA double helix as being akin to the *sutratmas, pindas, ragas* and *varnamalas* depicted in Hindu cosmology, artistic theory and linguistics. Neurobiology proves the life-enhancing and intellectually stimulating value of aesthetic experiences for the brain through the dopamine release they trigger. Beauty and goodness as the *Upanishads*, Plato and Aristotle, among many others, taught, are interrelated and are now known to trigger in the beholder a multiplication of synapses which, in turn, augment logical abilities. In that sense those, virtues are not a matter of subjective opinion as many contemporary theories argue, even though most ancient schools of wisdom teach that people must be educated to recognize and like them from childhood.

As Plato wrote, the young human cannot, from the outset, have correct reactions. He (and she) must be trained to feel pleasure, attraction and dislike towards things that really are pleasing, attractive, repugnant or dislikable. What is more troubling is what recent studies in the functioning of the brain have shown: decisions that seem spontaneous and freely taken, actually flow from "brain noises" that dictate them, so that, in effect, as many ancient psychological doctrines held, there is no such thing as individual free will. We and all our actions are shaped by our environment, our past (our *karma*, in Indian terms) and an unidentified power that seems to be the source of all manifestation or, in terms of Sankhya philosophy, the combination of *Purusa* and *Prakriti* or cosmic consciousness and nature.

Scientific exploration is thus gradually raising in front of us, a mirror or traditional wisdom, and many of its pioneers of the last hundred years have been influenced by, and are sometimes deeply involved, in the study of ancient Taoist, Hindu and Buddhist texts to which they have acknowledged their debt. Truly great scientists are aware that reality cannot be reduced solely to its material, measurable components or to its representations, just as a forest does not consist of an accumulation of timber logs, contrary to what technology makes many believe. Guenon defined the technocratic age as "the reign of quantity" and Tolstoy, like most traditionally inspired thinkers, had a similar view on it.

What we need is an epistemic and gnostic Renaissance, a true Enlightenment, in the an esoteric spiritual sense, of which the positivistic, literal interpretation predominant in the last three centuries in the West was a travesty.

BIBLIOGRAPHY

Lewis, C.S. *L'Abolition de l'Homme* (French translation), Editions Raphael, 2000.*The Abolition of Man*, 1974.

Goethe J.W. von, *West Eastern Divan* (translated by E Dowden), M Dent & Sons Ltd., London and Toronto, 1941.

Keith A.B., article on "Righteousness, Hindu" in the *Encyclopedia of Religion and Ethics* (vol. X).

Keats J. "Ode to a Grecian Urn" (in *Great Odes of 1819).*

Guenon R. *The Reign of Quantity and The Signs of the Times.* Sophia Perennis. 2004.

Coomaraswamy A. "The Bugbear of Freedom, Equality and Democracy" in *The Betrayal of Tradition, Essays on the Spiritual Crisis of Modernity.* Harry Oldmeadow, editor (2004).

Panikkar R. *The Vedic Experience, Mantramanjari.* Motilal Banarsidass. 1994.

Harmonizing Tradition and Modernity: A Conceptual View

K. RAGHUNATH

THE RATIONALE AND CONTEXT FOR this event and its timing is as follows: societies and nation states have, as a rule, assigned a fundamental role to evaluating the relevance of traditional cultures in their present and future. This preoccupation is reflected in a continuous and ongoing process of self-examination, which has been a central, integral part of their evolution and development. This involves a thorough study and exploration of traditional cultures all over the world, with the objective of understanding and discovering whether and how their knowledge systems and ways of life and thought could be relevant to our present and future concerns. In recent years, this exercise has acquired a special and sharpened focus, prompted by the recognition, that the milieu to which it is addressed is a world that is undergoing a revolutionary transformation, a process appropriately summed up by one of our scholar-participants in the following words: "Our world is now being shaped in a novel fashion by the powerful force of the technologies of communication and transport, of globalization in wealth creation, information, commerce and popular culture as well as global threats to the well-being of nations, societies and individuals."

Over the last few decades, this has thrown up an entire range of closely interrelated and fundamental, critical global issues and challenges—political, economic, societal, cultural, inter alia, relating to the role of the state and government and of political leadership; the composite tasks of ensuring effective governance, democracy, the rule of law, human rights and equity and justice; the challenge of coming to grips with the massive problem of poverty, and in this context, of building prosperity for all, making the benefits of wealth creation and technological progress available to all, ensuring that GDP growth translates into real development, sustaining quality of life and the human factor, especially in health, education and social welfare, also safeguarding the all-pervading values of ecology, that is overall sustainable development; and at another level, building a rational, democratic world order, which provides for a structure of bilateral and multilateral cooperation for all-round benefit, as well as protection of the security and welfare of nations and their citizens, against dangers such as natural disasters and the menace of globalized terrorism. These terms are shorthand for trends and events that are all too familiar and which loom large in our environment and deeply condition the lives of nations and people everywhere. Overarching this process is the historic development of "an uncontrolled deluge of money, ideas and things tending to obliterate traditional knowledge and indigenous culture, wherever it flows", as put incisively by one of our scholar-participants. It is not as though there is any lack of will and effort in meeting these challenges. Indeed, we are living in an era marked by a forceful display in the world as a whole, of energy and imagination, of resilience in finding answers, as well as the capacity to survive and thrive. Thus, with reference to the overarching category of culture, to once again quote the scholar referred to above, "the will to a universal monoculture is opposed by forces that act to scatter and disperse this energy and transmute it in the service of local, particular and creative purposes. The contemporary world is the chaotic result of this dynamic."

Having said this, and with due care in not over-dramatizing the global challenges we face, the fact is that they are indeed very serious and we have not as yet found satisfactory answers. Arguably, they are becoming more critical and even coming to a head. One senses that every generation sees itself as living in an age of revolution and crisis, but the current experience of crisis could, with good reason, be seen to be more intense, traumatic and far-reaching that anything in the past. The theme of "mankind at the end of its tether" has been repeated age after age, but it rings today with more urgency than ever before. Objectively viewed, this situation is the consequence of historical evolution, set in motion by our own omissions and commissions, and we need, more than ever before, to invoke every possible source of inspiration and insights to help rectify it. One cannot presume dogmatically that traditional cultures, that is their knowledge systems and ways of life and thought will provide all the answers; but one can proceed on the clear indication that they could.

We need to begin with a clear understanding of key terms, above all, of culture, tradition, traditional cultures and civilization. It is submitted that one does not need a ponderous definition exercise, considering that to a great extent, common sense itself provides this understanding. Further, the discussion itself is meant to bring forth clarity on this subject. Culture could be seen as a composite totality of knowledge systems and ways of life and thought. This implies that it has an overarching, all-encompassing character, and is the heart and foundation of political, economic and societal thought and activity. If this formulation is agreed on, it would suggest a basic weakness in the current effort and engagement with the critical global challenges, referred to above. This means this engagement involves a rigorous political discourse, first on the political themes noted above, second on a parallel discourse at the economic level, and third, in the realm of culture. One senses that the overall effort is vitiated by the inadequate interrelating of the first two levels of discourse with the third. This would be an important question in our enquiry.

Proceeding logically, a workaday understanding of civilization (or state, nation and society) on the one hand, in relation to culture on the other, is that the former is the vessel and the latter the content. This implies that every civilization, state, nation or society has its own unique culture, traditional as well as contemporary (more accurately, a continuum over these time categories). This would apply to the West as much as to the non-Western world, and the exercise of examining the relevance of traditional cultures to the present and future would involve traditional cultures in the former as much as in the latter. Thus, logically speaking, Western Europe applying this prescription to its Norse, Anglo-Saxon or Celtic/Gaelic past should be seen as equally valid with India and China invoking their Confucian or Vedic past, even if this logic is obscured by the fact that the West European traditional ages noted above do not have the hoary antiquity of the Eastern traditional ages. At the same time, having noted this for mental clarity, the common perception that in talking about traditional culture and examining its relevance we are referring essentially to non-Western civilizations, is understandable because they have retained much more of their tradition than the West has. In reality therefore, the relevance exercise is, in fact, been focused on non-Western civilizations.

Thus, evaluating their tradition with reference to the requirements of the present-day world, was perforce a task of crucial, compelling importance for the movements for national independence in Asia, Africa and Latin America over the last century and a half, including the decades that followed independence and liberation, which were devoted to establishing modern nation-states. This process involved the posing of fundamental questions on the meaning of categories such as tradition and modernity, and the extent and nature of the posited dichotomy between the two, of national and cultural identity, and, indeed of the very concepts of civilization and culture. Because of the authenticity and intensity of their engagement, the evaluation of tradition in the emerging and emergent nation states of Asia, Africa and Latin America was marked by independence of mind, rationality and maturity of judgment, and, by all accounts, offered valuable contemporary perspectives on the civilizations of the non-Western world.

One could say that the Western world went through a comparable exercise, in an earlier era, but its self-image as developed over the last three centuries or so, could be described as being based on the judgment and a clear sense that they had graduated out of tradition, in their historical evolution from the medieval period, through the Renaissance, on to the Age of Reason, the Enlightenment, and beyond. This transition was strongly reinforced through the Industrial and Scientific-Technological Revolutions; having thus transcended tradition, and entered the phase of modernity, they did not need to examine their traditional cultures in a manner comparable to Asia, Africa and South and Meso-America. Their imperial and colonial domination of the non-Western world would no doubt have reinforced this approach. To be sure, there was a serious and continuous thread of dissent, but the mainstream, establishment

European perception, was, from all indications on the lines outlined earlier. Tradition and traditional cultures were of course, seen as important but the focus was on the non-Western world. Driven by the same energy and curiosity that led to the voyages of discovery and the scientific and industrial revolutions, the West, particularly Europe (including Russia and East Europe), has over the last 200 years produced a substantial body of scholarship on non-Western cultures, covering a wide range, from the humanities—languages, literature—to the social sciences—sociology, anthropology, history. This effort reflects a recognition that the non-Western world also represented rich and highly developed civilizations, with monumental accomplishments, from which the West had much to learn. At the same time, the prevailing framework for the study of non-Western civilizations was that they were relics, entities which were live and vital in earlier epochs of history, which were disjointed from the present, rather than as constructs and entities that could be, or needed to be, related to the present. They were regarded very much as the contents of a museum, admittedly of absorbing interest and worthy of specialized, lifelong scholarship, but in a compartmentalized manner, isolated from the concerns of the modern world. The underlying sense and ideology was that the civilizations of the non-Western world constituted a secondary stream, subsidiary to the mainstream civilization of the West, that is Europe and its affiliates; the distinguishing feature of the latter was that they represented a largely seamless continuity of the past, whereas the normal progress and evolution of the non-Western world had been irrevocably disrupted. This paradigm hampered the development of a balanced and accurate global understanding of the idea of culture and civilization, as applied to different countries, and, in particular, of the relevance of tradition.

The big story on the subject is the progressive emancipation, over the last century, from the constricted paradigm recapitulated above. This trend was slow in the making; in retrospect, the growing realization that all civilizations should be seen as parallel streams, with equal intrinsic significance—a manifestation of the classic aphorism, "We are all equidistant from infinity." Implicit in this perception is a sense of the unity as well as the diversity of the civilizations of the world. In the felicitous phrasing of the late Dag Hammarskjold: "Diversity respected within the framework of an even deeper respect for unity." This is a concept far removed from that of the homogenized, universal monoculture sought to be imposed on the world.

Equally important is the understanding that in viewing history, one should not dichotomize the past from the present, or even the unknown future, i.e., time present, time past and time future are best seen holistically as a composite—as a continuum. Time in itself does not render an idea or event passé. By extension of this principle, "modernity" is not necessarily a function of the passage of time. That is to say, there are societies, which were chronologically ancient, but were in their behaviour, at a given point, modern as we would construe the term today. Conversely, there are several examples of societies that are contemporary and modern by virtue of chronology, but retrograde in their outlook. Time and chronology could well be obscuring the unity and indivisibility of historical movement.

This guideline is accurately recapitulated in the, aphorism, "The past is not dead; it is not even past." It should of course be clarified that this rehabilitation of the past should not become a justification for revivalism or obscurantist manipulation of history. The call is for a rational approach to history, giving it its due place as a substantive factor in the present day.

These unities and, equally importantly, the continuities of space and time are reflected in the fact that despite the obstacles of geography and politics, civilizations, communities and societies have indeed interacted, throughout much of history, over land and sea, through trade, migration, pilgrimage, territorial conquest, promoting dispersion of ideas and value systems. Obviously, this was on a much smaller scale than in today's milieu of instant, all-embracing communication, but it suffices to illustrate the perspective outlined above. In this regard, one should note the point made in the concept note, that the civilizations of Asia, Africa and South/Meso-America predate the rise of Western civilization. The latter has been influenced by the intellectual and cultural aspects of the older civilizations over a long period of time.

This historic transformation could justifiably be attributed, in a basic sense, to a widening human awareness and awakening. In more rigorous and specific historical terms, the initial impulse could be seen in a sense as a trend of serious self-questioning within the West, starting from the late 19th century, prompted by the experience of social turmoil and internecine war, challenges to and the ultimate liquidation of Empire, (a process that might well have been obscured by an assertion in the Establishment, of Western primacy, and of the maxim that there is nothing to be learnt from the non-Western world—the Macaulay paradigm). The emergence of a new world of sovereign, independent nation states in the non-Western world created the conditions necessary for an enduring change of perceptions. This helped bring about the realization that learning from the older civilizations of the non-Western world would no longer be as from a vantage point of self-sufficient Orientalist superiority, but from a more vulnerable, receptive position. In more recent decades, this awareness has been consolidated by the ever-increasing globalization of the exchange, not only of goods and services and technology, but equally important, of ideas and value-systems, by the steadily expanding mutual exposure of East and West. Underlying this is the process, which is both cause and consequence of globalization, of the sustained growth, especially over the last three decades, of overall national power in the countries of Asia, Africa and Latin America, and the coming of age of the much-heralded multipolar world, offsetting and balancing the conventional big powers. The far-reaching character of this transformation is tellingly indicated, by recalling that as late as the 1970s, the prevailing, conventional wisdom was that the division of the world between developing and developed countries was an "end of history guideline"; for understanding the international system. For good measure, it was added that the gap between them would progressively widen, with the implication of inbuilt global tension and crisis; the trend over the succeeding decades has happily been to the contrary, with the economic and total national weight of the developing world increasing steadily. The shorthand for this is "shift in the structure of power from West to East". In fact, this shift involves not only the East, but Asia, Africa and South/Meso-America as a whole. This should not be viewed simplistically as a re-assertion of independence by the ex-colonial world and an acknowledgement of this reality by the West. This should not be seen simplistically as a case of the tables having been turned on the West. More accurately, it is a move in the direction of an equalization and rectification of unbalanced perceptions, and, above all, the emergence of a more unified, holistic view of world civilizations as a whole.

It is to be noted that the exercise taken up at this conference, while designed to focus on traditional cultures in the non-Western world, the broader, universal canvas set out above should be kept in mind.

Our large paradigm and framework as summed up in the concept note is that the older civilizations of the non-Western world have maintained a considerable measure of continuity in spite of their turbulent trajectories and the political and economic dominance that they have been subject to over time. They have also retained and sustained their inherent values and traditions together with knowledge systems woven into popular culture, which are intricate and rich enough to attract scholarly study. Now they are poised to rearticulate the relevance of their values in the contemporary era, and in the shaping of the future.

To complete this narrative the following paragraphs reproduce, with some additional comment, the depiction in broad brush strokes of the distinctive character of the large civilizations of the non-Western world, which is contained in the concept note.

Africa is a prime example of unity in diversity, marked by a truly wide geographical spread and a truly rich, ethnic, linguistic variety, and at the same time unified by a common African personality, constituting a pan-African civilization and a shared African sensibility, whether it is in the territorially large countries in the North, relating closely to each other, or the honeycomb of countries south of the Sahara, also closely knit into an African ensemble. One recalls Dag Hammarskjold's words, visiting Somalia in 1960, that the newly independent nations of Africa "could share in creating an international world, a world of universality and unity, which could save not only the personality of Africa, but the personality of each country, each group in this wonderfully rich continent. You can create and you will create the African personality, as part of the picture of mankind today." Egypt and the other countries of the Maghreb are unique, in that geographically and culturally, they straddle Africa and the Arab world, and have interacted substantively with both. Egypt has played a pivotal role for millennia as a creator and disseminator of culture and its civilization has a long history of continuity along with change.

West Asia is heir to the powerful classical civilizations of the Levant, Turkey, Mesopotamia and Persia. Each of them has a unique presence and resonance, continued in the modern nation-states of the region. They have also nurtured a wealth of traditional cultures, which have retained their vitality in the contemporary world, and a study of these would be an essential part of this exercise.

Asia (other than West Asia) is characterized by the emergence, over a very wide geographical area, of large, distinctive civilizations and cultures, each with its own strong identity and centre of gravity. Despite the striking, diversity among these countries, there have been from, the very beginning certain deep seated commonalities and a convergence. They are all joined as if in a honeycomb and attached to each other. It has seen the play of centripetal as well as centrifugal forces, which have been disruptive at one remove, but also enriching and unifying. Of particular significance to understanding the Asian civilizational ensemble is that the civilizations of Asia have a traditional, and sound commitment to plurality—plurality of perception and world view, and plurality with a capacity for dialogue. There is a distinct Asian sensibility, which also allows for multi-identities. In the context of global interactions, as one scholar participant puts it, "the civilizational repositories of Asia would be a great additional resource."

South and Meso-America are home to numerous ancient civilizations (Pre-Columbian, such as Maya, Aztec, Olmec, Inca). Each of them represents a rich source of philosophical concepts and insights, highly relevant to this exercise (eg., concepts of time and space), which are valuable inputs, for the conference proposes to focus for the most part on the cultures of Peru, Mexico and Brazil. In each of these, there is a distinct South/Meso-American sensibility, which has been modified through accretions—layer upon layer, over a long course of time (in particular the all-pervading Hispanic and Portuguese influence). Perhaps, the key question is how these civilizations, facing intense challenges, have been able to absorb new elements and change, and yet maintain their character through many historical moments.

We also need to consider including the civilizations of North America—of the American Indians—which could be seen as belonging to the same large family as South and Meso-America, and which is also a storehouse of rich traditional cultures.

The global milieu recapitulated above provides for the nurturing of an intellect which is steeped in the positive cultural content of one's own civilization (using the term culture in the inclusive sense emphasized earlier), and at the same time is ready and indeed keen to relate in a cosmopolitan spirit to other civilizations. This enables reflection on the fundamental question of how the rich cultural traditions of the non-Western world, i.e. their rich and varied knowledge systems and their ways of life and thought, and their overall wisdom, can be brought to bear on finding insights and answers to the totality of the fundamental, critical global issues and challenges highlighted earlier.

The proposed conference is intended to bring together intellectuals in the academic world and elsewhere, from Asia, Africa, South and Meso-America as well as from Europe and North America, to address this large theme.

There have been conferences held over the past decade on this broad subject. We would reemphasize the critical need to revisit these concerns with new vigour and clarity.

Report on the Proceedings

NALIN SURIE

An International Conference on "The Relevance of Traditional Cultures for the Present and the Future" was held at the India International Centre from March 24-26, 2014. The conference was organized by the IIC-Asia project and the Indian Council for Cultural Relations. The conference was attended by 30 delegates from Greece, Ghana, Hungary, UK, USA, Lebanon, Nepal, Ethiopia, Brazil, Sri Lanka, Japan, Afghanistan, Vietnam, Argentina, Mauritius, Egypt, Senegal, Russia, Indonesia, Mexico, China, Benin and India. The delegates represented the older civilizations as well as those of European origin. Participants from Iran and Republic of Korea, who had confirmed, did not attend.

A concept note for the conference had been circulated in advance and the purpose was to bring together intellectuals from these countries who have reflected on the fundamental question—"Whether, given the long civilizational histories of their countries with their rich and varied knowledge systems and cultural traditions, do they still have a meaningful and significant role to play in the contemporary world and more importantly in the world of the future?" This, in the context of the shift that has evidently begun to take place in the structure of power from the West to the East and/or North to South.

The conference was held in the backdrop of the widely expressed feeling that modern civilization, as it has evolved is facing crises on several fronts.

The conference was structured around an inaugural session wherein Kapila Vatsyayan, Chairperson of the IIC Asia Project, introduced the conference. The Inaugural Address was delivered by the Chief Guest, M. Hamid Ansari, Vice President of the Republic of India, while N. N. Vohra, Governor of Jammu and Kashmir and Life Trustee IIC, gave the Presidential Speech. Thereafter, there were four sessions covering participants from Africa, Asia (two sessions), Latin America and Europe, respectively, and a fifth open discussion session. The conference concluded with a Valedictory Session at which the Rapporteur presented his report on outcomes and highlights of the discussions. The Valedictory Address was delivered by Karan Singh, President, ICCR.

At the inaugural session, the representatives of the IIC and the ICCR noted that this was a seminal conference that was dealing with a profound subject. The Chairperson of the IIC Asia project explained that this conference represented the fifth phase of work undertaken by the IIC-Asia project since its inception in 1993. She clarified that the objective this time was to place the developing world in the context of the ongoing international political and economic discourse and drew a distinction between two separate tendencies, viz., the Earth and the Globe. There was tension between these two tendencies because of the undue focus on GDP considerations. She noted that developing countries are homes of old civilizations, multiple identities, of the continuity of oral traditions, knowledge systems, etc.

The Vice-President of India in his incisive address, raised a series of questions to which the Conference should seek answers and gave a number of examples to underline that traditions are indispensable, that they do not impede forward movement of societies but actually lend authenticity to them. He stressed that tradition and modernity are not antipodes, that the examination of the past has to be critical rather than adulatory and must steer clear of imagined glory, and must not be an incentive for chauvinism. He suggested the need to rethink modernity by criticizing it from within, in its own terms and thereby enriching it. His speech was warmly acclaimed and set the tone for the discussions that followed. The Governor of Jammu and Kashmir, in his thought-provoking speech, added several new dimensions to the issues under discussion. He asked whether the past can contribute to finding solutions to the challenges facing the world today, including for instance, that of internal insurgencies in different parts of the world, overcoming the problems inherited from colonial systems of education and imperial thought, changes required to the framework of the international economic system and its impact on defence and other policies. He felt that the concept note was quite comprehensive but was not sure whether a shift in power had actually begun. He underlined that the tradition in India and Asia was of brotherhood and living in peace, that pluralism as defined in the concept note was badly needed today. He stressed that in today's world the capacity for dialogue needs to be enhanced. His views were greatly appreciated and served as an important guidepost for the discussions that followed.

In Session 1, presentations were made by Mohamed Salmawy, Wafaa Taha El-Saddik (both from Egypt), Elizabeth W. Giorgis (Ethiopia), Akosua Anyidoho (Ghana), Ousmane Sene (Senegal) and A. Parsuramen (Mauritius). The Session was chaired by O.B. Joseph Yai of Benin who introduced the discussants and also summarized the discussions at the end. After the presentations and the Q&A sessions, the following consensus opinion emerged:

1. The conference was a major initiative.
2. There is a need to redefine both modernity and tradition.
3. The preservation of the centrality of language especially in the African context, is important; also the need to safeguard lesser-known languages.
4. The importance of strengthening oral traditions across the board.
5. The importance of diversity and plurality in nation-building.
6. Modernity must devolve around the individual culture of each country. Tradition is not exclusive but can be inclusive.
7. There is a need to sustain the tradition of resilience in old cultures.
8. Museums should be used for the virtual recreation of tradition so that they do not become relics of fragmented cultures. Further, Egypt's example of setting up a museum for children was worthy of emulation, and

9. Ways and means should be devised to share our traditions with other cultures and civilizations, for instance, by establishing an Institution of Asian Tradition in Africa.

The delegate from Mauritius suggested that Africa should hold a conference to follow up the present one.

Sessions 2 and 3 covered presentations by Asian scholars. Session 2 was chaired by Sri Hastanto (Indonesia) and presentations were made by M.A. Kamawal (Afghanistan), Samira Hanna El Daher (Lebanon), Wen Haiming (China), Atsushi Ibuki (Japan) and Lokesh Chandra (India).

Session 3 was chaired by Samira Hanna El Daher and presentations made by Le Thi Minh Ly (Vietnam), Sri Hastanto (Indonesia), S Goonatilake (Sri Lanka), Abhi Subedi and Tulasi Diwasa (both from Nepal) and Aditya Malik (India/ Germany).

Following extensive discussions during the two sessions, the following main issues emerged on which there was broad confluence of views:

1. There is no need to have traditional culture oppose modernity. Traditional and Western cultures/modernity can be synthesized.
2. A nation cannot cease to exist unless you destroy its culture.
3. Advances in technology can potentially have an adverse impact on traditional cultures but the latter can and have adapted.
4. Traditional cultures also have an impact on Western cultures.
5. There is a need to create a "better world". Diversity and respect for cultures are of paramount importance. Tolerance is not enough, for it represents acceptance at the lowest level. We need to seek clues from traditional cultures.
6. There is a need to go back to the basics. The soul cannot be reached through the computer.
7. It is critical to use new technologies for sustainable development. Culture must be harmonized with the latter.
8. The trinity of knowledge, science and space is essential to sustain traditional cultures and their relevance.
9. To create something new, it is necessary to reach out beyond the existing cultural boundaries and ideas.

10. There is a need to find ways to win hearts and minds in a timeless manner.
11. The criticality of plurality and the affirmation of diversity were stressed.
12. There is a serious need to move away from glorifying consumerism, sex and violence.
13. We need to guard against the tendency to focus on comparing the dark side of Western civilization against an idealized version of ancient civilizations.
14, Tradition does not offer solutions to all problems and should not always be idealized. Its link to ethics should, though, be stressed. Tradition as understood in India, i.e. *parampara*, is not a static state. The latter would imply an end of tradition.
15. Modernity, like other formulations, is given to a multiplicity of interpretations. It is a time concept; covers, ideas (dynamic) vs. ideology (static). It has to be dynamic and lead to constant innovations in life, in technological structures, etc. Modernity should mean a better life for all of humanity.
16. The importance of incorporating the study of cultural heritage in schools was recognized.
17. As the balance of power shifts, the East needs to take the initiative to sustain it. Such shifts of power can be healthy.
18. New technologies are changing the way we do things. They are even impacting our mental processes.
19. Can we transcend humanity in search of ethics? This requires further examination.
20. Culture is all-pervasive. There is connectivity among cultures in different parts of the world reflected for instance in the theatre.
21. The continuity and fluidity of traditional cultures provides a liberating influence.
22. The importance of the study of the "language of silence" and non-verbal communication.
23. The crisis of modern civilization, sources of fragmentation, the notion of "selfhood" and seeking "common ground" needs greater attention and study.

24. Power should be shared for the betterment of humanity.
25. We live in a broader world; we cannot live in isolation; cannot have atomization. Man has to be at the centre of the discourse.
26. Culture is universal and exists at many levels, in time and space, and has to be kept alive for humanity. People should not be culturally homeless.
27. Lastly, there exists some cultures of "indefinition" in some parts of Africa.

Session 4 was chaired by Faust Godoy (Brazil) and presentations were made by Maria Del Carmen Valverde Valdes (Mexico), Hugo Novotny (Argentina), Y. Andreadis (Greece), Sergei Serebriany (Russia), Geza Bethlenfalvy (Hungary), Emma Clark (UK) and Tom Cheetham (USA). The chairman also presented a paper.

The session saw the presentation of seven fascinating papers that covered the Mayan/Meso-American, the Latin American, the Indo-European, the Greek, the Russian, the Divine in Art and philosophical perspectives of the subject of the conference. Given the variety and diversity of the presentations, I will not try to project outcomes in this section of the report, but will simply highlight some important takeaways.

1. The specificity of Latin America; essentially, two official languages and perhaps one semi-official religion that makes communication and interaction that much easier.
2. Maya culture is indigenous and not traditional, that its practice is still very much a reality albeit in changed circumstances through a process of constant adaptation to change. That, time and space cannot be separated in Maya culture. Its vision incorporates a neverending sequence of creation and destruction.
3. Expansion of any one culture cannot be at the expense of another and the need for a habitual change towards a new culture of non-violence, dialogue among civilizations and respect for diversity of cultures. Related to this, the need for a New Spirituality.
4. Fourth, Brazil is the melting pot of the South. This gives rise to its own set of issues/problems, including that of multi-identity. There was animated discussion on this proposition.

5. In so far as traditional culture is concerned, in the process of its adaptation and survival, individual decisions have to be taken because of the process and pressures of globalization. But, there are non-negotiable core spaces.
6. The importance of inter-cultural dialogue as exemplified at this conference, including horizontal communication among non-European cultures.
7. The need for a new universal contract among humans and between mankind and nature.
8. The need for abstraction, imagination and permanent reinterpretation in our study of the subject of this conference, and
9. Tradition is a living reality and the principles that underline it evolve and adjust but are based on timeless wisdom.

Session 5 was chaired by Kapila Vatsyayan and presentations were made by Come Carpentier and K. Raghunath, both from India. Carpentier's presentation included issues such as defining tradition its preservation even at the cost of being anachronistic. He pointed out that traditions are often controversial and have a negative impact although they can also help contain tensions. He recalled that the period of Enlightenment in the West was subject to dual interpretation. He referred to the Freemasons and their impact on the development of human rights. He called for the need to seek connection points between traditions and the Supreme Truth. That saving a tradition was not enough; it needed to be corrected and reinvigorated. Finally, there was need to move away from the concept of Western Enlightenment.

Raghunath noted that modernity was not related to time and asked whether it was feasible to resolve the gap between tradition and modernity. Does modernity allow us to take a new look at tradition? The impact of religious structures had to be considered. For instance, is there a special aura around them? He argued that culture was all pervasive; it could be taught. There was, in this regard, continuity over space and time. There were also good things in the West. As for the issue of modernity, the matter is in our hands and we must find our own answers.

An animated and open discussion followed these two presentations. These were seen as having brought in a sense of balance in the discussions at the conference.

The final Valedictory Session was chaired by Kapila Vatsyayan. After the Rapporteur delivered his Report, the Valedictory Address was delivered by Karan Singh, President, ICCR. His address was wide-ranging and profound. He began by stating that he agreed with the outcome of the discussions as presented by the Rapporteur. He recalled the IIC-UNESCO project on Tradition and Modernity held 50 years ago. The crisis in the world community persisted. We face a vanishing past and an indeterminate future with problems such as fanaticism, terrorism and inequality confronting us. In addressing this crisis, the development of cultures was critical. Traditional culture needed to be defined. He saw no conflict between chanting Vedic verses and listening to rock n roll and hip hop music.

Karan Singh recalled that the Global South was not always poor. Indeed, it is the riches of the latter that attracted the attention of free-booters and others. The South had again to develop and articulate its cultures and perceptions to add to the richness of global society and make due contributions to Asia, Africa and Latin America. The links among the South that had been shattered by colonialism had also to be restored across the board. Further, the importance of oral traditions should be stressed. In India, the latter had been central to its persistence as a civilization.

Despite outstanding achievements in science and technology during our lifetime, the world is full of tension, turmoil, inter-religious strife, poverty and degradation, huge income inequalities, global warming, etc. Karan Singh recalled that in addressing these issues we must draw upon our traditional cultures, which are of permanent value. The latter should be preserved, but simple glorification of these is not acceptable. There is a need to, critically reassess and reappraise traditional cultures. He recalled in this context the work of the Inter-Faith Movement. The clash of civilizations must not become a self-fulfilling prophecy. There should instead be collaboration among them.

In conclusion, Karan Singh noted that in the 21st century, the world cannot afford the luxury of fanaticism. Truth is one though the wise call it by different names. We must think, work and achieve together. There should be no hatred among us. The current century offers a great opportunity for this.

The vote of thanks on behalf of the foreign participants was given by Akosua Anyidoho of Ghana. She announced that there was a need for a follow-up conference and that Africa would take up the baton in this regard. Details would be conveyed at a later date. This decision was received with applause. She also conveyed the special appreciation of all the participants for the outstanding contribution of Kapila Vatsyayan, Chairperson, IIC-Asia Project for conceptualizing and organizing the conference and guiding its deliberations.

The vote of thanks on behalf of the organizers was given both by Kavita Sharma, Director, IIC, and Satish Mehta, Director General, ICCR.

Valedictory Address

KARAN SINGH, PRESIDENT, ICCR

AFTER THE BRILLIANT ENCAPSULATION BY Surie, I really do not feel there is very much left to say. I agree wholeheartedly with almost all the conclusions that you have reached. It is a great privilege to have such a distinguished group of academicians and intellectuals here at the India International Centre, which has become one of the major intellectual hubs in Asia, if not in the world. My only regret is that due to other commitments I could not spend any length of time with you, and I was not able to learn first-hand from so many distinguished people around the table. I have not had time to prepare a paper, but I would like to share with you some general views on this whole question of tradition and modernity. If I recall correctly, Kapilaji, 50 years ago when IIC was created, there was a UNESCO project on Tradition and Modernity which was undertaken by C.D. Deshmukh in IIC many years ago. "Tradition and Modernity" remains a perpetual question.

We live in an age of great turbulence and turmoil, where the past is disappearing and the future is struggling to be born, and we find ourselves precariously poised between a vanishing past and an indeterminate future. At a time like this, there is a quest for cultural certitudes, for cultural personalities, for cultural ideas, a quest which often takes us back into the past. Unfortunately, this often derails of our thinking and regresses into fanaticism and terrorism.

As Kapilaji said, culture is an essential ingredient of the human race. The human race as it has developed over the last half a million years has involved gradually the development of various cultures. Now the question that you have raised in your seminar about relevance or otherwise of traditional cultures also raises a semantic problem. What is traditional culture? I begin my prayers in the morning by reciting some verses from the Rig Veda which is 5,000 years old. Would you call that an indigenous culture, or would you call it a traditional culture still alive? These are the same verses that were chanted 5,000 years ago in the same accent, because they have come down by oral traditions to the present day. So a lot of what we do is, based upon what we could call tradition. But I do not see how that in any way prevents me from enjoying rock and roll, which I listen to for an hour or so every day. The question is whether there is necessarily a conflict between traditional Vedic chanting and postmodern music.

So how do we define tradition and what particular problems arise from trying to define it? Many of these were encapsulated by the Rapporteur. Let me just say two or three things. First of all, it is useful to remember the so-called Global South was not always poor. In fact, it is estimated that sometime, perhaps in the 14th century, China and India between them produced 40 percent of the world's GDP. It is our riches and not our poverty that attracted the unwelcome attention of free-booters, fanatics and iconoclasts, and finally, of colonialism. This is tremendously important, because as a result of four centuries of colonialism the whole area has been impoverished. The great Latin American empires, the great culture of the Mayas and the Incas were full of gold; they were not poor. India, too, was a rich country.

So I think, first of all we have to get rid of this idea that we are poor, Third World countries. I dislike the term "Third World". Who are the Westerners to assume to themselves the First World, push all the former Communist countries into the Second World, and then we are all given a third class certificate, as it were? In fact, we were building great temples when the Europeans were cautiously emerging from their caves.

I am glad nobody used the term "Third World" in front of me because I get very angry at that. One of the traditions we set up in our IIC-Asia Project was that we invited only Asian scholars. Western scholarship is outstanding; in fact, in many ways it is more effective and more comprehensive than modern Eastern scholarship. But we did this because we wanted Asians to meet each other. Many delegates who came here to this room said that this was the first time they had met a delegate from another country which was next door to them. I am glad that the bulk of the participants are from Asia, Africa and Latin America. This is not, as I have said, to denigrate the scholarship of the West, but simply to stress the fact that we have got to develop our own perceptions now, and we must be able to articulate our cultures in such a manner that it adds to the richness of the emerging global society.

Whether we like it or not, we are moving into a global society. Science and technology is shooting us into the global society, shouting and screaming as we may be, and therefore we have got to see that in the emerging global society, the formerly suppressed peoples of Asia, Africa and Latin America are able to make their due contribution to the new society that is developing. Let it also be remembered that colonialism not only suppressed many of the traditional cultures, it also shattered the links between the countries. For example, Indian influence spread to South and Southeast Asia two thousand years ago. Angkor Wat, the greatest temple in the world, was built a thousand years ago at the same time our Rajarajachola Temple was being built in Tanjavoor—built by Indian inspiration, maybe by Indian artisans along with local artisans. Hinduism spread throughout South and Southeast Asia, as did Buddhism. But as a result of colonialism we got cut off. Therefore, our relations with Myanmar, our relationship with Thailand, our relationship with Cambodia, were shattered.

The same thing must have happened in Latin America and in Africa. So that is something we must now re-establish. And this whole IIC-Asia Project, which Kapilaji is now so brilliantly leading, is designed to re-establish the links, the intellectual links, the cultural links, the spiritual links between the peoples of Asia, and in this conference we have added Africa and Latin America. All three, although they are very different, have nonetheless been through the same sort of experience and, therefore, we have a lot in common. Our cultural heritage is largely based upon oral traditions, which are tremendously important. The oral tradition in India, particularly, has been central to our persistence as a civilization because all our sacred texts have come down to us orally. The Vedas were reduced to writing only by Max Mueller in Oxford in the 19th century. Before that, thousands and thousands of verses with their correct pronunciation and intonation came down by memory. So the importance of the oral tradition in our cultures should never be underestimated.

There have been astounding scientific developments in our own lifetime. We have seen the world transformed by them, whether it be sub-nuclear particles or space travel or instant communication. Everything has changed and is changing. If there is one certainty in the world today, it is that change is going to speed up with each technological generation. But despite all the improvements done for the human race, the world is full of tension and turmoil, of inter-religious and intra-religious strife, of wide spread poverty and deprivation. While the very rich live in great luxury, the very poor live on the verge of starvation. There are still millions of people, may be two billion people, on planet earth who live on or below the poverty line. Is it not a shame and a disgrace to the human race that when there is so much material wealth going around, there are still people who are denied the minimum inputs necessary for a decent civilized existence?

Look at what is happening in environmental destruction, man-made global warming, the rising oceans, melting of the ice caps, species extinction, arms trafficking, drug trafficking, human trafficking, which is most shameful of all. So we have all these very negative factors before us along with all those unparalleled achievements of science and technology, and unprecedented levels of well-being for huge numbers of people.

In this situation, how are the traditional cultures relevant? This is the point that you have raised and I think that I would answer that in this way: I would say that there is a lot that is of value in our traditional cultures, and that they should remain with us. If we lose it, if we lose our language, for example, or if we lose some of our noble traditions, the world will be very much poorer. On the other hand, an uncritical glorification of our past cultures is also not acceptable. For example, if a culture teaches untouchability, are we going to accept that? If a culture supports slavery, are we going to accept that? If a culture practices human sacrifice, are we going to accept that? If a culture imposes female circumcision and puts women in a subordinate position, are we going to accept that? We are not. We cannot say that because these are part of our traditional cultures, therefore we are going to accept them.

This is a significant point. We must realize because very often people swing into this, glorifying the past without realizing the terrible weaknesses that it had. But on the other hand, our traditional cultures—if they teach us to respect elders, if they teach us to honour the earth and the environment, if they teach us human brotherhood, if they teach us love for our neighbours, if they teach us unity of all religions, these are all positive values which we should certainly adopt. In other words, what is needed is a critical re-assessment and re-appraisal of traditional cultures so that we can move towards a creative symbiosis between tradition and modernity. That is how I would sum up my reaction, my response to this seminar.

There was a seminar on Asian Values and I would like to give an example. I recall that on one occasion I was in New York and my good friend Carl Sagan, the great cosmologist, said to me: "Karan, I am teaching in Ithaca, would you like to come to one of my classes?" I went with him and I noticed that at the end of the class, two boys were sitting with their legs up on the table in front. Now nobody thought that it was strange or that they were misbehaving. But I was shocked beyond belief, because for us, for children to sit in a classroom with their legs on the front table is unthinkable. Now you can call that an Asian value, if you like, or you can call it old-fashioned, but you know there is something in it. I mean, if you see a teacher, you cannot point your leg at him and sit there with your legs on the table.

Again, I went to an international students' function where there was a musical performance and a harmonium had to be brought onto the stage. One boy was pushing the harmonium with his foot on the stage, and a girl suddenly ran up and immediately picked it up, because for us to put a foot on a musical instrument would be a sort of sacrilege. It is not superstition but because music is such a glorious gift to humanity it has to be treated with respect. I am just mentioning these examples to say that there are certain attitudes, there are certain Asian, maybe African, Latin American attitudes and customs that perhaps can teach us a lot. On the other hand, we have a great deal to learn from the West. Therefore, this will always have to be a continuous two-way dialogue.

Before I close, I want to say a few words on the Interfaith Movement, a movement designed to bring together people of different religious persuasions in a harmonious dialogue, not to prove the superiority of any other one religion or the other. It began in 1893 with the first Parliament of the World Religions in Chicago where 6,000 delegates from around the world assembled and where Swami Vivekananda, who was a powerful advocate of Vedanta, made a very dramatic impact. Then in the 20th century a large number of Interfaith organizations came into being, including one which I head worldwide called the Temple of Understanding. In 1993, a hundred years after the first Parliament, the Second Parliament was again held in Chicago, and in the same hall where the first one had been held. In 1999, the Third Parliament, was held in Cape Town, South Africa, in 2004 in Barcelona, Spain and in 2009 in Melbourne, Australia.

The movement is designed, as I have said, to try and get people to understand each other because there are stereotypes in our minds with regard to other religions. Many of the religions, in the Jungian sense, are looked upon as "the other", as hostile and therefore something to be feared or hated. It is true that religion-based terrorism and fundamentalism have created havoc in the last 40 years, but we should be careful that we do not fall into a situation where Samuel P. Huntington's brilliantly argued thesis about the clash of civilizations becomes a self-fulfilling prophecy. We must move towards a confluence of civilizations rather than a clash of civilizations.

It is my belief that until there is harmony between and within the great religions of the world, there will never be peace on earth. However regretfully, the Interfaith Movement is still peripheral unlike the environmental movement, which moved rapidly into the centre of human consciousness. I was at Stockholm at the first UN Conference on Human Environment in 1972 as part of the Indian delegation led by Indira Gandhi. In that conference, there were only Olof Palme and Indira Gandhi, two Heads of State. In Rio, 20 years later, there were over a hundred Heads of State. They talk of Rio plus 20. That is incorrect. Rio was Stockholm plus 20, and that is now forgotten and everybody starts with Rio.

The basic thesis of the Interfaith Movement is the acceptance of multiple paths to the divine. We are tiny creatures on a speck of dust in the illimitable cosmos around us with billions and billions of galaxies, *anantakoti brahmanda* (infinite number of galaxies). Who are we to lay down that the illimitable splendor of the divine can appear only at this time, and at this place, and in this form? This is prima facie unacceptable. I can say that for me, my religion is the best and my formulation of that religion is the best. But I cannot say that because you do not follow that religion, you can be persecuted or blown up or killed or tortured.

Religion has had a mixed record in human history. Much that is great and noble in human civilization—music, dance, art and architecture, the glorious temples, and the cathedrals and scriptures—can all be traced back to one or the other great religions of the world. At the same time, more people have been killed and murdered and tortured in the name of religion, than in any other name. And the irony is that each religion looks upon "its" god as being very compassionate. I worship Lord Shiva—*karunavataaram* (the incarnation of compassion). The Muslims start their prayer with Bismillah Rahman e Rahim (the Lord, the Merciful, the Compassionate). The Christians believe that Jesus Christ mounted the cross in order to expatiate the sins of humanity. But in the name of religion, the most terrible events happen. We have to get over this in the 21st century. We can no longer afford the luxury of fanaticism, and that is why I feel that when we talk about culture, this is one point which should be stressed. There is this one line in the Rig Veda: *Ekam sadvipra bahudha vadanti* (the Truth is one, the wise call it by many names). Once this is accepted, we will find a great change in attitudes.

One can go on for a long time, but let me simply end by saying that the deeper the roots of a tree, the taller it grows. So we need to be rooted in the best of our traditional cultures but our branches must reach out. We are living in a moment of great change, of great possibilities. It is an exciting time to be alive because we are witnessing these extraordinary changes. The latest concept I learnt 10 days ago was neuro-plasticity. Neuro-plasticity implies something we, have known for thousands of years, that through certain practices including yoga and breathing, you can actually modify the neurotic structure of the brain. This is now being proved by scientific experiments. Is, that not exciting? Because we have known this for thousands of years that by certain breathing exercises, certain practices, you can actually come to new stages of consciousness. Consciousness research is cutting-edge science today. So there are all sorts of exciting possibilities. The question is, will we blow ourselves up before we get there or will we in fact, gradually integrate all these great discoveries, integrate all the great religions, integrate great cultures and move into a sane and harmonious global society? That is the question before us, that is the challenge before us all.

I am going to end with a quotation again from the Vedas, which exhorts us to work together, to achieve together, to think together and to work harmoniously. May there be no hatred between us.

Saha navavatu saha nau bhunaktu
Saha viryam karavaavahai
Tejasvinawadhitam astu
Ma vidvisha vahai

Contributors

Mohamed Salmawy, President, Writers' Union of Egypt and Secretary-General of the General Union of Arab Writers, Egypt

Wafaa Tha El-Saddik, Archaeologist, Art Historian; former Director-General, Egyptian Museum, Cairo

Elizabeth W. Giorgis, Director, Modern Art Museum, Gebre Kristos Desta Center and formerly Head, Institute for Ethiopian Studies, Addis Ababa

Akosua Anyidoho, Director, New York University, Accra, and formerly Chair, Department of Linguistics, University of Ghana, Accra

Ousmane Sene, Director, West African Research Centre (WARC), Dakar

A. Parsuramen, Founder-President, Global Rainbow Foundation, University of 3rd Age (Mauritius); formerly Member-Secretary, UNESCO Executive Board

Olabiyi Babalola Joseph Yai, former Chairman, UNESCO Executive Board.

Mohammad Amir Kamawal, Acting Vice-Chancellor, Kabul University

Samira Hanna El Daher, formerly Lebanese Representative on UNESCO Executive Board; Member, Lebanese Association for Inter-Cultural Dialogue

Haiming Wen, Assistant Dean, School of Philosophy at Renmin University of China; Assistant Director, International Centre for Chinese and Comparative Philosophy

Atsushi Ibuki, Professor at Toyo University, Japan; Specialist in the history of Zen Buddhism in China

Lokesh Chandra, Linguist and prolific writer; President, Indian Council for Cultural Relations

Le Thi Minh Ly, Member, National Heritage Council, and Director, Center for Cultural Heritage Research and Promotion, Hanoi

Sri Hastanto, Professor at the Department of Ethnomusicology, Indonesian Arts Institute, Surarkarta, Indonesia.

Susantha Goonatilake, President, Royal Asiatic Society of Sri Lanka

Abhi Subedi, Eminent Nepalese writer and theorist on theatre; Professor of English, Tribhuvan University

Tulasi Diwasa, formerly Professor of Folklore and Literature, Tribhuvan University, Nepal

Aditya Malik, formerly Fellow, Max-Weber-Centre for Advanced Social Science Research, University of Erfurt, Germany

Maria del Carmen Valverde Valdes, Centre of Maya Studies of the Institute of Philological Research, National Autonomous University of Mexico

Hugo Novotny, Independent Researcher, Argentina; author of *Humanist Basis for Convergence of Cultures* (2007)

Fausto Godoy, Brazilian diplomat and cultural historian

Yangos Andreadis, specialist in comparative aesthetics and dramaturgy; Emeritus Professor, Painteion University, Athens

Sergei Serebriany, Director, E.M. Meletinsky Institute for Advanced Studies in the Humanities, Russian State University, Moscow

Geza Bethlenfalvy, formerly Research Fellow in the project of Altaic Studies of the Hungarian Academy of Sciences; formerly Director, Hungarian Cultural Centre, India

Emma Clark, Senior Tutor and Lecturer, The Prince's School of Traditional Arts, London

Tom Cheetham, Biologist, Philosopher' Fellow, Temenos Academy, London; author of four books on the imagination and the meaning of Henry Corbin's work for the contemporary world

Come Carpentier de Gourdon, writer on comparative philosophies and religions; Convener of the Editorial Advisory Board of World Affairs: the Journal of International Affairs

K. Raghunath, former High Commissioner to Nigeria and Ambassador to Russia

Nalin Surie, Director-General, Indian Council of World Affairs; former Indian Ambassador to China and High Commissioner to UK